1970

ok may be kept

The Secret Battle for Israel

The Secret Battle for Israel

COLONEL BENJAMIN KAGAN

TRANSLATED FROM THE FRENCH
BY PATSY SOUTHGATE

FOREWORD BY BRIGADIER GENERAL
DAN TOLKOWSKY, ISRAELI AIR FORCE

THE WORLD PUBLISHING COMPANY
CLEVELAND AND NEW YORK

Published by The World Publishing Company
2231 West 110th Street, Cleveland, Ohio 44102

Published simultaneously in Canada by
Nelson, Foster & Scott Ltd.

FIRST PRINTING 1966

Library of Congress Catalog Card No.: 66–24991

Printed in the United States of America
by American Book–Stratford Press, Inc.

Contents

Foreword by Brigadier General Dan Tolkowsky   xi
Biography of Benjamin Kagan   xiii
To the Reader   xv

PART I   IN THE UNDERGROUND

Chapter 1   On the Edge of the Abyss   3
Chapter 2   The Shameful Abandonment   11
Chapter 3   To the Rescue!   19
Chapter 4   The Arab Peril   29
Chapter 5   The Quest for Airplanes   34
Chapter 6   The First Successes   41
Chapter 7   The Battle for the Highways   52
Chapter 8   The Great Departure   59
Chapter 9   The State of Israel Is Born   65
Chapter 10   The Djihad   69
Chapter 11   From the Four Corners of the
                Earth   78
Chapter 12   The First Score Against Albion   90
Chapter 13   The Story of the B-17 Flying
                Fortresses   97

Chapter 14	Film Production on a Grand Scale	107
Chapter 15	Operation "Dust"	116
Chapter 16	The Wind Shifts	122
Chapter 17	Victory	133
Chapter 18	The Day of Reckoning	145
Chapter 19	Adding Up the Score	149

PART II   THE NATIONAL FRONT

Chapter 20	Israel Faces Her Problems	157
Chapter 21	Paris	161
Chapter 22	Return to London	167
Chapter 23	The Arms Race	172
Chapter 24	"Impossible" Is Not in the French Vocabulary	177
Chapter 25	Still a Piston-Engined Air Force	185
Chapter 26	Disappointments and Surprises	190
Chapter 27	The Hesitation Waltz	195
Chapter 28	The Philosophy of Revolution	202
Chapter 29	A Question of Honor	210

PART III   "KADESH"

Chapter 30	True Friends and an Occasional Ally	223
Chapter 31	The Averted Menace	232
Chapter 32	The Theft	239
Chapter 33	The Pitfall of Suez	250
Chapter 34	Downhill to War	260
Chapter 35	The Decisive Days of October	270

PART IV   THE SINAI CAMPAIGN

Chapter 36	And They Have Taken Off Again	279

The Secret Battle for Israel

FOREWORD

by Brigadier General Dan Tolkowsky

THIS IS a tale of imagination, resourcefulness and high adventure, a story of participation in the making of history and, above all, in a war of survival; like many a war of survival in history it may well have to be refought. It is also a story of the surprisingly unorthodox inception and growth of a military air force. The Israel Air Service, later to become The Israel Air Force, first went into action in 1948 equipped with a motley collection of transport and miscellaneous light aircraft adapted for military use. It underwent a series of transformations that enabled it to go into battle in October 1956 flying modern Mystère IV jet-fighters. This eight-year period of intensive training and organization of an air force, beginning with the War of Independence and ending with the Sinai Campaign, represents one of the many facets of Israeli endeavour. One of its lesser known but no less unusual aspects is that of the acquisition of aircraft for the Israel Air Force, in which Colonel Benjamin Kagan was intimately concerned. If there is a moral to be drawn from this fascinating tale it is that few things are impossible, given a just cause, the will to fight for it, and a modicum of luck.

BENJAMIN KAGAN

1914–1933. From Russia to Palestine

Benjamin Kagan was born on the 5th of December, 1914, at Dineburg, in Russia. Son of middle class Jewish parents, he was raised in the atmosphere of French enlightenment which then reigned at the heart of the Russian bourgeoisie, nourishing its liberal and socialist ideals.

At the outbreak of the Russian Revolution, his family left Russia and took refuge in Poland, at Bialystok. There, in a Polish State School conducted by Jesuit Fathers, he completed his secondary education.

Anti-Semitism was rampant in Poland at the time. Benjamin, an ardent Zionist, joined the Zionist-Socialist Movement and, in 1933, despite the opposition of his family, left home for Palestine. He was only eighteen years old.

1933–1945. The Sorbonne and the Commandos

Having become a member of the Haganah, the Jewish organization for self-defense, and on the point of being arrested by the English, Kagan was forced to leave Palestine in 1936. He reached France and went to Paris where he studied at the Sorbonne until war was declared.

He enlisted in the Polish Army which was formed in France during that period, and crossed the Channel to England after the Armistice of June, 1940.

Soon, the revelation of the Nazi persecutions led him to enlist in the Commandos, in which organization he fought throughout the war. His participation in many different raids —notably on Monte-Cassino—earned him the honor of being one of the few Jews decorated by General Anders.

1945–1949. For the Freedom of Israel

At the end of the war Benjamin Kagan asked to be repatriated to Palestine where, upon arrival, he rejoined the ranks of the Haganah.

Meanwhile the English authorities suspected him, as much because of his activities in that country before the war as because of his military history, of belonging to a terrorist organization. He was arrested on numerous occasions and subjected to long interrogations which, however, never resulted in his imprisonment. Being a journalist by profession, he knew how to defend himself during interrogation.

This persecution by the police lasted until 1948 when the battle for the freedom of Israel began, that exalting epic which he lived through and relates here.

Today he is a colonel in the Israeli Air Force and an officer of the Legion of Honor.

TO THE READER

This book is not an official document and does not reflect the opinion of the Government of Israel or its services. It is not based on any documents held by the Ministry of Defense of that country. I have simply endeavored to reconstruct most of the facts about the underground, adding my memories to those of my comrades. I have spent many long evenings comparing notes with them. In any case, during that period nobody had time to put down in writing what he was living from day to day. For the years 1950–56 I used my own notes only and not official documentary evidence.

COLONEL BENJAMIN KAGAN

PART ONE

In the Underground

1

On the Edge
of the Abyss

IN PALESTINE November 15, 1946 is just a day like any other. The men of the Jewish underground movements carry on the fight; the British troops and the Palestine Police continue their arrests, break up riots in the streets, and strictly enforce the curfew. But, for the immigrant who landed during the night as well as for the British soldier who was just issued his ticket home, this day becomes confused with the fulfilment of a dream.

For me, this was a day of work like the others, subject to the routines of the newspaper. Since the end of the war I, too, had been dreaming, but only of big headlines. To get my name on the front page of a large foreign daily I was ready to leave at any moment, for anywhere, legally or not. I wanted to become an international reporter, but I also was anxious to remain a good Jew. So I was straddling a fence.

Since my return here in 1945, I had constantly been in this dilemma, knowing perfectly well that, sooner or later, I would have to make a decision.

In London, my old wartime friends were convinced that I was writing history with a machine gun, and not with a pen.

The police officers in Palestine likewise refused to believe that my only goal was to become a good reporter.

I had not forgotten my last visit to their headquarters. It is always disagreeable to be awakened at six in the morning by two policemen, and be led off to that station. The incident had earned me, it is true, the esteem of my neighbors; at that time to be arrested by the police was an honor. But whatever my old buddies from the Commandos might think of it, I subsequently resolved to stay out of trouble.

Alas! One glance at the newspaper that morning of November 15th told me that I was in trouble.

M.1.5 WATCH OUT FOR HIM. . . . Under this headline the local papers reprinted an account published in the London *Daily Graphic*. It related that a certain Benjamin Kagan, ex-sergeant in the Commandos, who had been awarded the Polish Cross for Valor in Italy and upon returning to Palestine had joined the secret Jewish organization known under the name of the Stern gang, had recently left Palestine and was now in Paris en route to England.

I was stupefied. My name, at last, had made the front page. But certainly not for the reasons I had hoped. Who could be responsible for this absurdity?

This account, at any rate, was clearly aimed at me; there was no other Benjamin Kagan in the Commandos and, while not having won the Polish Cross for Valor, I had all the same been decorated on the battlefield by General Anders.

I did not know I had any enemies besides the Police Department. Could this be a way they had found to get rid of a bothersome reporter? For, without knowing about my contacts with underground groups, they still did not appreciate my articles, as I knew only too well. In short, to all appearances it must be a charge rigged by the police.

During my service in the Commandos I had learned quite a few useful things; one being, when danger strikes react at once. After reassuring my family who were convinced that, this time, I would really be arrested, and after rejecting the advice to seek refuge in one of the agricultural communities, I called on the Public Information Office where I raised merry hell, demanding the personal intervention of the High-Commissioner to bring this matter to light.

The official I spoke to did not know what to say. He promised to refer the matter to the Government House.

I next telegraphed my friends in London to deny the account in the *Daily Graphic*, and then I prepared to face the police. I must admit I was having a marvelous time.

The "fortress," as we called it, was protected by a tangle of barbed wire and guarded by two armed guards and about twenty parachutists. At the information desk, I asked the officer-on-duty what one had to do to give oneself up. He did not understand exactly what I meant. No one in Palestine had ever had that idea. So I repeated my question, adding that I was suspected of belonging to the Stern gang. The confusion caused by my statement was worth seeing. I was literally carried up to the Chief Inspector's office on the fourth floor. With great calm, this inspector asked exactly what was the significance of my little joke, which he considered to be in poor taste. I did not feel very proud of myself, but there was no turning back now. Accordingly, I translated the information about me that had appeared in the press into English for him and I accused the police of having invented the story out of whole cloth.

I accused; the inspector denied. It was a curious reversal of roles. I warned the inspector that I planned to sue the *Daily Graphic* for defamation, that I had demanded to be heard by the High Commissioner and that I intended to institute proceedings against the police. Plainly, the inspector hardly appreciated this situation. In the end, I declared that I would be willing to forget the incident if the police consented to print an official denial of the article in question.

A half an hour later I left the building with the formal promise of the inspector that such a statement would be sent to my lawyer.

This is the kind of thing that was going on in 1946 in Palestine. Less than a year after the end of the war, the same people who had lived, worked and fought side by side were at each other's throats. What had become of the Balfour Declaration and the British promise of November 2nd, 1917, "to view with favour the establishment in Palestine of a national home for the Jewish people."

This Declaration had at last opened the way to the realization of an old dream, inspired by love of Zion—a dream which a nation persecuted for centuries had never been able to forget throughout its long exile. What hope, in effect, lies in the simple words spoken from year to year during the Easter celebration: "Next year in Jerusalem!"

On the eastern coast of the Mediterranean, not far from the point where Europe joins Asia, a new Palestine was being born. It covered 10,157 square miles, an area smaller than Belgium. "A land of wheat and barley, of vineyards and fig trees," the Bible described this Promised Land during the forty-year trek of the Jewish people across the desert. But the Palestine of yesterday was now just an arid region, eroded, parched. The indifference of a long line of conquerors had left it a particularly hostile country; the hills were nothing but rockpiles; the valleys were nothing but polluted swamps. The sands from the sea like the sands from the desert had invaded the last of the arable land. The southern half of this country, squeezed in between the Mediterranean Sea and Jordan, had actually become a desert, the Negev, whose southernmost tip ends at the Gulf of Aqaba, on the Red Sea.

All the same, Palestine concealed a hidden wealth of potentials: first the sunny climate which has nurtured all Mediterranean cultures, and secondly its mineral resources, which were to intrigue the English.

The first Jewish immigrants encountered no organized hostility from the Arab population, which watched with amused indifference the incomprehensible efforts of these pioneers to drain the swamps and irrigate the deserts. But the new social concepts upon which the Jewish settlements were founded soon began to displease the big landowners. They saw in them, quite rightly, a threat to their ancient feudal regime. However, the most serious opposition to the Balfour Declaration did not come from the Arabs but from their masters, the autonomous officers of the British Mandate who dreamed of an Arab Empire under British domination and saw in the Declaration an obstacle to this grand dream. Very quickly, the British administration allied itself with the Arab landowners who, by fallaciously invoking Muslim religious zeal, had no trouble arousing the Muslim masses against the Jews.

Since 1921, the Arabs had been staging major riots. Immediately, the British Administration flooded London with alarming reports of Arab resistance, and soon the British Government published a White Paper denying the very basic concept of a Jewish homeland in Palestine, and sharply curtailing immigration.

Being the victims of these first riots, the Jews in Palestine realized that they could only exist if they organized their defense. Thus the first self-defense organization, the Haganah, was founded, comprising the entire Jewish population of Palestine. It was given a political structure, the Jewish Agency.

An illusory peace reigned for seven years. In 1929 the country was again bloodied by strife instigated by Amin-el-

Husseini, the Mufti of Jerusalem. England took advantage of the occasion to release herself from the last obligations born of the Balfour Declaration, and the local administration in Jerusalem announced that not a single Jewish immigrant should be allowed to enter the country.

Seven more years went by. The Arabs triumphed until, following Hitler's rise to power, the British suddenly authorized a higher immigration quota. The Mufti responded with arson and murder. This time the Jews realized that simply organizing their defense was not enough to safeguard their rights. They would have to take the offensive. They were abetted by circumstances; during that time of exceptionally strained international relations, London was anxious to maintain peace within her family of possessions. Influenced by a young English officer, Orde Wingate, the organization of shock troops recruited from among the young members of the Haganah was set in motion. Objective of these groups: to strike at nests of Arab terrorists. So the Haganah got its striking force, the Palmach, which became the nucleus of the future Israeli army.

But the rioting nevertheless continued. London proposed dividing the country. The Jews were not hostile to this idea and were willing to enter into discussions, but the Mufti rejected the proposal. In May, 1939, Great Britain released a second White Paper which limited immigration for the next five years to 75,000 men and deprived the Jews of the right to buy land. It was a complete Arab victory, Britain coming to terms with Arab extremists. Churchill spoke out against these decisions, calling them "a betrayal," and "a petition in moral bankruptcy."

Then the war broke out. The Jews could not combat a people who were fighting against Hitler's armies, so the whole Jewish population lined up on the British side, while the Mufti offered his services to the Nazis, Egypt tried to come to terms with the enemy and a pro-Nazi revolt broke out in Iraq.

One might logically have hoped that at the end of the war Britain would revise its attitude in regard to Palestine. It did nothing of the sort. Mr. Bevin, the Foreign Secretary, reverted to the policy of the last White Paper, despite American intervention. President Truman, in effect, had asked His Majesty's Government to authorize entry into Palestine of one hundred thousand Jews. Mr. Bevin replied that he could not strip Europe of its Jewish population. . . . In reality, he was trying to assure Great Britain's popularity among the Arab countries, where oil was flowing like water.

This time it meant revolt, unanimously. The Haganah, of liberal tendencies, embraced the majority of the population. It organized clandestine immigration, directed the sabotage of British installations, but condemned the taking of lives. The Irgun Zvai Leumi, a military organization issuing from the right wing of the Zionist movement, on the other hand recognized the law of retaliation, and indiscriminate reprisals were the result. The members of the Irgun were relatively few in number, but well organized. Even fewer were the Sternists, dissidents of the Irgun and promoters of terrorism. They held ambushes, firing on sight at any British subject.

The Jewish Agency, which officially represented the Jewish population in Palestine, condemned the actions of the Irgun and the Stern group. But the British, in their zeal to quell the revolt, did not discriminate between the Haganah, the Irgun and Sternists. And it was the Haganah that General Barker, officer commanding British Forces in Palestine, decided to crush during the summer of 1946. From all over the country Jews were herded into concentration camps, their settlements searched and their arms seized. The General won a good victory and the British illustrated magazines showed photographs of the General entering an arms cache. What the

General overlooked was that although two thousand Jews were neutralized by internment in concentration camps, tens of thousands of others living in cities or settlements were still all active members of the Haganah. The two thousand who had been detained were released, moreover, after long weeks of incarceration.

What had been gained? The Irgun and the Sternists were left free to intensify their acts of violence, which led to harsher reprisals and more violence.

The Shameful Abandonment

THE NEW PALESTINE could count three large cities: Jerusalem, built on the flanks of the mountains of Judea where the pines rise from among the wild flowers; Haifa, on the slopes of Mount Carmel which plunge into the sea; and Tel-Aviv, spread out along a vast beach on the Mediterranean. It was this last city which particularly attracted the British soldiers stationed in Palestine. Its movie theaters and bars allowed them to forget their troubles.

The Gat Rimon Bar was one of the few places left where British officers still mingled with the Jews. There David served drinks to the "Poppies" of the Airborne Division, the reporters of the world press and the few Jews who remained faithful to their pub. There words flowed freely, the soldiers displaying their complete ignorance of the situation and their belief in the infallible British policy.

Occasionally a few of them might timidly plead the Jewish cause, but that was rare. It must be said that most of these soldiers had only recently arrived in Palestine. They had not known the Jewish community during the war years, when the British soldier was regarded as a friend and warmly received in every Jewish household. The soldiers of 1946 had landed in Palestine while terrorism was raging; for them the Jews were nothing but gangsters, the assassins of their comrades. It would have required long and difficult explanations to make them change their opinions.

On that same November night with the bar almost empty, a typical incident occurred. The British soldiers had not been allowed out of their camps because a mine had exploded the previous day in the path of a truck transporting seven British policemen and three airmen; the long list of terrorist victims had grown longer.

Suddenly, a burst of explosions nearby mingled with cries made all in the bar rush outside. About twenty men of the British Mobile Police Force were demolishing a bar down the street. A shot was fired in our direction, forcing us to seek safety inside the bar. For more than half an hour, the quarter was left open to destruction, the police going at it to their hearts' content. The intervention of the Military Police was needed to put an end to their rampage. I cabled my newspaper: "Four civilians hospitalized in critical condition. Twenty-nine suffered minor wounds. No soldiers took part in the Police action which was finally broken up by the Military Police." I imagined with satisfaction how my "friends" on the Police Force would bless me for that last remark.

A week went by without any notable incidents. It had been my intention to spend a few days in Jerusalem when events forced me to leave suddenly for Haifa; a new drama was unfolding.

A refugee vessel transporting about 4,000 Jews immigrating to Palestine had been hailed on the high seas by a British destroyer and ordered to alter course for Cyprus. The answer from the immigrants had been explicit: "We come from concentration camps in Europe. We refuse to exchange them for British camps. We will fight for our right to live."

Since the immigrants refused to obey, there was nothing to do but let the ship proceed to Haifa. During the crossing two other British destroyers had drawn alongside the refugee ship, which had been renamed "Knesset-Israel" (Jewish Community).

What were the British going to do? Deport the refugees by force upon their arrival at Haifa? Wait for the decision of the Supreme Court to which the refugees had appealed? Watching the police string barbed wire along the docks of Haifa, I had, for my part, no longer the slightest doubt as to the British intentions.

On Tuesday November 26, 1946, at midnight, the police and the army surrounded the port. The next morning, troops occupied most of the trouble spots in the city, while the police patrolled the streets. Nobody in Haifa went to work that day. All the stores were closed, and the factories deserted.

Finally the refugee ship entered the harbor with its destroyer escort. It stopped near the wharf where the deportation ship for Cyprus was moored. From the topmost masts of the "Knesset-Israel" the Zionist colors were flying.

Everything seemed calm. One could see, on the decks of the ship, men, women and children, motionless, contemplating the troops drawn up on the jetty. Were they still hoping against all hope?

Suddenly, orders were shouted out and the British soldiers began marching toward the gangway. Quickly they were on the deck of the ship. For a moment, one might have thought that the immigrants were going to surrender without fighting back. But suddenly, just as a soldier took hold of a young boy to lead him off, resistance broke out and the most heterogeneous assortment of missiles began to rain down on the soldiers. Surprised, they retreated back to the dock. They soon made another attempt, protected now by helmets and armed with billies and iron tent pegs. They were pushed back a second time. The third attack took place under a hail of machine gun bullets fired over the heads of the immigrants; one man was killed, however, and another wounded. A few soldiers succeeded in gaining the deck of the ship; then a free-for-all broke out.

The officers in charge realized that this forced deportation, code named Operation "London," was going badly: they would never succeed in getting the immigrants off the ship unless the troops attacked the vessel under cover of fire. On the other hand, firing on unarmed men, women and children would be murder, pure and simple. There remained one other method, less brutal and quite effective. They tried it. New orders were given. The troops retreated to return this time equipped with gas masks, and a shower of tear gas bombs fell on the ship.

The resistance ceased quickly. It was the end. Although the press had been authorized to enter the barbed wire enclosure, I left the port. I had seen enough.

The soldiers had only been following orders, but they were not very proud of themselves. Apparently the officers did not feel much better. As for me, I was ashamed. I was ashamed to have stayed there like a stranger, an indifferent spectator, without making a move, while those of my race were fighting to become human beings again.

The following Friday was a day of mourning for the whole country: we had just learned that the Supreme Court, made up of British judges, had upheld the deportation order.

The consequences were not long in coming. The next night a police station was attacked in Jerusalem. For 45 minutes the city was a battlefield. In the darkness, soldiers and policemen fired at random.

On Monday, December 3rd, a jeep carrying four soldiers blew up. Two more met the same fate in the days that followed. The score: one dead, two wounded. Finally, a truck loaded with explosives was run into a military camp; the blast killed two and wounded 30.

These senseless acts, these blind murders revolted the whole Jewish population and, politically, they were a grave error. In spite of the indignation I had felt at the incidents at Haifa, I could only approve without reservation the words which came to us from Basle where four hundred delegates representing the Jewish communities of nations had met for the first Zionist Congress since the war. They were an unequivocal condemnation of the campaign of violence which debased the struggle of the Jewish people for the liberation of Israel. But, also at Basle, David Ben Gurion took the floor to resolutely demand the independence of the State of Israel: "We are not beggars asking for charity. We are reclaiming that which is our due."

Meanwhile, a small liner hit a reef and sank off the coast of Syrina with 800 immigrants destined for Palestine aboard. All succeeded in reaching the nearest island but then found themselves in dire need of food and medicine. The R.A.F. and the British Navy answered their call immediately. At the Ekron military airfield, near Tel-Aviv, men of the R.A.F. and the much hated 6th Airborne Division worked all night loading three planes with supplies. The grudges of the day before were forgotten. At four in the morning the planes took off. Braving death in adverse weather conditions and poor visibility, the pilots located the island in the midst of an archipelago of a hundred little reefs difficult to distinguish one from another. Flying at low altitudes, they finally found the refugees in a valley hidden among the arid hills. Six tons of provisions were promptly parachuted into the valley. Three days later a British ship came to pick up the castaways.

His Majesty's Government ordered the ship to proceed to Cyprus. But when it reached the port of Cyprus, the immigrants refused to get off and, once again, tear gas had to be used.

Pity and politics decidedly make bad bedfellows.

The holidays at the end of the year brought an ephemeral truce, but the people were profoundly demoralized. The British Government seemed incapable of adopting a constructive solution to the problems it had to face. Furthermore, the British had addressed an ultimatum to the Jewish Agency demanding, within a week, the arrest of members of terrorist organizations whom they wished to bring to justice. Did they actually imagine that the population would lower itself to this kind of informing?

Neither the draconian measures sanctioned by General Barker nor the threat of martial law produced the desired result. Men who, until then, had condemned terrorism, began to ask themselves if perhaps violence was not, after all, the only language the British understood. What was the meaning of the perpetual temporizing, of the measures they were threatened with? Did Mr. Bevin think that by means of ruthless repression one could impose on a broken people a solution that would satisfy the Arabs?

The British Foreign Secretary proposed a plan that was rejected by both the Jews and the Arabs. It involved a sort of compromise for a period of five years, after which Palestine would become an independent state. The entry of a total of one hundred thousand refugees would be authorized. The country would be divided into cantons, but only districts with a Jewish majority at the time of the proposition would be considered Jewish territory. And what would happen after that? Partition of the country or a Judeo-Arab war? Mr. Bevin's reply was: Final arbitration by the United Nations.

Finally, on February 26, 1947, Mr. Bevin conceded defeat and advised his government to place the problem of Palestine before the United Nations at once. In his speech to the House of Commons he expressed his unreserved opposition to the principle of a Jewish Homeland.

A few days later, as a ship transporting fourteen hundred refugees went aground near Haifa, a wave of terror swept through the country. It accounted for twenty dead and thirty wounded. A declaration of martial law ensued. Operation Hippo was under way.

The regions falling under martial law were subsequently completely cut off from the rest of the world. All communications were paralyzed. The mails, telegraph and telephone services ceased functioning. Food was brought in by military convoy and a strict curfew was imposed.

Tel-Aviv seemed like an abandoned city. Every vehicle was searched by patrols and the jittery soldiers were trigger happy. Even for a journalist armed with a curfew pass it was dangerous to circulate in the streets.

In London, Mr. Churchill, shouting angrily, asked the House of Commons how much longer this disgraceful state of affairs would continue before a decision was made.

The state of siege, which had gone into effect the beginning of March, stretched into two weeks. Then the British had to admit to the fact that the siege was an unexpected windfall for the Irgun and the Sternists: in the deserted streets British soldiers made easy targets.

As all Jews wondered what the next turn of events would be, Great Britain was preparing her report for the extraordinary session of the United Nations which was to open during the summer of 1947. But how could one believe in a rapid solution when Great Britain declared that she would not consider herself bound by the decision of the United Nations? Mr. Bevin's true intentions were becoming clearer and clearer. Not only did he not have any intention of abandoning the British Mandate over Palestine, but he hoped on the contrary to have it ratified by the Assembly of the

United Nations. He was counting on the fact that no other nation wanted to be on bad terms with the Arabs, or more precisely with the oil of the Middle East. He also felt that no other people wanted to take up the "burden" of liquidating the Jews in Palestine. Great Britain, he thought, would have a free hand in the long run.

As a prelude to the session of the United Nations, 27,000 new refugees were deported and four young Jews, members of the Irgun, were hanged in utter secrecy in Acre Prison; two others committed suicide before they could be executed.

Did the British Government decide to prove its resolution and determination or deepen the impression that the Palestine problem was "unworkable" by aggravating the situation? The hangings were a senseless act for who knew better than the British that it would not deter a single Jew in Palestine from action. If Mr. Bevin was asking for violence, violence of every description he got. And the security measures brought the development and reconstruction of the country to a standstill.

3

To the Rescue!

THE STORIES going around at the time about the drama of the Jewish immigration could not but fire the imagination of any young Jew, whatever his nationality.

Numerous Jewish pilots and technicians of the American Air Force asked themselves why only use ships for this purpose. The subject was the topic of passionate discussions among the members of the Zionist Movement in Los Angeles, and the most ardent defenders of an air route were Leo Gardner and Sam Lewis.

Leo Gardner was the son of a Los Angeles rabbi and had been raised to respect the old traditions, but he had always be interested in aviation and, during World War II, had first served as a flight instructor for primary flying, then as a pilot in the American Air Force.

Sam Lewis had also grown up in a religious family and, also from a very young age, had dreamed of being a pilot. All the money he was given or earned he spent on flying lessons. Then the war gave him his chance to realize his dream of braving the skies at no cost at all.

When the peace was signed, Leo became an expert on precious stones, while Sam went to work for a transcontinental airline.

Leo and Sam had been friends since childhood. They had never lost track of each other, and the possibility of using planes to transport Jewish immigrants to Palestine had been for some time their principal topic of conversation.

Having perfected a plan for air transportation, Sam and Leo decided to submit it to the Jewish Agency in New York. Their idea was favorably received, and the Agency proposed to Sam that they be put in touch with a man who shared their ideas. This interview turned out to be a pleasant surprise for Sam: his interviewer was one of his old flying companions, Al Schwimmer, currently working in the aircraft industry. During the war he had served in the U.S. Transport Command. His bravery had been cited several times. He did not like to evoke his war memories although he had to his credit some quite remarkable exploits.

Until 1947, Al had never been concerned with the Jewish problem in Palestine. But, that year, he made several trips to Europe for T.W.A., and there came into contact with Jews who had been freed from the concentration camps. In talking with them, he learned of their dream: to immigrate to Palestine. He also became aware of problems he had never known existed. Like many other young Americans, Jewish or not, hopelessly in love with liberty, he could not comprehend Great Britain's policy in Palestine. And, he knew perfectly well, men like himself could be of inestimable service to the Jewish cause.

Full of enthusiasm, he presented himself one day to the offices of the Jewish Agency in New York. There he revealed his intention of creating a system of clandestine immigration by air. His proposal was revolutionary, for the transporting of immigrants, clandestine or not, had always been effected by boat. Al's declarations were carefully recorded and verified. It was a known fact that numerous British spies had tried to infiltrate the clandestine immigration organizations; confidence must rest on absolute certainty. After his meeting with Sam, they were asked to draw up a specific plan of their project, including all the technical and financial details.

Leo and Sam saw their dream taking shape. They met frequently at the latter's apartment. Sustained by cups of coffee served by Jean, Sam's wife, they stayed up late into the night pouring over maps which covered the rug of the spacious living room. Little by little, their project gained weight, density, reality.

For his part, Al, with the help of two of his old flying companions, Ray Salk and William Sosnov, tackled a particular aspect of the project: the purchase and reconditioning of scrapped transport planes.

They knew that the Government of the United States was selling off its gigantic stock of war materiel at prices that could not be beaten: from one to two per cent of the real value. Thus a Curtis C-46 Commando sold for $5,000, a Constellation for $15,000. Of course, these planes could not be put back into service until they had spent a long time in a repair shop. For an overhaul of this nature there were two possibilities: to either approach a firm like Lockheed which could take over the overhaul of old machines, or to set up a repair shop. The last solution was more complicated, but without a doubt more economical. Al and his friends adopted it, convinced that they would succeed.

In the meantime, the UN Commission left Palestine. It must be noted here that, during their session in the summer of 1947, the UN had appointed a commission charged with finding a resolution of the problem of Palestine. It had stayed for a month and a half in Palestine, and was returning to submit its report to the Assembly. By majority vote, the Commission had decided that the only solution to the problem lay in the partition of the country. But their decision had yet to be put to a vote in the UN.

The leaders of the Haganah could hardly fail to grasp the meaning of a declaration made at the time by the British delegate. This honorable gentleman pointed out that Great Britain could not shoulder the responsibility of enforcing the partition. So the Haganah was obliged to get ready for a showdown with the Arabs.

For some time, a group of young members of the Haganah, former pilots in the Allied Forces, had urged the leaders of that organization to create an air force without further delay and sought funds for the purchase of airplanes. Their plans, to tell the truth, met with little favor from these men, who were all getting on in years and were suspicious of new ideas. However, after a number of secret meetings and urgent petitions, the question was submitted to David Ben-Gurion, who gave his approval to the project. A new section of the Haganah—Israel's future Air Force—had been born. This took place in October 1947.

The decisions had been made, and approved, yet everything still remained to be done. The only planes at Haganah's disposal at that point were the few training planes belonging to the Palestine Aero-Club and some small private planes. These might be used for observation, but that would be the extent of their usefulness.

At the same time the Haganah was sending one of its men, Yehuda Arazi, to the United States on a mission to obtain arms.

During his overseas stay, Yehuda heard about Al Schwimmer's project, which naturally interested him highly; a fleet of planes would offer tremendous possibilities in transporting arms. He asked for and obtained an interview with Al.

The two men met at the Empire Hotel. Al, suspicious, studied his new acquaintance carefully. Since it was very hot in the room, Yehuda had taken off his jacket and Al noticed

MI spenders. This displeased

old saying that you should

belt and suspenders at the

took effect, and Al relaxed.

se infinite possibilities filled

ganah with enthusiasm.

the necessary funds and,

good his promise.

64's and three Constellations.

required a complete overhaul

ns. A new organization took

nd other specialists. A base of

operations was established Burbank, California, and the organization took the name of The Schwimmer Aviation Company.

The maintenance base set up, the first task was to fly the acquired aircraft to Burbank. The C-46's were located at Ontario, California and the Constellations at the same Lockheed Terminal. The C-46's had been grounded for months without being maintained and to fly them over in their existing condition was rather a risky job. But then the entire game upon which Al, Leo and Sam embarked spelt danger every inch of the way. The harshness with which the British handled illegal immigration did not encourage hope that they would hesitate to fire at an airplane carrying these very same immigrants. There was no time to waste in preparing the aircraft at Ontario for a flight according to safety requirements and Leo and Sam, helped by Bill Gerson, U.S.A.F. Reserve Major, Harold F. B., retired U.S. Marine Air Force Colonel, and Al Auerbach, Lt. Commander U.S. Air Force, ferried the C-46's, wheels down to Lockheed Terminal. The Constellations did not present such a problem since they were simply towed.

The B-6 area seethed with work under the sunny Southern

California skies. A fifteen feet blast fence, which blocked the air blast caused by aircraft propellors when the engines were being run and ground tested, protected the area from the prying eyes of the curious. A small wooden shack was dragged over and placed at the very end of the blast fence, forming the anchor point and office. The men worked hard, yet morale was high and a good joke or story was always provided by Willy, who helped ease many entanglements with his highly developed sense of humor.

Simultaneously, Leo and Sam, were kept busy flight testing and retraining the pilots. The recruiting of air crews was no simple matter. The Jewish veterans of World War II had by now gone into business, married, had children and carried obligations which could not easily be shaken off. Nevertheless, a number of them answered the appeal.

An additional task and problem to solve was the training of thirty young Jewish volunteers from Palestine who were currently studying in the United States.

A young Jewish girl, Eleanor Rudnick, daughter of one of the richest meat cattle breeders in California, had a private airport south of Los Angeles: several Stearman-type airplanes were regularly used for a crop-dusting and spraying business. When approached by the organization, Eleanor Rudnick agreed to make these planes available to the training crews. Furthermore, using her personal influence with wealthy families of the Jewish community, she was able to find lodging for the future pilots of the Israeli Air Force.

The Schwimmer Aviation Company now had a most urgent need for a legitimate front in order to carry out its transport operations. A certain Irvin Shindler, nicknamed Swifty, who directed a small private airline in New York called Service Airways, Inc., came to mind. Swifty agreed to join the plot. The organization duly bought up his company. To give the enterprise the appearance of carrying on its normal activities several old employees of Service Airways Inc. were retained and were kept occupied with preliminary negotiations for commercial freight and passenger contracts.

All the activities of the organization were, of course, under the direct control of a branch of the Haganah in New York and under the personal direction of Yehuda Arazi.

One morning, Al Schwimmer received a telephone call from Yehuda informing him that a Jew from Honolulu, a secondhand dealer by trade, had an opportunity to get us various spare parts for aircraft engines and also perhaps arms. ARMS! It was a very touchy subject. The men had volunteered to fly immigrants but not to smuggle arms. The FBI discovery of a Haganah TNT shipment in New York Harbor put a real scare into everybody.

Yehuda's phone call was an order. Al called in his friends for consultation. First they required our arms expert and then they needed somebody not directly connected with the Schwimmer Organization in order not to jeopardize the whole project if things went wrong. Somebody suggested Hank Greenspun. An ex-Major of the 8th Army, Hank surely knew something about arms. Leo and friends hopped into a twin-engine Cessna and flew over to Las Vegas, where they landed at mid-day. Although on that very night Hank was scheduled to start the operation of a radio station into which he had put much effort over a long period and quite a lot of money, he did not hesitate to drop everything and join up. He told his surprised wife that he was leaving immediately.

Hank went directly to Honolulu where he was joined by Willie. Some days later Al received word from them that four-hundred 0.50 caliber aerial machine guns with large quantities of spare parts, packed as aircraft engines and forty-five spare engines had left Honolulu and could be expected in Los Angeles soon.

Since there is no customs between Hawaii and continental

America, it was easy, when the cargo was unloaded, to divert it to an abandoned dockyard where the crates were swiftly emptied of their contents and then burned. The arms were dispatched to various warehouses whose owners were sympathetic to the Zionist cause; the forty-five engines were moved to Burbank.

Two days later, agents from the FBI raided the air base at Burbank—they had been ordered to check our shipments: they had received information from Honolulu about the actual contents of a certain cargo destined for the United States. Al Schwimmer answered all their questions with the utmost calm. The FBI agents searched the premises and then left, not having found anything suspicious but, actually, not fooled either. They had come too late, but knew perfectly well that there was a link between the machine guns and Schwimmer Aviation Company which became, by the way, the object of an intensive investigation.

It became obvious that operations originating from an American base would in the future be doomed to failure. However, an airport in Panama had already attracted our attention. Tocumen—that was its name—had cost the Panamanian Government nine million dollars but Panama did not own any airplanes and foreign airlines, wary of the legendary political upheavals of that country, preferred to use All Brook airport, located in the American zone. For some time the Panamian Government had been looking around the United States for an aviation company in a position to take an interest in Tocumen and use it. It had actually just signed a contract along those lines with a certain Harvey B. Harvey, a friend of Swifty's. It was just the thing. The Panamanian Government was presented with a plan of an international operation of two-engine and four-engine airplanes, to which it promptly agreed. The new company was called *Lineas Aereas de Panama* (LAPSA) bearing registration numbers RX.

The three companies—Schwimmer Aviation, Service Airways and LAPSA—enabled the hiring of personnel without FBI interference, and the transfer of aircraft from American to foreign registration when needed, offering a solid operational front.

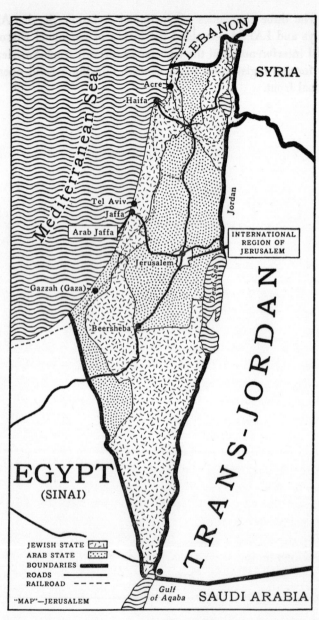

The partition plan presented in the United Nations Resolution
of November, 1947

4

The Arab Peril

EVER SINCE the United Nations decision of November 29, 1947, calling for the partition of Palestine had been broadcast throughout that country, the Arab attacks against the Jews had multiplied.

"Since the Jews have bought the United Nations for dollars," the Arabs preached, "it is the sacred duty of the Arabs to plunge the Middle East into a sea of blood."

The British authorities had previously appointed Amin el-Husseini to be the Mufti of Jerusalem, that is to say the final arbiter of all important questions concerning the Muslim religion in Palestine. He had been for some time the real leader of the Arabs in the Middle East. A fierce opponent of the Balfour Declaration, the Mufti rapidly changed from merely refusing to cooperate with the Jews, to active hostility, becoming the high priest of Arab antisemitism. Liberal Arabs who favored cooperation became the victims of brutal repressions; Husseini did not hesitate to use the weapons of terror against his own people.

Between 1920 and 1939 the Jews had had to suffer many attacks from the Mufti's organized bands. At the outbreak of World War II, Amin el-Husseini and his friends found in Hitler a willing ally. They stepped up propagating the hatred of the Jew so attuned to Nazi doctrine throughout the Middle East. Their dream was to solve the Jewish problem in Palestine and the Arab nations as Hitler meant to solve it in the Axis countries. To convince the Arab masses, he spread the legend that Hitler had been converted to Islam!

The defeat of Hitler should have also been the defeat of the Mufti, but it was nothing of the sort since the dream he embodied still lived—to exterminate the Jews. Husseini had under his command thousands of Arabs armed either by the British or by neighboring Arab nations. He benefitted from the support of Egypt, Transjordan, Syria, Iraq and Lebanon, who had undertaken to supply him with arms, money and men. The Arab troops were trained by former Nazi prisoners-of-war who preferred not to return to Germany.

Everyone the Arab countries had in the way of fighting men, assured that the war against the Jews would be a picnic, rallied en masse to the call of the Mufti. Dressed in English uniforms, European clothes, or their traditional long robes, they went into battle in their headdress, the "kefiya," a white or colored veil knotted with a black cord around their heads. On the whole, they were an undisciplined force, certainly galvanized by the Mufti's call, but above all lured by the prospect of looting. They were almost always accompanied by their wives who were "armed" with numbers of sacks; operation looting followed close on the heels of any favorable tide of battle.

From then on, on the craggy hills of Galilee; among the sparse olive trees; across the pastures below where shepherds played old folk tunes on their flutes; in the valley of Jezreel, that drained swamp where wheat now grew in profusion; in the valley of Jordan where palm and banana trees stood together by the Sea of Galilee perfumed with laurel; along the Mediterranean coast as on the shores of the Dead Sea; in the awesome Negev Desert where the farming settlements formed little islands of green in a sea of sand and rock; everywhere, throughout all of Palestine, one cry echoed: "Death to the Jews!"

In the very land where their only thought was to rebuild their home, the Jews thus heard the same death cry which had followed them across Europe and had just been silenced there, and after what slaughter!

It began on the 30th of November, 1947; an Israeli bus was ambushed that day and several Jews were killed. On December 2nd Arab mobs attacked the old Jewish Quarter in Jerusalem and looted and burned Jewish property without intervention on the part of the British Police.

In the Negev, the young Jews who tended the irrigation ditches had become friendly with the Arab inhabitants of the nearby village. On the 10th of December, this excess of confidence cost them their lives.

On December 11th, ten men of the Haganah were killed on their way to a settlement near Jerusalem. A few days later, soldiers of the British-commanded Arab Legion attacked motorists on a highway and killed fourteen young boys. On the 16th, the passengers of a truck were assaulted near a military camp occupied by the British, who refused to give aid to the wounded.

All over the country, villages and settlements were sacked and looted. Even without reckoning the loss in human lives, these devastations were a terrible ordeal for us; the villages and settlements, which had cost us so many sacrifices, were our great source of pride.

All of ancient Jewish civilization has its roots in the land; our holidays, our laws and our poetry drew their inspiration from the labor of the fields. Coming back from the ends of the earth where the great dispersal had taken us, our dearest thought had been to seek a new expression of the old agricultural civilization of the Jewish people. Many forms of planting and cultivating had been put into practice by the men of our villages in a passionate search for better ways to a new happiness. Some had decided to realize their dream of socialism, making everything communal property in the attempt to reclaim the now sterile land. So it was in the *kibbutzim*. The land belonged to the community; each person had his own room but shared the dining room and living room with his comrades. The profits from manufacturing as well as from the land were held in common. A nursery took care of all the children, and a collective kitchen prepared all the meals. But alongside the *kibbutzim*, the *mochavs*, villages where the community was limited to mutual cooperation among small landowners, struggled and prospered as well, with the men maintaining independent family lives. Since in the *"mochavs,"* sometimes the farm work and all the buying and selling were done collectively, one saw the development of a formula that was a compromise between the *kibbutzim* and the holding of private property.

The peasants of Israel were not warriors. Their only desire was to live in peace on their land. But, as soon as they felt their safety threatened, they took up arms.

The situation, from a military point of view, was not favorable to us. Our settlements were scattered all over the country, usually far from each other and often strategically surrounded by Arab villages. They made so many easy targets for attacks by the Mufti's forces. The fighting, moreover, cut off all communication with the cities. Soon, help could only be sent to them by air.

The few aircraft we had at our disposal were assigned to transport supplies and arms. They also took care of evacuating the wounded. But our machines were based at two airfields controlled by the British; before carrying equipment to its destination we first had to smuggle it onto the field. Besides that, we ran the risk of seeing our planes sabotaged by the Arabs without the British lifting a finger to stop them. To be in a better position to defend our planes, we decided to concentrate them at the Tel-Aviv airfield, also occupied by a British transport unit. In order to do this we had to obtain the authorization of the British Department of Civil Aviation. After some maneuvering, we obtained it.

An inspection of the landing strip revealed that some work needed to be done. We mobilized a team of workmen on the spot, even though it was the Sabbath. Time was short. The British soldiers at first stared in amazement at these Jews furiously working on the Lord's Day, and then they came and helped us! In one morning the job was finished, and we were able to land our planes the next day.

The first light "squadron" of the Haganah's Air Service—for the moment the entire Air Service—had been created. The boys decided to rule the squadron by democratic election of a squadron leader once a month, but the H.Q. of Air Service did not like the idea and a commanding officer was appointed.

The Quest for Airplanes

THE TASK imposed on our planes was heavy, far too heavy; calls for help came in from all over, and it was impossible to answer them with the slight resources at our disposal. At all costs and with the utmost urgency, we had to find more planes.

At first, we had the idea of approaching the merchants who dealt in British surplus, clothes as well as scrap metal and parts from dismantled airplanes. Fortunately, they were on the best of terms with the British officers and, with money, thought they could get whatever they wanted. However, when it came to aviation equipment, their contacts netted nothing at all.

The general staff of the Air Service then decided to enter into direct negotiations with units of the R.A.F. under the cover name Aviron Company, an airline created by the Jewish Agency.

One of our men, Alex Zielony, himself a former officer in the R.A.F., went to Ekron airfield, a British base located 38 miles south of Tel-Aviv, where he learned that soon several "Austers," light communications planes, were to be put up for auction. He was granted permission to examine the machines and, the minute he saw them in their hangar, realized that they exactly suited the immediate needs of our Air Service, even though they were in bad condition.

When public notice of auction was made, the Aviron Company was invited to participate in the bidding. The terms of sale required filing certain official documents plus a financial guaranty on a specific date in Jerusalem. Unfortunately, the road to Jerusalem had been cut off by the Mufti's forces—burnt cars and dead bodies were painful evidence of Jewish attempts to break through. The Jewish population of Jerusalem was in dire distress—there was no food or water; no telephone connection could be relied upon since the telephone exchange was operated by Arabs and all conversations were tapped. There was only one way to reach the city—to run the road in an armored car. Alex agreed to give it a try and, to the utter amazement of the British, at the appointed hour placed the necessary documents on the desk of the officer-in-charge in Jerusalem, who received him warmly. During their conversation, Alex remarked that in view of the rather deplorable condition of the planes being auctioned there hardly could be offers other than that of the Aviron Company, and so why not conclude the matter without further delay?

Taking Alex at his word, the officer asked him to make an offer then and there. Alex mentioned a figure. The officer demanded more. Alex knew that the important thing was to settle the question even if it meant spending a few thousand pounds too many. But on the other hand he did not want to reveal how anxious we really were to get these planes. He therefore proposed to the officer that they halve the difference. The Britisher accepted, on the condition that the entire sum be paid that very day, within the space of two hours, since it was noon and the offices closed at 2:00! To get together £14,000 in that short a time represented, at that period in Jerusalem, a veritable *tour de force*. But with the help of the Jewish Agency, it was done and, at 1:50 Alex appeared at the major's office with the required amount. When half an hour later Alex left the Major's office with sale documents properly signed, the Major remarked: "Say, how is Aviron going to transport the aircraft out of Ekron."

Shipping the planes presented a difficult problem indeed. A convoy of trucks on the road between Ekron and Tel-Aviv would surely attract the attention of units of the Arab Legion which would certainly reserve their special brand of welcome for them when they returned loaded with airplanes. It was necessary, all the same, to attempt the operation. Members of the Haganah were duly mobilized and twenty trucks accompanied by an armed guard left for Ekron to load the machines. Our men had orders to finish the job in twenty-four hours and to fight if necessary.

The convoy carrying the planes left Ekron at dawn without running into any trouble. A little later, an order came from Jerusalem to the officer commanding the base; the sale had been canceled and the trucks must be unloaded immediately. But it was too late; the trucks, and the planes, were already far away.

At Tel-Aviv, the sub-assemblies of the Austers were hidden in the cellars of Sarona, the old general quarter of the police. Re-assembling them proved to be child's play for our specialists.

The acquisition of the Austers was an unexpected stroke of luck, but we soon realized that, short of having real combat planes, we could never create an effective military force. Our men were therefore sent all over the world to seek out planes and pilots.

Freddie, another ex-pilot and colonel in the R.A.F., first tried his luck in England. He hoped that his old comrades would come to our aid. But he was wrong. The general atmosphere was hostile to us, and the embargo regulations imposed by the British government made export almost impossible. It was a great shame, for one could find on the British aeronautical market whatever one wanted, from light training planes to heavy bombers. But Freddie did not give up. First a bona fide company had to be found which had the right to use all types of planes commercially. There was no shortage of either pilots or mechanics, British Jews, ex-members of the R.A.F., and even non-Jewish volunteers. Freddie formed a small nucleus of men. A few training planes and four light bombers, not very modern, were bought. But how to get them out of England? Our fellow conspirators, who were amateurs at this dangerous game, soon attracted the attention of the British Security Service, who could do nothing, however, since no illegal action had as yet been attempted. Our men were quick to realize that they were being watched, and we began a game of "cat and mouse." The first thing our men did was to divide themselves into two groups, one for the training planes, the other for the bombers. The planes themselves were dispatched to two separate airports. It was a simple plan, almost naive. The group working with the training planes was ostensibly supposed to be readying them for a flight to Europe. Those assigned to the bombers were to do the least possible amount of work on them so as not to attract the attention of the authorities.

The plan succeeded. While the attention of the Security Service was focused on the training planes, the bombers, purchased by an air transport company from the Far East, took off as legally as you please en route to Singapore.

Unfortunately, Freddie did not have much luck from then on. At Nice, one plane had to be abandoned after a forced landing. At Brindisi there were mechanical difficulties causing a delay of several days. The take-off for the island of

Rhodes went smoothly but, upon landing at Rhodes, a surprise—Greek soldiers, fully armed, surrounded the planes and all our men were arrested. They were accused of being Communists. It was a serious accusation at that time when Greece was in the throes of a civil war.

The coup had been well staged by agents of the British Secret Service. Our men, overconfident, had mistakenly thought they were out of danger when the coast of England disappeared over the horizon. Their itinerary had been folowed, however, and the few days' holdover at Brindisi had given the British time to learn the truth. Unable to act in Italy, they had notified the Greeks that a group of international Communists was on its way and that its planes were destined for the guerrillas. So our men were arrested and the planes seized. The make-up of the crews seemed to confirm the accusations; English, Palestinians—en route to Singapore—all this seemed suspect.

The men were subjected to interrogation but the Greeks could not make up their minds whether they were genuine Communists or not. They called upon the British Military Mission for help and a British Military Police Colonel arrived. During the conversation with the "prisoners," the colonel thought the name of one of them sounded familiar. It was Dan Tolkowski, until recently the Commanding Officer of the Israel Air Force. The Colonel knew Tel-Aviv and Dan's parents quite well. Their son could not be a Communist. Next morning Dan was called in by the Greeks and told that he was free. Inquiring about the fate of the others, he was told that they were still under suspicion. But after a few days all men were released, but the planes remained confiscated.

Freddie's second attempt, this time in Europe, had more success. The American Air Force in Germany had released fifty Norseman transport planes which were to be sold by the American Government. These single-engine planes, capable of carrying a ton of freight, were not interesting for an air transport company, but suited us perfectly for carrying supplies and ammunition to our settlements. Unfortunately, it was evident that the Americans would not agree to sell us these planes. Our search for an acceptable buyer led to Spain, where a fictitious airline was created, and twenty Norsemen were able to be purchased. With the complicity of the French authorities, some of these planes received permission to land at French airfields from where our volunteers, arriving from America, England and South Africa, were to fly them to Palestine. The other planes were distributed throughout various Dutch and Italian airports. By the end of the war for independence, seventeen Norsemen had reached Israel. Each of their pilots could by then recount a veritable odyssey of adventures.

South Africa seemed to offer an opportunity for more immediate success. Hundreds of Jewish volunteers there were pestering the representatives of the Haganah. They wanted to leave immediately for Palestine, leaving behind their homes and the lives they had made for themselves. Nothing one could tell them about the difficult life that lay ahead served to discourage them. One of the most accomplished was an ex-Lieutenant in the South African Air Force, Boris Senior. The son of a wealthy family, he had been one of the first South African pilots to volunteer for Palestine. He soon took on a single task, sending us every airplane he could get his hands on. An attempt to send about twenty fighter planes by sea having failed, he decided to fly a Bonanza commercial plane from Johannesburg to Tel-Aviv himself. Another pilot, Cyril Katz, offered to accompany him in another Bonanza. The British Security agents suspected something was afoot, but were unable to take action. For their part, the South African authorities could hardly oppose the whim of two young men who proposed to tour Europe by air.

And so, one fine morning, the two Bonanzas took off from Johannesburg. Their flight plan was a daring one; they not only had to fly over all of black Africa, but also would have to land at two Egyptian airports.

The Johannesburg-Pietersburg flight took place without incident. But during the flight to Lousaka, in Rhodesia, Boris lost sight of his companion. Hours went by, and still Cyril's plane did not appear. It became obvious that something had happened to him. Boris, despairing of his fate, was going to alert the authorities when the commandant of the airfield transmitted a message to him from an outpost of the Bush Police near Zambezi who reported that Cyril had had to make a forced landing. Without wasting a moment, Boris hired the services of a mechanic and went in search of his friend. "I never flew so low in my life," Boris recounted. "The view we had of the Bush and the wild animals was splendid. . . ." All at once they spotted the plane sitting in a field and Cyril, surrounded by natives, gesticulating frantically. Boris made a landing. Cyril's plane was beyond repair. There was nothing to do but leave it in the Bush and go in search of trucks to carry it. But, in taking off, Boris' Bonanza also was crippled, and the two men had to walk nine miles on foot, find shelter in a police outpost, and ultimately return to Johannesburg.

Boris, however, did not give up the cause. A few weeks later a new Bonanza was bought and, one day, Boris landed at Luxor, in Egypt! There he was received by the local authorities with all the honors due a rich and eccentric tourist. Then he took off, pretending to be headed for Beirut. He landed, of course, in Israel, in a settlement in the Negev.

It was not so simple, however, to then convince our soldiers in the Negev that he was a Jewish volunteer, and not an Englishman in the service of the Egyptians.

```
WWW
6
/\/\/\/\
```

The First Successes

DURING THIS TIME, in Palestine, the situation was getting worse from day to day. From the north, from the south, from the east, from the hills around Jerusalem, the Arabs were attacking. Units of the Arab Army of Liberation, under the command of Fawzi el-Kawoukji, were preparing to cross the Syrian frontier. This adventurer, a self-styled general, began his military career under Lawrence, leader of the Arab Revolt of 1915–1918. An officer in the army of Faycal of Iraq, a mercenary in the special Eastern forces in the service of the French, military chief of the Syrian Revolution and of the Revolt of the Druzes against the French, Kawoukji had allied himself with the Mufti of Jerusalem since 1929. The command of the Army of Liberation had been offered him in return for his services in the "Holy Wars" against the Jews. In Syria and Lebanon, the newspapers gave enthusiastic backing to the troops which had been organized and equipped by the governments of those countries, and held themselves in readiness for an invasion of Palestine.

All our hopes of seeing the Arabs turn away from the Mufti had vanished. All those Arab "friends" who, only a few months earlier, had done business with the Jews of our villages, even those who had been patients of Jewish doctors, as well as Arab workmen who were members of unions founded by Jews, all of them, almost without exception, had turned against us. They were not motivated by fanaticism; many of them acted from fear of their fellow believers and some of them from cupidity.

Only the 21,500 Druzes of Israel and one Bedouin tribe refused to follow the Arabs. The Druzes lived in about twenty villages in Galilee and Carmel. They had broken away from Islam in the 11th century. Establishing a separate community, they had chosen to build their future with us, counting, quite rightly, on the fact that in an independent Israel they would be free citizens and would enjoy the rights which Muslim domination had denied them. Their attitude was a consolation to us, but of little import.

In order to survive, it was imperative that we have arms.

We had placed a great deal of hope in support from the United States, but that hope was soon dashed. The United States decided to place an embargo on all arms destined for Palestine. Agents of the FBI were assigned to watch seaports and airfields. At the same time the British were at liberty to supply the Arab states with all the arms they pleased.

There were several explanations for the attitude of the United States toward us, the principal one being that American diplomats and agents of special services were under the influence of their English colleagues. And these, it seems, still lived in the wake of T. E. Lawrence's ideas, haunted by the dream of building an Arab Empire which would be under the domination of Great Britain. The Americans had been led to believe that the Jewish community was living out its last days and that aid uselessly offered to the Jews would mean the definitive loss to the West of the oil resources of the Middle East.

The measures taken by the FBI proved to be relatively effective, but rather less so than one might have thought. Our men were a very determined lot. Among them numbered Jews, of course, but also non-Jews, often veterans of the last war, and sometimes young boys whom recent events had won over to our side.

The brains, the moving force behind the Haganah in the United States was now more than ever Yehuda Arazi.

At first glance, it seemed hard to imagine that so much lay behind that smiling exterior. Always impeccably dressed, fluent in several languages, Yehuda, with his mane of white hair, resembled a European intellectual of great distinction far more than the head of an organization dealing in contraband arms. But when he gave an order, enforcing it with his piercing look, no one seemed to be inclined to question it.

Born in Poland to a lower middle class family, he was still a very young boy when he came to Israel. He dedicated himself body and soul to serving the Haganah.

He was not an expert in armament, but he knew its value in a country where the life of every man was constantly threatened. A person of prodigious intelligence and imagination, he had, besides, the ability to use his talents consciously. Deeply sincere and honorable, he was able to win the respect not only of his friends but also of the arms merchants with whom he was dealing, not one of whom ever took advantage of him. He lived long enough to see victory for Israel and, at his death recently, thousands of people came to pay tribute to his memory.

It fell to him to outwit the FBI. To him and to his men, many of whom had left lucrative and comfortable positions to place themselves under his command.

However, not even Yehuda's fertile imagination could foresee that, in our hour of need, help would come not from the United States, but from Czechoslovakia. That is, nevertheless, what happened.

Among the many sympathizers who had rallied to the

Jewish cause, Masaryk and Benes had been the most loyal. Before 1939, at a time when anti-Semitism was rampant throughout central Europe, Czechoslovakia had remained a haven where the words liberty and democracy still had some meaning.

I will never forget my first stay in Prague, in December of 1936. It had snowed the night before. The quays along the River Vltava, the narrow streets lined with ancient houses, all evoked illustrations of the Middle Ages and one almost expected that at any moment one of the countless alchemists who had walked these streets might rise up out of the past. In the old Jewish cemetery I spent many hours deciphering the inscriptions, half-eroded by time, and the guard informed me that in 1254 a decree of King Ottokar II had accorded the Jews full legal status, made the desecration of a Jewish grave punishable by death, and allowed the Jews to bear arms to defend themselves when necessary. After wandering through the streets all day, I found myself in the evening in a little café where the dancing went on until dawn. Many Jews made it a habit to go there. Nobody bothered them, nobody asked them questions. What a difference from the oppressive atmosphere that reigned over all the other cities in Central Europe!

Perhaps we had these images in mind when, two years later, abandoned by everybody, we decided to seek help from the Czechoslovakians.

When questioned as to our chances of success, Dr. Otto Felix Doron, a Czechoslovakian Jew residing in Palestine, answered: "The Communist Party perhaps might help us, Masaryk probably not."

During that period, in effect, the Communist Party saw in the Jewish community of Palestine a progressive force opposed to the colonial policies of the British in the Middle East. Masaryk, on the other hand, was fighting against the growing power of the Communists and leaning towards the Anglo-American Bloc. It was therefore logical to suppose that he would not dare to openly oppose the policies of the West. Also, if the Czechoslovakian Communist Party decided to come to our aid and was willing to take the first steps, perhaps the liberal and democratic elements of that country would rise above their fear of antagonizing the West.

However, neither the Communists nor the Liberals dared to get involved, while at the same time considerable quantities of arms were being furnished by the Czechs to the Syrians (arms which, by the way, never reached their destination, thanks to the efforts of our sabotage networks in Italy). When we reproached them for supplying these arms to Syria, the Czechs claimed that it was a simple commercial proposition with no political overtones whatsoever.

Political contacts having failed, we decided to approach the arms manufacturers directly. After endless negotiations, we finally won them over and signed our first contract guaranteeing a shipment of machine guns, rifles and ammunition at the going price. Payment was to be made in dollars.

Subsequently, our relations with the Czechs became much more friendly. We succeeded in extracting a promise from them that in the future they would no longer send arms to Arab states, which they even publicly denounced as aggressors. Without a doubt, the neutral line the Kremlin followed with respect to us facilitated our efforts with the Czechs. Moscow observed their actions without approving or disapproving, leaving them free to act.

Once the contract had been signed, another problem arose —that of transporting the arms. Since Poland had denied us transit rights through the port of Gdynia, the only remaining solution was to send the cargo across Hungary to a Yugoslavian port. An emissary was dispatched to prepare the groundwork. The Yugoslavians were not hostile to us, and had proved it in the past by doing us several favors, but it must be admitted that the prospect of shipping a cargo of armaments from one of their ports hardly pleased them. Their relations with Moscow were fairly strained, and they were afraid the Cominform would accuse them of trafficking in arms with the West. Nevertheless, our envoy, who had many friends among the Yugoslavians in power, succeeded in convincing them to come to our aid. And they even agreed to do this without exacting money in return. Did they foresee that before long Yugoslavia would find herself alone in the world and did this bring them closer to us? It is quite probable.

Hungary having, for her part, granted a right of transit, we arranged to send the shipment down the Danube from Bratislava to Vukovar in Yugoslavia, and thence by rail to the port of Sibenik.

It was certainly a long journey. Why, one might ask, did not we use the Constellations and C-46's we had in the United States? We had considered doing that, obviously. But such a plan required above all having a base of operations in Europe. Again it was Yehuda Arazi who took charge of the problem.

Operations from Europe required landing rights and an operational base. Italy seemed to be the most suitable country for such an operation. Our airplanes needed modifications and the fitting of a passenger interior. Even LAPSA could not transport passengers in military cargoes. The large Italian aircraft industry was idle; workers were out of employment and the Italian Government viewed with favor a foreign airline offering work. Yehuda, consequently, approached a small private enterprise located in Castiglione del Lago whose owner, Mr. Angelo Ambrosini, had played a fairly important part in the aviation world under the Fascist regime. However, in spite of this, he had always hated the Nazis and had never forgiven Mussolini for his pact with

Hitler. Ambrosini was wealthy, and as aviation was still his great passion he devoted a good part of his income to building models of airplanes.

Ambrosini was quite aware of the problem of Europe's Jews. Yehuda did not try to hide the truth from him and openly admitted that our planes would not only carry men but also arms into Palestine. Ambrosini was not at all alarmed, and declared that he would place the airfield at Castiglione del Lago at our disposal.

Meanwhile, in the United States, Service Airways, with the help of LAPSA, had put together a dozen flight crews. But we had to redouble our precautions to make sure the Jewish Agency did not find itself implicated in recruiting volunteers for, coincidental with the aggravation of the conflict in Palestine, a campaign of calumny had been launched in the United States by certain pro-Arab or simply traditionally antisemitic elements who would have had it believed that the Jews were smuggling contraband war materiel for the benefit of the Russians!

Our men therefore had to carry out their assignments under the cover of the most diverse facades. In New York, for example, Steve S., former radio operator in the American Navy, worked under the cover of an organization called Land and Labor for Palestine, although land was actually the least of our worries. With the help of several Canadian war veterans, he succeeded in extending his operations to Canada. In Los Angeles, Leo Gardner, never at a loss for stratagems, had secured the complicity of a movie producer. He had even set up a recruiting center right in the middle of Beverly Hills, in the offices of the producer.

All this time, at the base in Burbank, we were still working feverishly. Our old military planes had been transformed into transport planes which met the American authorities' requirements for civil aviation. All that remained was to get them out of territorial United States.

The date of departure had been set for the month of March, 1948. A C-46 and a Constellation, piloted respectively by Leo Gardner and Sam Lewis, were going to attempt to reach Europe, and then Palestine. LAPSA applied to the State Department for an export license for Panama, and Service Airways for one for Italy.

On March 6th, at Telebord, in New Jersey, after passing customs inspection, the C-46 took off for Europe. The first stop was Goose Bay, Labrador. After having breakfast and refuelling the plane, they took off again for B.W.1 Greenland. Strange as it may seem, B.W.1 was a U.S. Army base which offered the C-46 full service. From there the flight took them to Iceland, Shannon, Ireland, and Geneva.

Al was following the progress of the flight from the New York office.

"One of your planes is reported missing somewhere between Geneva and Rome. Could you give us the names of the crew members?" The call came from a daily newspaper. Other calls soon followed: "What was the destination of the plane? Exactly what type of outfit are you running? Who was on board the plane?"

One can well imagine the veil of gloom and the feeling of disaster which descended upon Al and our men. The inquiries confirmed that the C-46 took off from Geneva for Rome but never got there. None of the Italian civil or military airports reported the airplane. None of the radio stations heard any distress signals. The C-46 just disappeared. Al was already thinking of breaking the bad news to the families but, hoping against hope, decided to wait one day more—perhaps the airplane landed in Castiglione del Lago and Leo had just forgotten to notify the authorities. In his heart he doubted this—would Leo disregard the basic laws of the civil aviation code, knowing that absence of such notification would create an outcry the world over? The suspense came to a sudden end when one of the crew members telephoned New York to reassure his father, who notified Al without delay. All was well; on March 9th, at nightfall, the plane had landed at Castiglione del Lago. But, since the airport did not have a control tower, the landing could not be reported.

A bitter disappointment lay in store for them. The airport at Castiglione proved to be impractical for planes such as C-46's and Constellations which needed much longer runways than it offered. Furthermore, the ground was not firm enough and our planes, heavy to begin with, could never have taken off with a cargo from that terrain which gave beneath their weight.

The crew therefore requested and received permission to land temporarily at Perugia. Leo would have liked to leave without further delay for Prague where the C-46 was impatiently awaited, but to do this might have permanently jeopardized the departure of the planes still grounded in the United States. In effect, if the FBI found out that a C-46 had crossed the Iron Curtain, it would most certainly have blocked the departure of the planes still remaining in California.

Therefore, the C-46 waited at Perugia.

In the meantime, the Haganah learned that a freighter carrying 6,000 guns, ammunition and explosives purchased by the Syrians in Czechoslovakia was steaming across the Adriatic towards Syria.

The crew of the C-46 received orders to bomb the ship on the high seas and sink it. It seemed simple enough, but Leo and his men well knew that in reality it would be quite a problem. They strongly doubted the effectiveness of a bomb which would have to be home-made and then thrown out of one of the C-46's portholes as though it were a simple hand grenade. The bomb had every chance in the world of missing its target; the ship would get away, but the plane flying at such a low altitude would have been easily identified and would be seized upon landing, seriously compromising operations under way in the United States.

Most of our men agreed with Leo, and were against transforming the C-46 into a makeshift bomber. Nevertheless, the plane took off and circled the Adriatic for hours. But it did not find a trace of the freighter. Our informatives soon told us that it was still in a small Yugoslavian port from which it would sail the evening of March 30th.

On the 3rd of April we located the freighter in the port of Molfetta, near Bari. It was within our range. A daring plan was worked out; it involved riveting a time bomb to the ship's hull. The bomb had been made by our men and hidden, along with an inflatable raft, under the false floor of an American truck used for our transport of illegal arms. Painted yellow, large black letters on its side announced that it belonged to a DDT exterminating service. It therefore aroused no suspicion. Our plan was simple. The truck was to carry our men to a little beach near the port and, from there, in the raft, our sabotage crew would try to get to the ship and attach the bomb which was to sink it. The risks were great: first of being surprised by an Italian patrol, and then of being spotted by the ship's crew which stood watch day and night.

Our first attempt proved to be a total failure. An English torpedo boat had entered the harbor and its searchlights constantly swept across the waters. Our raft had to turn back. Our men had gotten nowhere, but at least had learned that the raft was maneuverable enough to get quite close to the ship, close enough for our divers to be able to fix the bomb to the hull.

The next day, the torpedo boat sailed for the open seas; our men decided to try their luck the night of April 10th. The raft left the beach around 10 o'clock at night, a night so clear that one could not help expecting the worst. However, the raft got up to the ship without being discovered and our men were already far away when, several hours later, an explosion woke all the inhabitants of the little town; the freighter had sunk with its cargo.

When, a few months later, the Arabs chartered an Italian ship to salvage the precious cargo of arms sent to the bottom, our men hailed it at sea and brought the arms back to Israel. So the arms from Czechoslovakia finally reached a destination!

During this time, the Constellation piloted by Sam Lewis had left the United States. Its arrival in Panama was an event. Hundreds of Panamanians, who had not seen an airplane at Tocumen for a long time, hurried out to the airport to admire it.

The Battle for
the Highways

AFTER FOUR MONTHS of combat with the Arabs, we had not lost one of our settlements or villages. Then the Arabs changed tactics, from then on concentrating their efforts on our lines of communication; they hoped to isolate settlements or villages which they could then besiege and force to surrender. The battle of the roads began.

A single road led from Tel-Aviv to Haifa, but, as this region was in our hands, travel posed few problems. From Haifa, one road went to Galilee and another to Jerusalem. Both crossed an area where there was much danger from attack by the Arabs, who saw in the rich settlements of Galilee easy prey. It was in Galilee in 1920 that Arab bands had wiped out the Jewish settlement of Tel-Chai, whose defenders under the command of Joseph Trumfeldor, all fell in combat. Furthermore, in Galilee, our farming communities in the valleys and hillsides were open to attack not only by local bands but also by the Arab Army of Liberation across the Syrian frontier. The plight of our settlements in the Negev was even more desperate. In that region, where the majority of the population was Arab, our villages were entirely dependent on help from Tel-Aviv.

A single road also went from Tel-Aviv to Jerusalem and its neighboring settlements. This twisting road, winding through thickly wooded hills, lent itself perfectly to ambush. Very few convoys indeed succeeded in getting through without mishap. Bab el-Wad, located on the section of road where most of the attacks were launched, even became the subject of a song praising the courage and sacrifices of our men.

On Saturday, March 26th, 1948, a convoy of armored trucks attempted to run the barricade on the road from Jerusalem to bring help to Kfar Etzion, a settlement of great strategic importance besieged by the Arabs.

Two earlier attempts to rescue this village had ended in a bloody drama. On the 16th of January, twenty-five members of the Haganah had fallen into an ambush. Every last one of them had been killed and their bodies so horribly mutilated that it was impossible to identify them. Photographs of this massacre were being sold in the streets of Arab cities for the benefit of the War of Liberation. On March 4th, another group of seventeen men had had to do battle with an enemy numerically vastly superior. There again, the Arabs massacred them and left seventeen mutilated bodies along the road. We were therefore on our third attempt to get through to Kfar Etzion.

This time, the convoy reached its destination without incident, but on the return trip fell into an ambush. For a day and a night our men kept fighting. They counted seventeen dead and many wounded when British troops arrived on the scene and proposed a truce whose terms were that our men surrender their arms and trucks until they reached Jerusalem, where this equipment would be returned to them.

The Jews accepted. But as soon as the British were in

possession of our weapons they handed them over to the Arabs. Was it neutrality or betrayal?

The population had not yet recovered from the blow when a new one fell on the country. Forty-two soldiers of the Haganah were killed while transporting provisions destined for the settlement of Yshiam, in Galilee.

Towards the end of March, the settlements in the Negev region found themselves completely cut off from the rest of the country.

The Air Service did what it could but very little could be achieved with the airplanes available. Nevertheless, the drivers of the convoys breathed with relief seeing the Auster in front of them checking the road and reporting Arab ambushes. Whatever regular supplies and communications there were, were due to the Air Service.

We wanted to do much more, so to enable them to take part in the battle it was decided to arm the airplanes. At first, the pilots only had hand grenades at their disposal. Then we supplied them with bombs of wildly varying quality put together entirely by amateurs. When the first bomb of fifty kilos emerged from the workshop, the crew members eyed it with considerable anxiety. It was in the shape of an egg, fitted with a time fuse which one released by pulling a wire. "How do you drop this thing?" one of the pilots inquired. The armament engineer, who was an American, answered: "You just push it." "Push, Push . . . Pushkin," marvelled the pilot, and from then on, bombs of 125 lbs. were nicknamed "Pushkins," which seems a rather poetic term for an instrument of death. It was certainly a dangerous thing to handle, but our pilots were happy to at last have an offensive weapon, whatever it was, as long as it could serve to beat the enemy and help out their comrades.

Among the astonishing deeds of this period there is one

which deserves special mention. Somewhere in the south of the Negev a convoy had been attacked. It was reported that two men were wounded. There was no doctor in the vicinity and, since the road was under fire from the Arabs, the wounded could not be taken to a hospital. One of our pilots, Pinchas Ben Porat, received an order to fly a doctor into the settlement where the men of the attacked convoy had taken refuge. When the little plane landed in a hail of Arab bullets, one of the wounded had unfortunately just died, and the other had already left for the hospital in an armored truck. But just then a message came in reporting that the neighboring settlement of Nvatim had just been attacked.

"I asked the settlers to get me a machine gun," Pinchas recounts. "One of the boys of the village offered to be my machine gunner. I took on a load of grenades. Then I ripped off both doors of my plane to give my gunner, whom I strapped into his seat, room to maneuver. And I set up the gun so the propellers would not interfere with its action. Then we took off. A few minutes later we were flying over the Nvatim region, where the Arab bands were attacking. We opened fire, with great success; before long the enemy was in flight."

Little by little, by using ingenuity, we succeeded in building up the armament of our planes. We assembled an assortment of equipment to be adapted to the wings and fuselage for carrying and launching bombs. With a few changes, a small transport or pleasure plane could be made capable of carrying six 125 lb. bombs, four under the fuselage and two under the wings. But while our pilots lacked neither courage nor initiative, they had to make do with the most haphazard arms, and their field of action of necessity remained very limited. Furthermore, they always ran the risk of an encounter with the R.A.F. who had orders to shoot down any civilian plane caught dropping explosives. And, at that time, we were hardly prepared to engage in combat with the R.A.F.

The attacks directed against our lines of communication brought the Arabs their first real victories. Correspondents from foreign newspapers appeared to share the Arab opinion which held that the defeat of Zionism was imminent. An important British daily even published an article ridiculing our efforts to form a Jewish army. It claimed that of the 90,000 men the Jews said they had under arms, in reality there were only 3,000, all volunteers, poorly trained, and hardly equipped at all. This newspaper was wrong; we did not lack men, only arms.

All the same, our general staff made plans for Operation "Nachshon," which was to open up the road to Jerusalem.

We first rounded up all the arms we could find, but needed many more. Since we did not know exactly when the freighter carrying Czechoslovakian arms would arrive, or when the C-46 grounded in Italy would be able to take off, the order was given to find more planes at any cost.

Thus an exorbitant deal was made in Geneva with U.S. Overseas Airlines, a private American company. And, on March 31st, a Skymaster DC-4 carrying a cargo of arms left Czechoslovakia. The crew, with the exception of two men, was made up of non-Jewish Americans.

For the landing, we had chosen the field at Beit Daras, an old airfield built by the British in the south and out of commission since 1945. But since the landing was to take place in the middle of the night, we had to see to the emergency installation of an entire system of markers and lights which the airport had been completely stripped of. This was done in haste, and in secret so as not to attract the attention of neighboring Arab villages or the British authorities. A mobile installation on trucks was readied, and units of the Palmach were deployed in nearby colonies to assure the protection of the operation; there was nothing left to do but wait for news from Europe announcing the departure of the plane.

The DC-4, after a non-stop flight, landed in the middle of the night without the slightest trouble. We unloaded its cargo—cases containing 200 guns, 40 machine guns and ammunition.

During the unloading, an Arab band occupied a police post located at the other end of the field, which had been handed over to them by the British. But the Arabs and the British, informed of the deployment of the Palmach in the area and fearing an attack, barricaded themselves inside the post without even trying to find out what was going on a few hundred yards away.

The plane took off again for Czechoslovakia where another shipment awaited it, also destined for us. This time, however, our luck ran out. On their arrival in Prague the crew members were greeted by envoys of the American Embassy and interrogated. Thus ended the escapade of the DC-4, and the State Department for the first time had confirmation of the arms shipments from the Czechs into Palestine.

However, two days later, the freighter we were impatiently awaiting entered the port of Tel-Aviv; the *Nora* brought us a stock of 200 machine guns and 4,300 rifles. By the end of the day the arms had been distributed to the units whose mission was to open the road to Jerusalem.

On April 6th, Operation "Nachshon" was launched. It ended to our advantage. A great wave of hope swept over our soldiers, strengthening their faith in our final victory. The decisive turning point of the battle was marked by the death of the Arab chief Abd el-Kader el-Husseini, killed in the course of an attack on his fortress, Castel, which dominated the outskirts of Jerusalem.

On April 13, a convoy of 178 trucks loaded with 550 tons of provisions entered Jerusalem. For the first time, in the course of this battle, our few small planes had effectively supported the units on the ground. The most important battle of the struggle for the highways had been won.

VVVV
8
MMM

The Great Departure

THE FLIGHT of the C-46 to Italy and of the Constellation to Panama had not gone unnoticed. The surveillance of the FBI kept on our organization tightened. The activities of LAPSA and Service Airways became the targets of investigations by various American governmental departments. Certain personalities, whose sympathies we had gained, advised our men to remove our planes as soon as possible from territory controlled by the United States.

After a period of feverish work and despite the constant surveillance of the FBI, on April 9th four Commando C-46's, their crews fully manned, were ready to leave the United States. Five other planes of the same type were to follow.

The flight leader of the four C-46's of the first wave of departure was U. S. Navy Lt. Commander Hal Auerbach, holder of the Distinguished Flying Cross and the Croix de Guerre. Like many other crew members, he had left a well-paying job to fight at our side. His was one of the best paying, that of inspector for the Civil Aeronautics Administration of the United States.

In the fight for Israel, Hal had found a new reason for living. For months, under fire from both the Arab Legion and the Egyptian Army, he had supplied the besieged settlements in the Negev by air and dropped bombs to stop enemy tanks and troops.

On April 9th, having completed last-minute preparations, he telephoned the Customs Office in Philadelphia and alerted the authorities to the imminent departure of four airplanes. They requested that he delay the departure until an inspector could get there. Finally, around seven o'clock in the evening, an official appeared at the field in Melville. He said he had been ordered to prohibit the planes' take-off and refused to give any explanation, deliberately ignoring questions put to him by our men who were thoroughly exasperated by his attitude. Finally, driven into a corner, he admitted that they were suspected of carrying arms aboard their planes.

Commander Auerbach then called the offices of LAPSA in New York and apprised them of the situation. An hour later, several Customs officials turned up with more detailed orders: no take-off, no boarding the planes, no unloading of anything at all from the planes.

Discouraged, our men left the field. Later that evening, however, they held a conference with the Customs officials and representatives of LAPSA who had hurried to the scene. But these talks were futile.

The next day was Saturday. First thing in the morning Commander Auerbach, accompanied by his men and the representatives of LAPSA, once again went to the Customs Office in Melville. But it seemed that, that day, no one in the office knew anything about the matter. It was clear that they had decided to delay the departure of the planes indefinitely by administrative evasiveness. But that was to misjudge not only our men's stubbornness, but also their thorough knowledge of the law.

Commander Auerbach began by announcing that neither he nor his companions would leave the offices of Customs until they had obtained permission to take off. At his instigation, the LAPSA representatives telephoned their lawyer in New York asking him to begin legal proceedings against Customs for abuse of power. This maneuver of intimidation immediately had quite an effect; several officials in uniform appeared in the offices. From then on, for two full hours, a veritable debating match took place. The Customs officials insisted on their right to detain the planes, without much success, for our arguments were at least as well-reasoned as theirs.

Finally, tired of arguing, Customs agreed to a compromise. Since in any case, they declared, Commander Auerbach would have to put down in Miami for refueling, the authorization to leave American territory was actually in the hands of the Miami Customs. The Commander at once smelled a trap; the whole comedy would undoubtedly be repeated at Miami. He chose a course of action on the spot; to force the Customs men into an immediate decision he announced his intention of making a non-stop flight to Jamaica, outside territorial United States.

The Customs officials had not expected this decision; once again they sidestepped the issue. They would only consent to the departure of the planes if Commander Auerbach could obtain authorization from the main Customs Office in Philadelphia. But the Commander did not see it that way. The point of departure of the planes, he reminded them, was Melville and therefore, logically, it was up to the Melville Customs to grant the authorization to take off.

After endless consultations on the telephone, Customs gave in, weary of the fight, and at last the authorization the Commander wanted was issued. He had, in the end, almost had to wrench it out of them by force.

The four C-46's left Melville on the evening of April 10th. Three of them reached Kingston, Jamaica, without incident. The fourth, piloted by Commander Auerbach himself, had to make a forced landing at West Palm Beach to refuel. The Commander had every reason to expect new difficulties. He had been warned in Melville that if he made a stop in American territory he would have to request permission to leave the country all over again. But all went well and he was able to get to Jamaica where the first three planes were waiting for him.

Two days later, the five other C-46's left Los Angeles. Due to bad weather conditions they had to land at Tijuana, on the Mexican border, where they were grounded for a week. On take-off, one of the C-46's, overloaded, crashed to the ground. The pilot Captain William Gerson was killed instantly. The accident unfortunately focussed the attention of the American press on the activities of LAPSA.

The eight unharmed planes arrived in Panama where, again, they did not go unnoticed. The presence and the activities, in Central America, of young American aviators had its intriguing aspects for the FBI. Although it had no proof against LAPSA, it had nevertheless suspected it of illegal activities for some time. Panamanian officials were urged to open an inquiry into the subject. The Government agreed all the more readily since a feverish atmosphere gripped Panama at that period, on the eve of elections. The people were accusing the Government of selling out the country to the Americans.

An armed guard was accordingly posted around the field. But it was hard to determine whether the guards had been put there to protect our men from the populace or to keep the planes from leaving the area.

In the meantime, another contract had been signed with the Czechs, and as of April 23, 1948, our Air Service was augmented by ten Messerschmitt ME-109's. A special clause assured our pilots of a training period in Czechoslovakia. It also guaranteed the assistance of Czechoslovakian specialists in reassembling the planes which would have to be disassembled for the transport to Palestine. Furthermore, the Czechs gave us the option to use Czechoslovakian National Airlines' Dakota DC-3's for transporting spare parts, but not arms, since the Dakotas had to put down in Athens. The C-46's grounded in Panama were therefore indispensable for the transport of planes and arms. But, for these planes as for the Constellations, an intermediary base was essential, and Yehuda Arazi, who had left the United States, succeeded in obtaining landing rights in Sicily.

The airport selected, at Catania, happened to be under Italian military control. Two of our men therefore presented themselves to the authorities as representatives of the LAPSA and Service Airways companies, requesting permission to examine the field and the installations to see if they met with the requirements of their companies. They stressed the fact that since they used large planes, twin-engined C-46's and even four-engine Constellations, LAPSA and Service Airways would be in a position to offer jobs to the local workmen. In a region where work was scarce, this possibility aroused enthusiasm and the affair was quickly concluded.

From then on, the airport at Catania became the base for our future operations. On May 8th, the planes remaining in Panama left the airport at Tucumen for good and landed in Catania.

The State of Israel Is Born

I WILL NEVER FORGET the day of the 14th of May, 1948, when, in the Museum of Tel-Aviv, David Ben-Gurion announced the creation of the State of Israel. No other event can ever erase that moment from my memory.

Those of us who were there wept, I confess. We were not only Jews of Palestine, we were also survivors of the vast Jewish community of Europe, refugees from the most gigantic massacre the world has ever known. Our friends and relatives had died in the flames of ghettos or in the gas chambers of Nazi extermination camps. And, if the State of Israel came into being that year of 1948, it was in a large measure due to those dead, to the tragedy the Jewish people had lived through. When in November, 1947, the world upheld our claims, it acted not so much because it recognized our historic right to the land of Israel, but rather because it bore the guilt for the massacre of millions of Jews, accomplished with almost total indifference. For the facts must be faced. Did the Polish Resistance make the slightest effort to prevent the extermination of the ghettos during the uprisings? What did the Hungarians do to protect their

Jewish community? In France, were not Jews often arrested and turned over to the Germans by the Vichy police? And did not the Nazis recruit their most expert butchers from among the Ukranians?

Another fact, even more significant: in 1940, part of the Jewish community in the Balkans could have been saved if it could have found refuge in Palestine. But what did the British Government do at that time? On November 11, 1940, three ships carrying 2,000 Jews from the Balkans were hailed at sea off the Palestinian coast by the British Navy and brought into the port of Haifa. The next morning, an official communiqué from the British Government proclaimed: "His Majesty's Government would like to express its sympathy to the refugees from territories occupied by German troops. But, being responsible for the administration of Palestine, it is obliged to see to it that the laws of the land are respected. At the moment a recrudescence of illegal immigration would be likely to result in regrettable incidents and might prove to be a serious threat to British interests in the Middle East." Nothing could be more respectful of regulations or more hypocritical; as for the interests in question, they apparently had more importance than 2,000 lives. Further measures were taken by the British to deport refugees to the island of Mauritius. On November 25, the immigrants chose to scuttle their ship and 252 men thus lost their lives.

A year later, 769 refugees left Constanta on board the steamer *Struma;* the British having refused to welcome them in Palestine, they asked for hospitality from the Turkish authorities, who sent them back to Rumania. The ship sank in the Black Sea. There was only one survivor.

The British, decidedly in a mood for issuing proclamations, had explained in a special communiqué: "The High Commissioner fears that admission of these Jews into Palestine would provoke tension in our relations with the Arabs and most particularly with the Arabs of Iraq." A shabby excuse and a gross miscalculation, for nothing further could halt the march of history in the Middle East or curb the will to independence of the Arab peoples. At any rate, neither the millions of Jews who died, nor the closing of the gates of Palestine to those condemned by the Nazis prevented the anti-British *coup d'état* of April 2, 1941, in Iraq, or the appeal to Hitler for help that followed. Quite simply, the British Government had a bad conscience and felt the need to justify itself.

I was thinking of all that as I listened to the now historic words of Ben Gurion proclaiming the founding of the State of Israel.

At that very moment, to the east, in the heart of the hills of Hebron, twenty-five miles from Jerusalem, the last flames of a vast conflagration still licked at the ruins of Gush Etzion which had recently been the scene of a particularly bloody drama.

Gush Etzion, defended by about four hundred settlers, was a strategic point of the highest importance; its resistance could mean thwarting the Arab Legion's plan for the lightning conquest of Jerusalem.

On May 12, the Arabs launched an extensive operation in this area. A few telegrams briefly retrace that tragic day:

12:15—"We are being bombed continually. Our situation is desperate. The Arab Legion's tanks are within 300 yards of our walls."

12:53—"Arab troops advancing on Kfar Etzion (one of the four colonies of the region). We have dead and wounded. Moshi, our commander, is among the dead. We are lost unless planes come to our rescue."

And, a little later, "Enemy tanks have entered Kfar Etzion, which is resisting hopelessly."

That was the last telegram received from Gush Etzion.

After the enemy tanks entered Kfar Etzion, each of the settlements had to fall back on itself for the final resistance.

To rescue our settlements, our Air Service had done the impossible with their pathetic resources—light planes which suggested tourism rather than war. We dropped supplies, ammunition and bombs exactly as you get rid of a thing by throwing it out the window. Two of our pilots, headed for Kfar Etzion, met their deaths in the mountains of Judea. Both were veteran pilots who had fought the war in the R.A.F. They were representative of the type of young Israeli who had known nothing of life but combat, sacrifices made in the name of a future liberty, sacrifices in the ranks of the R.A.F. or the British Army, then those in the Haganah or the Palmach. They were the same young Israelis who organized the defense of the *kibbutzim*, committed acts of sabotage against the British, and in Europe organized illegal immigration. They formed the nucleus of the young Israeli army which was so poorly equipped and dressed in makeshift uniforms, a khaki shirt and pants and, instead of a helmet, a sort of woolen cap that looked like a sock.

On May 13th, at dawn, covered by fire from their artillery, the Arabs delivered their final attack. In Kfar Etzion, already fallen, they blew up every house. Three Jewish settlers appeared waving a white flag and the over-excited plunderers shot them down forthwith. With great effort, an officer of the Arab Legion somehow managed to impose calm on his ranks, then he asked the last Jewish fighters to give themselves up. He lined up his prisoners against a wall with the intention of photographing them but, at that moment, an Arab with a machine gun leaped forward and cut them down in a burst of fire.

After this exploit, the officers of the Legion completely lost control of their troops. It turned into a carnage. Twenty women who had hidden in the cellar of an apartment house were massacred by raging Arabs with hand grenades.

In Jerusalem, when reports of what had happened at Kfar Etzion came through, negotiations were begun, with the help of the Red Cross, to prepare for the surrender of the other three settlements. On May 14th, Gush Etzion surrendered; 160 of its defenders had died in combat, 240 were taken prisoner.

Following the decision of the United Nations to divide the country, British troops had begun to evacuate Palestine. Only a few detachments were still stationed at Haifa. A group of English deserters, former members of the police force for the most part, at that time founded the British Fascist League which vowed to support to the end, in their struggle, "the knightly sons of Arabia come to free their country from the yoke of the wandering Jew."

This poetic passage is not included in a gratuitous attempt at effect; it is an excerpt from a tract distributed in Palestine by the British Fascist League.

The Djihad*

ON MAY 15TH, in a large-scale operation, five Arab armies totaling 120,000 men, supported by their air power, invaded Israel.

At the same moment, the Secretary-General of the Arab League declared: "This will be another war of extermination which will be talked about like the Mongol massacres and the Crusades." Under the banner of Islam, as at the time of the Great Conquest, the Arab troops felt assured of an easy victory. Furthermore, did not the Koran promise eternal paradise to those who died in battle against the infidels? And the Mufti upped the reward: the victors would divide Jewish women and Jewish property among themselves.

Given the Arab superiority in numbers and in arms, most foreign observers doubted that Israel could survive. The overall situation indeed was extremely troubling. The first front to the north, that of the Lebanese Army, did not worry us too much; the Lebanese frontier runs through a mountainous region from the Mediterranean Sea north of Galilee to Metula, a small city located at the juncture of the Syrian frontier.

The Lebanese Army, a fighting force not exceeding 10,000

* In Arabic: the "Holy War."

men, equipped with artillery and outdated armored cars, had only two possible invasion routes into Israel through which an armored car could pass—the coastal road to Haifa, and the road from Metula. Also, to reach the coastal road, it would first be necessary to destroy or cut off the Jewish settlements along the frontier.

Besides, Lebanon, a veritable mosaic of races and religions, entered into the "Holy War" with no enthusiasm whatsoever. The Christian majority in Lebanon, surrounded like us by a sea of Muslims, feared as much as Israel being swept by the tide of an Arab victory.

The Syrian front was more alarming. The frontier we shared with Syria, which extended along Lake Hule and the Lake of Tiberias until it joined the Transjordanian border, had no natural defences. The Syrian army, 20,000 men with artillery and tanks, personified by the "veterans" of the "Special Troops of the East" which the French had created, was animated by a vigorous religious fanaticism. In the "Djihad" against Israel, it advanced under the banner of Salah al-Din.

The Syrian plan of attack aimed at destroying the settlements—Mishmar Hayarden, Ein-Gev and Degania—which guarded the city of Tiberias and access to the highways to Haifa and Tel-Aviv. It seemed an easy task; the positions of the Syrian troops were situated on a chain of high hills overlooking the settlements.

As for the Jordanian Army, the Arab Legion, a force of 40,000 men, entirely motorized, equipped with tanks, armored cars and artillery, presented an even greater danger. These well-trained, well-disciplined troops were flawlessly commanded by former British officers. And, with the help of Great Britain, the Arab Legion already occupied the interior of the country from Jerusalem to the coastal plane of the Mediterranean. Attacking simultaneously from outside and from the very heart of our territory, the Legion was a formidable menace.

The task of the Iraqi Expeditionary Corps was to reinforce the Arab Legion. Its 5,000 men of mediocre quality did not have any heavy arms. The immediate objective of the Iraqis was the valley of Jordan between the Syrian sector and the Jordanian front (from there, the Jordanian frontier extended along the shores of the Dead Sea to the Gulf of Aqaba and the British military base).

Finally, the Egyptian Army, which numbered 40,000 men, for the Palestinian expedition activated a special corps made up of 10,000 men of the regular army and 15,000 volunteers recruited "for the deliverance of our Palestinian brothers." This special corps was motorized and equipped with tanks, armored cars and heavy artillery.

The Israeli-Egyptian frontier being protected to the South by the desert which separates Egypt and Palestine, the Egyptians needed a base for feeding and concentrating their troops close to our border. El-Arish, in the Sinai Desert, with its military airfield, was the ideal base. From there, in a parallel action, two motorized columns were to advance, the first along the coastal highway from Gaza to Tel-Aviv, the other along the route to Beersheba where it was to join up with the Arab Legion.

On May 15th, British troops still stationed in Palestine and Jordan, in Egypt and Cyprus, were put on the alert. His Majesty's Government could not, after all, permit the total extermination of the Jewish population in Palestine.

For extermination was, alas, foreseeable. We had neither an organized army nor heavy arms. The battle could only be fought by the population itself—men, women and even children—with only light arms at its disposal, and in insufficient quantities. And our armored vehicles were nothing but trucks hastily armor-plated in our machine shops.

On May 15th, Egyptian fighter planes, Spitfires, went into action to support the Arab forces; our settlements and even Tel-Aviv were bombed. The pilot of an Egyptian plane shot down by our machine-gun fire confirmed that in the air we would also be up against a strong opponent: Egypt had forty fighter planes, four bombers and four transport planes; Syria had ten fighter-bombers and four transports. Compared to ours, this array of air power was overwhelming.

It became more urgent than ever to establish an air lift between Prague and Tel-Aviv for transporting arms and the ten Messerschmitts Czechoslovakia had agreed to let us have. The purchase of these fighter planes was an important event for Israel at the time. The C-46's and the Constellation received orders to take off for Prague. Following new negotiations, we were even able to acquire in addition two Skymaster DC-4's.

But it was out of the question to keep Prague as a base of operations, since the British and American Embassies in Czechoslovakia interested themselves in our activities with an alarming solicitude. Fortunately, the Czechoslovakian Air Force was able to put at our disposal the old German airfield at Žatec, long out of use. We gave it the code name "Zebra."

The Arabs were attacking.

Although the Lebanese troops were stopped by the first settlement they encountered—the motorized column with its armored cars did not even attempt the road to Haifa—on the Syrian front the fighting soon became fierce. Our settlement Mishmar Hayarden ("the guardian of Jordan") fell after four days of pounding from enemy artillery and attacks day and night by the infantry, the cavalry and six Syrian tanks, where heavy losses were suffered.

The settlement of Ein-Gev, the second Syrian attack point, found itself in a very poor strategic position. Built on the shores of Lake Tiberias, Syrian batteries mounted in the hills held it under fire from virtually invulnerable positions. As a result, it was subjected to heavy artillery fire for several hours, whereupon the Syrian commander sent out his tanks and artillery in the hope of taking it by assault. But the tanks were blown up by our mines or disappeared into deep trenches which had been cleverly camouflaged. The Syrian soldiers, now without support and under fire from our light arms, retreated in disorder, abandoning their dead and wounded. The following night, in a daring sortie, a group of the defenders of Ein-Gev penetrated the enemy positions and demolished their artillery and vehicles.

The third Syrian attack, this time against the settlement of Degania, failed in the same way. As before at Mishmar Hayarden and Ein-Gev, the assault was proceeded by heavy artillery bombardment. Then, protected by their tanks, the Syrian troops moved forward. They came within a hundred yards of Degania, but there the tanks were forced to stop at the trenches and the infantry was mowed down by our automatic weapons. Seized with panic, the Syrian soldiers fell back, abandoning their tanks which our women and children blew up with grenades.

Holding our own on the defensive in the north on the Lebanese and Syrian fronts, we decided to attack in the center, against the Arab Legion positions. Our objectives were rapidly taken, with the exception of the fortress of Latrun, where our losses were very heavy. But the most difficult ordeal had just begun—the battle for the city of Jerusalem. The Legion occupied the old city and the citadels and walls around it which dated from the Crusades. Furthermore, the old city of Jerusalem was Arab, while the Jewish quarter was an isolated neighborhood where for generations pious Jews had clung to the narrow streets. To lend them support, we were able to infiltrate through the Arab quarters a few dozen soldiers, all vounteers, who were not unaware of their probable fate. The Jewish quarter was the immediate goal of the Legion.

After our defenders had rejected appeals to give themselves up without fighting, the Legion undertook to destroy the quarter with shells, house by house. Even though a counter-attack launched from outside the city to come to their rescue failed, the survivors still held out, but without hope.

Our settlements to the south, encountering the Egyptian forces moving up towards Tel-Aviv and Beersheba, were in a similarly desperate situation. Built in the middle of the desert, the settlements had no natural defences whatsoever. Completely isolated by enemy troops, their defenders knew very well that their survival depended solely on their own courage and ingenuity. Negba, Yad Mordachai, Dorot Rouchama and Kfar Hadarom, all had been relentlessly bombarded by tanks, artillery and by air. For the moment, despite all this, assaults by the Egyptian infantry had been repulsed. But how many more days would they be able to hold out?

The Egyptian Air Force deployed its planes in lively actions in many areas. Even our base at Ekron underwent heavy bombardment and several of our planes were seriously damaged.

Fortunately, a sense of direction and the science of navigation were not exactly the strong points of the Egyptian pilots. Thus, one morning, four of their Spitfires attacked an R.A.F. airfield, the last not to have been evacuated by the British. Three planes were destroyed on the ground and the Egyptians, apparently carried away by their success, decided to have another go at it the following day. But this time the R.A.F. was prepared. A blistering welcome greeted the Egyptians, costing them two Spitfires.

The besieged villages and settlements, deprived of water and arms, desperately called for help. Our only means of saving them was to use our Norsemen which could carry a ton of freight and land in short distances. But they were still in France and Italy. Our friends in Paris and Rome duly received the order to take off come what may and however they could.

Buzz Beurling and Leonard Cohen, two of our most brilliant pilots, accordingly took off from the airport at Urbe, near Rome, but, alas, their plane crashed.

Buzz Beurling was a Canadian hero whose exploits during the war had become legendary. George "Buzz" Beurling was not Jewish. He had joined our ranks simply because he thought our cause was just. We were particularly proud and touched to count a man of his caliber as one of us. His death hit us all painfully. Meanwhile, in Rome, the Canadian Embassy did not seem to share our sentiments. It requested that we turn Beurling's body over to them so that it could be buried at dawn, in anonymity, judging that any publicity about the funeral would be undesirable. We refused. We wanted Buzz to be buried with all the honors we could give him. A telegram from Beurling's father decided the question. He knew his son had joined our ranks and he placed the responsibility for making funeral arrangements with the representatives of Israel. Every member of the Zionist colony in Rome followed the procession, paying a last homage of gratitude to the man who, while not a Jew himself, had embraced the cause of the Jewish people. The Italian Government was represented, and the Italian Air Force conferred military honors on Beurling's remains.

The second pilot, Leonard Cohen, born in Liverpool, England, imbibed Zionist ideas since his early childhood from his parents, who immigrated to Palestine. Young Leonard went to school in Haifa and fell in love with the city and Mount Carmel. Back in Liverpool at the university, he joined up at the outbreak of war. Released from the R.A.F., he married and had two children and a steady flying job. It seems that he made up his mind to stay in England but the United Nation's declaration brought home to him the sense of duty to his real fatherland and so he cabled his parents that he was coming back to fight. He was buried beneath Mount Carmel, which he loved so much and whose beauty he praised in poetry.

Meanwhile, at Žatec, airfield Zebra was in a fever. The first fighter aircraft was ready to be shipped. But the news of this fatal accident was a great shock to everybody and the loading of the ME-109 was done in an atmosphere of gloom, as nobody could explain the accident and sabotage was suspected.

On May 20th, in fact, a DC-4 left Zebra for Israel. On board was not only a disassembled ME-109, but also two fighter pilots of the Israeli Air Force, the first two to have completed their training course in Czechoslovakia.

The same day, we signed a contract with the Czechs guaranteeing us delivery of fifteen new fighter planes. From then on, a regular service, an air-bridge, operated between Czechoslovakia and Israel. Every day, one or two planes took off from Zebra, bringing us arms and fighter planes.

During the night of May 24th, two of these planes came upon particularly dramatic landing conditions. The weather had been very clear all day and normal radio contact had been maintained. But, just as the airfield at Ekron came into sight, a heavy fog rose. The pilots were alerted that the equipment in the control tower was too rudimentary to effectively direct a landing under such conditions; rags soaked in gasoline were placed along the runway and lighted, and our searchlights attempted to pierce the skies.

One plane succeeded in landing safely. The second headed for the airport but was unable to make out the field even though it was lighted by the burning rags. The fog was too thick. The control tower then ordered the pilot to head for the sea and then head back for the field, maintaining a certain altitude just above irregularities in the ground. These instructions reached the pilot normally, but suddenly radio contact was interrupted.

At the airfield, they waited in vain. Rescue teams were sent out to search the surrounding area, but not a trace of the plane was found. It was feared that it might have landed in Arab territory.

At dawn, however, the crew of the lost plane appeared at Ekron, exhausted by a long hike. Only the navigator, Moses Rosenbaum, was missing. The men had suffered bruises and traces of burns.

Following instructions, the plane had turned back toward the base, but it had gradually lost altitude and, suddenly, had crashed into a hillside. The next day, in the place indicated by the survivors, among the debris of the burned shell, crushed by the motor of the disassembled pursuit planes, was the body of Moses Rosenbaum.

This man had been a navigator in the American Air Force. During the Italian campaign, he had made contacts with the men of the Jewish Brigade. One conversation had led to another, and he had finally decided to settle in Palestine after the war. At first he had returned to his engineering studies; in this capacity, he thought, he could best serve the cause of a country which had a great need for engineers. But destiny had thwarted his desire to build a future in peace and he had become a soldier like so many others. Also like so many others, he had paid with his life for his attachment to the cause he had chosen to serve.

From the Four Corners of the Earth

ALTHOUGH OUR OPERATIONS were shrouded in strict secrecy in order to avoid the prying eyes of the various intelligence agents and correspondents, an article appeared in the *Chicago Daily News*, signed by a certain Nat A. Barrows, who revealed to his readers "an amazing story of world-wide repercussions." One learned in it that a deserter from the Israeli Air Service had disclosed the existence of secret air traffic between Czechoslovakia and Israel, and that Israeli air power therefore owed its vitality to substantial aid from the Soviets. He added that more than three hundred Soviet officers were in Israel and that the Czech-Israeli air lift was used not only for the transport of arms but also for ferrying young Israelis into the U.S.S.R. where they were given intensive military training. According to the author of this article, all this had been confirmed by American agents who had learned the truth under circumstances reminiscent of a cloak-and-dagger spy story.

There were no Soviets in Israel. But we knew all about the famous Mr. X., author of these revelations which the *Chicago Daily News* reporter had picked up. This X., or more exactly

L., not to name him outright, had given us good reason never to forget him.

For some time, actually, great pressure had been brought to bear on our men, pressure in which money played an important part. Considerable sums had been offered to our foreign volunteers in return for information about our real activities in Czechoslovakia. They had always refused the money.

One day, however, we learned that one of our men was planning an alarming plot—to seize one of our planes and escape in it to a foreign country. At the time we were hardly in a mood to take this rumor lightly, and with good reason; we ourselves were daily hatching more or less serious plots to hijack planes from the enemy.

In the utmost secrecy, an investigation was begun. It was learned that a bartender had overheard a most revealing conversation between two young women of questionable virtue during which one of them announced her intention of selling all her possessions since she was on the point of leaving the country. She let it be understood that "everything had been arranged by her friend," and even added that "it will make a good story for the newspapers." The bartender knew about the girl's past relations with British officers and he knew that, now, she cultivated our foreign volunteers just as assiduously. He confided his suspicions to one of our investigators who had no trouble making the young woman's acquaintance, and soon found out that she was on very intimate terms with one of our men, a certain L., a mercenary pilot who did not inspire anyone with much confidence. Ever since his arrival in Tel-Aviv he had given us trouble, categorically refusing to go on missions which did not suit him and finally demanding to be repatriated; a favor which we had refused him, for we well knew that no sooner free, he would hasten to reveal all the secrets of our operations out of Žatec to the first reporter who offered him enough money.

Our investigator rapidly came to the conclusion that L. really was planning to steal a plane and escape with his friend.

I must admit that at first I did not really believe this story. I suspected rather that L. would take the girl out in a boat in order to get for nothing what others had to pay for. But I changed my mind a few days later when two American volunteers came to tell me that one L. had offered to let them participate in a project which would bring them a large sum of money. They had obviously turned down the proposition. However, these two Americans were respectively a radio operator and a navigator. The pieces fitted together; since L. himself was a pilot, the three of them would have made up a complete crew. The airports were alerted. Two men were assigned to watch L. and his friend, but this surveillance brought nothing new to light.

We then decided to question the young woman, but she refused to answer our questions. Since we could not resort to methods used so successfully by other police forces, we were wasting our time. I then sent for L. in person. Our conversation evidently inspired a healthy fear in him for he gave up his plan. It must be said that thereafter he was the object of constant close surveillance and that at the first opportunity we got rid of him by sending him back home. That was treating him with great consideration; in other countries, many people suddenly disappeared for infinitely less serious reasons. We treated him with too great consideration, judging from the revelations he subsequently made to the reporter in Chicago.

L. was the exception which proves the rule. He was the only foreigner who made us feel that our work was really cut out for us. The others, mercenaries or volunteers, were not always easy to live with, sometimes having rather unique ways of amusing themselves, but they carried out their duties irreproachably. Our final victory is to a great extent due to them. And to this day, in Israel, we still talk with pleasure about their exploits.

Among the foreign fliers there were a number of Swedes. They were all tall, thin and blond, as tradition calls for. Upon arriving in Israel, they never seemed concerned about knowing why we were fighting, or even whom we were fighting. They had signed a contract, they were being paid to pilot our transport planes. They did not ask anything further and accomplished their work coldly but with a true professional conscience. Little by little, however, their attitude changed. They began to take an interest in our way of life and even got to the point of asking us about our aspirations and the meaning of our struggle and, although never quite warming to us, gave us some useful advice. I remember Chris in particular. One never saw him without his cane and his dog, with a woman on his arm. A pleasant companion, he was also a pilot of great brilliance. And the fact that he constantly borrowed money from everybody without ever paying back a cent of it in no way marred the friendship we felt for him.

Among our numbers there were also South Africans, for the most part men who had fought in their country's air force. Many intended to settle in Israel and certain ones actually did. Others never succeeded in adjusting to our way of life and preferred to go back home.

But, for sheer picturesqueness, no group could compare with the Americans. Among them were dedicated volunteers, mercenaries, and adventurers out for anything. No two were alike. Almost all of them had to their credit a past history that would make the most imaginative novelist pale with envy. The majority were American Jews, some professed the convictions of ardent Zionists; others were indifferent to our problems, but that did not prevent them from fighting passionately for our cause. They felt that they were Americans first of all, and they remained that way throughout everything. However, each time that the existence of the Jewish people was threatened, we could count on them; we would find them ready to fight, and in the front lines.

Finally, we had our English, who were a group completely apart. There were not many of them, but they were highly effective.

Among our volunteers from just about everywhere, there were, therefore, numerous elements which were not Jewish. I do not know why but this was particularly true in our Air Force. In other branches of service, the effective forces were almost exclusively Jews, volunteers or not. I do not have to dwell on the fact that these non-Jewish pilots received an especially warm welcome from the population of Israel which saw them as messengers of good will from the Christian world.

One of these non-Jews, a most curious personage, is still perfectly clear in my memory. N. was a fighter pilot so gifted that one would have sworn he knew how to fly a plane before he learned how to walk. The accuracy of his fire was extraordinary, although his style reminded one of a circus act. Since all things have two sides to them, N. counterbalanced his appreciable qualities as a fighter with a fault common to many heroes; he drank everything in sight, and drank it straight. And when he had been drinking, he completely lost control of his actions. Twice, we had hushed up scandals he had caused. However, on the day when, armed with a knife, he had pursued a mechanic across the mess hall, wrecking everything in his path, we were obliged to relieve him of duty.

I travelled with him as far as Marseille where other business took me and, before parting, we decided to have a last drink together. We were standing at the bar with some men from the crew of a C-46 owned by a private American company which had flown us there. We were talking about Tel-Aviv, and about the general situation in the Middle East, when one of the men of the C-46 made a remark whose anti-Semitic nature was not lost on N. who ordered him to take it back. The other saw fit to answer with another allusion in the same vein; it was to be his last. N. hurled himself at him, grabbed him up and tossed him out of the open window. N. was not drunk that night. He had not even finished his first drink; but the feeling of solidarity that bound him to his old comrades-in-arms could not tolerate racial prejudice.

Our land army was composed almost entirely of Jews who had either already settled in Palestine or, as volunteers, had come running from every part of the globe. Many were veterans of the last war or men who had fought in the Resistance in Europe. But others had never even held a gun before.

It is true that this was the first time, since the second century, that the Jews had united to defend their country. One had to go back to the years 132–138 to find an example of a war waged by Jews; at that time our ancestors, led by Bar Kochba, had routed the Roman legions, a victory without a future, however.

Our people then had to disperse to the four corners of the earth. Their new enemies could only be fought through keeping alive the traditions and faith of their ancestors. Enclosed behind the walls of ghettos, the Jews had to erect even higher, although invisible, walls around themselves to protect themselves from a hostile world. Their faith was their only defense. Upheld by it, thousands of Jews died impaled in Spain, as the first Christians had died in the Roman arenas.

Later, when the exterior walls of the ghettos were abolished, the spiritual wall remained. Freedom came too late to dissipate the hate, suspicion, and fear aroused by centuries of persecution. And this so-called freedom, what was it worth? Jews continued to die. Only the methods of killing them had changed. The sabres of the Russian cossacks replaced the stakes of the Spaniards.

With time, however, the Jews' attitude evolved. Influenced by the great modern revolutionary trends, the younger generations began to reject the philosophy of resignation and sacrifice which had been their fathers'. They refused to die passively, submitting to death without even having put up a fight, without having made an attempt at self-defense.

If it had not been for this new generation, the creation of the Haganah would not have been possible in Palestine. For if Jewish youth had had to conform to the religious and moral precepts of the Ancients, it would have simply allowed itself to be massacred. Fortunately, our young people understood in time that to an armed force one could only answer with an equivalent force, gun in hand.

The Haganah was able to procure its first arms only with the greatest difficulty. The young Jews had to hide them not only from the authorities, but also from their own parents who remained tied to nonviolence. Therefore the influence of the Haganah was not felt until the first young colonists had grown up little by little, and taking over from the Ancients were able to establish a national organization for defense. The difficult task of acquiring arms was entrusted to a small group, the "Rechesh." Each new gun obtained was watched over like a newborn baby. To the settler living in an isolated region, to the tractor-driver working alone in the fields, to the doctor who had to make his rounds in danger of ambush, guns at that time were as indispensable as bread or water. Unarmed, no one could be sure of living through the day.

The story of two of these young Jews of the Haganah will

show what kind of men they were; the two lives we are going to recount, similar to many others, are typical.

One was called Antek, the other Gideon. Both of them, after following very different and widely separated paths, had nevertheless come to the same conclusion, one which was to animate the Jews of Palestine from then on: that without arms, facing a determined enemy, there is no present and no possible future.

Antek was a mechanic, Gideon a pilot. The first was born in Warsaw, the other in Tel-Aviv. Antek had only been in Israel for six months. Both were about twenty and came from families of small shopkeepers, and both had had comfortable childhoods.

Antek spoke only Polish; his parents had wanted him to be an assimilated Jew. Gideon only spoke Hebrew: his parents' one desire had been to break all ties that bound them to the Russian city they had left.

Antek's childhood had been nourished with tales of the the battles waged, recently, by the first settlers in Palestine Brigade, and he had been taught to sing the Polish anthem. Gideon exalted in evoking the heroes of the Bible, and also in the battles waged, recently, by the first settlers in Palestine against a land lain fallow for two thousand years and against the Arabs.

When Antek was twelve years old, his parents gave a big party for his older brother who had just been admitted to the Faculty of Medicine in Warsaw where Jews, however, were generally considered undesirable. Antek's father had bought all the wine—some 2,000 zlotys worth. All his savings.

Then one day in December, 1936, it happened. Antek's father was going home accompanied by his older son. They stopped for a moment to chat with some neighbors. They talked about how things were getting harder—a wave of anti-Semitic propaganda against Jewish businesses had swept the country. They talked also about the University where the Poles kept the Jews segregated. "But lots of Poles come and sit near us," Antek's brother protested. The future doctor never spoke to his parents about the humiliations and bad treatment inflicted on him by his colleagues. While they were talking, suddenly, from heaven knows where, a band of Polish students surged into the street.

"Death to the Jews!" they yelled.

Rocks began to fly, breaking the window of a store. The police, who were called for help, stayed out of sight. The rocks were coming thick and fast now, and a few passers-by had fallen to the sidewalk, staining the snow with their blood.

"Father, get back!" Antek's brother cried, trying to protect him.

But it was already too late. The fanatical boys, the flower of Polish youth, had them surrounded. The young man stood up to his attackers, giving them blow for blow. Then the blade of a knife flashed, and in an instant put an end to his dreams of the future, forever. Antek's father never recovered from the death of his older son. Antek had to leave school to help his mother. He became a solitary, taciturn boy. All he now felt for the Poles, for all Christians, was hatred. Antek's father died a few months before the invasion of Poland. Then there was the din of bombs raining down on Warsaw.

Gideon, during this time, was spending his vacation near the Syrian frontier, in the settlement where his brother, the officer in charge of the regional section of the Haganah, lived. Gideon was burning with impatience to join one of the fighting units of the organization. He was only fifteen, but he was sturdy and courageous. Like all boys of his age, he had completed his military training and could handle a gun like a real soldier. The danger of running into a band of Arabs did not keep him and his friends from going on carefree expeditions through the mountains and valleys of the region.

Antek, in Warsaw, lived under the Nazi occupation. Decorated with the yellow star, he hardly dared to leave his house. The store had been closed for some time and, in order to survive, his mother had to sell off, piece by piece, everything they owned. There was hardly anything left of their possessions in the wheelbarrow he pushed before him when he and his mother had to proceed to the ghetto where all the Jews of Warsaw had been quartered. Antek already felt weary and old. Physically and morally, he was at the end of his rope. When he read the posters urging the Poles to fight against the Jews, he wished that he were already dead.

He and his mother had to make do with one room of a four-room apartment they shared with three other families. One of the families, notably, were Jews of the old order. As soon as they moved in, the father began to pray: "It is the will of God," he told his wife, who was weeping.

In Palestine, meanwhile, Gideon was doing his service in the Palmach. He was the leader of his squad.

Antek hated the apartment where he lived, but even more he hated the street. Without money or work, he and his mother only survived thanks to the public canteen. Never before had the Jews known such abject misery. People were dying in the streets—mostly old people but also young boys like Antek.

It was then that, in the face of death, an imperative will to survive took hold of Antek. He joined a group of young boys who had discovered an underground passage through which, at night, upon leaving the ghetto, they could get into the city. Armed with kitchen knives and iron bars, ready for anything, they stole everything in sight, especially food. One night, as they were breaking into a bakery, they were surprised by two members of the SS. Before the Germans even had time to reach for their guns, they were lying in a pool of blood.

Before the bodies of the two Nazis, Antek suddenly felt all his terror leave him. An irrepressible sense of satisfaction came over him; he had avenged the death of his brother, the death of his father, the deaths of all the Jews in the ghetto. And, that morning, Antek and his friends brought back not only food, but also two revolvers which they did not even know how to fire.

Then came the unforgettable summer of 1942. Two-thirds of the Jews in the ghetto were killed. Antek escaped extermination by hiding in the sewers. At eighteen, he became the head of one of the movements which were preparing for a final resistance.

At that moment, in Palestine, Gideon, who had taken flying lessons, asked his superiors for permission to join the R.A.F. After a period of training in Rhodesia, he was assigned to a fighter squadron which was based in Italy.

The massacre of the survivors of the Warsaw ghetto began in 1943. The ghetto was set on fire, but, for the first time, in the midst of the flames the Jews were fighting back fiercely against their assassins. And, as German bombers poured more fire into the ghetto, the Poles resigned themselves to the massacre: "How lucky that there isn't a wind," they said, "or else we might burn up too."

Antek and five of his friends succeeded in escaping from the inferno. Seriously wounded, he begged his companions to go on without him, but they refused. Miraculously, they reached a forest where they were joined by other groups of young Jews. From there, they conducted their own fight against the Germans.

When the war was over, Gideon, now an experienced pilot came back to Tel-Aviv. His parents hoped that he would resume his studies, but Gideon felt that he should devote himself to his new mission, the organization of clandestine immigration.

Antek, for his part, returned to Warsaw with the Red Army. He soon realized that the new Poland had in no way changed its attitude towards the Jews—anti-Semitism was still just as virulent. From the papers he learned about what was happening in Palestine. He thought about it for a long time. Then, one day, having made his decision, he went to West Germany where there was a transit camp for Palestine near Munich.

It was there that he met Gideon the pilot, who had come to ferry the immigrants. In spite of their different backgrounds, both shared the conviction that it was now up to the Jews to force their destiny. Later they met again, this time in the Israeli Air Force, to fight with real arms against the Arabs for the future.

The First Score Against Albion

THE FIRST ARAB ASSAULT had been stopped, but it is hard to imagine what the results of the fighting would have been without our air bridge.

Unquestionably we overestimated the potential of the invasion armies, since their soldiers as well as their pilots had had no combat experience and on the whole had no real desire to fight. But, with the support of artillery and tanks, even a poorly trained army can sample the fruits of victory.

To the south, in the Negev desert, our settlements, under attack day and night, were forced to surrender. Yad Mordechai and Nitzanim fell into enemy hands. For the first time since the fall of Gush Etzion, we lost ground. And, on May 28th, the old city of Jerusalem surrendered to the Arab Legion, our soldiers having either been killed, wounded or totally exhausted after 13 days of intensive bombardment. This loss was irreparable; even today we still are not able to take up life again in the old streets of our traditional capital.

At the British Colonial Ministry, the news from the Israeli front was savored with pleasure. They expected that any day now we would seek help from Great Britain.

Not one of His Majesty's functionaries, therefore, imagined that in our tragic situation we might still be thinking about acquiring airplanes in England. Was not the British territory stoutly defended against any attempts we might make? However, while the officials of the Colonial Office dreamed of a triumphal return to Palestine, a man dressed in an old overcoat, but wearing a brand new derby hat, got off a plane in London.

As everyone knows, the English have their own way of welcoming foreigners who want to stop over in England. The minute he sets foot on British soil, the foreigner is taken before an official who questions him about the purpose of his trip and his financial resources. Then the official consults a little black book where all the names of undesirables are listed. The foreigner is only admitted onto His Majesty's soil after having passed these two examinations. This procedure can take anywhere from five to twenty minutes. It leaves the new arrival with the disagreeable impression that, as soon as he lands, he is placed under police surveillance. Undeniably, during that period, persons carrying Palestinian passports were subjected to an especially severe interrogation.

Our man, Emmanuel Zur, duly presented himself; the questions came at him fast. He had prepared for them carefully. He stated and proved that, as a pilot for the Aviron company in Palestine, he had lost his job because of the turn of events, and that, subsequently hired by a French company to transport lobsters, he had been sent to England to buy planes on their account.

As his papers were in order, he was admitted. He found two Englishmen who, seeking more rewarding pursuits, became associates in the phantom company. A detailed plan for transporting live lobsters was submitted to the British authorities who, without reservation, gave their approval. The company had no difficulty in acquiring two "Rapides," small transport airplanes which were able to leave England.

They first landed at the airport in Toussus-le-Noble, in Seine-et-Oise. From there they reached Rome via Lyons and Nice, without incident. But, on the way to Athens, one of the planes was forced to land at Brindisi with engine trouble. It was Zur's own plane. Two Englishmen, with whom he had arranged the sale, were also aboard; they were to receive the balance due in Israel.

The trouble was not serious. All the same, they had to spend the night in Brindisi. The next morning, as Zur was having breakfast, a visitor was announced. It was the police inspector.

"They're going to confiscate the plane," was Zur's first thought.

However, the inspector did not ask questions about the plane. He merely wanted to take Zur's two companions to the police station. These two gentlemen had spent the previous night in a cabaret. Completely drunk, they had finally been thrown out. A taxi driver had taken them in hand and was going to drive them back to their hotel when an argument broke out which resulted in their throwing him out and driving off in his cab. The poor man complained to the police, and a strange chase began. Seeing that the police were following them, our Englishmen had forced open the window of an apartment and, terrifying the widow and her three children who occupied it, had hidden there. When danger had passed, they had quietly gone back to the hotel where they were staying with Zur.

Zur obviously did not want them to be arrested. He gave the inspector a healthy tip which got everyone off the hook, and the affair was settled. The plane finally took off and landed in Tel-Aviv.

The first delivery having been made, Zur returned to

London. This time, the English police was on its guard. Zur knew that the British authorities would not hesitate to throw him in jail if they could prove that the plane's destination had been Israel. The incident at Brindisi had aroused the Italians' suspicion and it was highly probable that the British ambassador had been informed of the affair. It would therefore be better in the future to avoid landing on Italian soil. It was proposed to make the stopover in Ajaccio, which was, to tell the truth, a dangerous solution; Ajaccio already was the secret rendezvous point for our airlift from Žatec. If the pilot was discovered, our whole airlift would be lost.

France, by the way, only gave us the right to land at the Ajaccio field on the specific condition that the real object of our operations never be revealed. Since the start of the clandestine immigration to Palestine, France found herself in a rather delicate position. She could not openly defy the Governments of the United States and Great Britain, but all the same she never missed an opportunity to be of service to us. Safe conduct across French territory was guaranteed to refugees from Germany on their way to small French ports where immigrants could find ships sailing for Israel. The police and the French Army even kept careful watch on these ports to frustrate any attempts at investigation on the part of British agents. France also supplied us with arms, using the cover of transacting business with some Latin American country. Likewise, landing rights were always assured us at French airports. We never had to furnish official papers, licenses or written orders. At the airport at Ajaccio, for example, the officer in charge welcomed with open arms all who gave him the right password. And when Commandant Latour later visited Israel, he spoke of his great pride in having contributed to the founding of our State.

France acted this way either out of friendship for the Jews, a friendship sometimes born in concentration camps or

Resistance movements, or out of animosity towards the English. Many Frenchmen had not forgotten the most recent political and military intervention by the British in Syria, which had driven France out of the Middle East.

Unfortunately, the veil of secrecy which for a long time covered the stopover at Ajaccio was soon lifted following two mishaps.

While one of our C-46's was crossing the Alps, flying from Žatec, one of its engines went dead. The plane, which was carrying arms in crates labeled "Glass," made a forced landing at the Italian military airfield at Treviso. The pilot, when questioned by the Italian authorities as to the purpose of his trip, refused to answer, simply stating that he worked for a certain Danny Agronski and that all questions should be addressed to him. Agronski, who was responsible for all operations in Italian territory, happily gave proof of his sangfroid. He was able to arrange things and, a few days later, the pilot received permission to continue his flight. But the cargo of arms had been seized and was not returned to us until several months later.

A short while afterwards, another C-46 also had to make a forced landing, but this time at Rhodes where the plane was immediately seized by the Greek authorities. And more seriously, the American ambassador received a detailed report on the incident. Then American agents, knowing perfectly well that a C-46 could not make a non-stop flight from Žatec to Tel-Aviv, uncovered the stopover at Ajaccio. The experience proved that it was very difficult to maintain complete secrecy. Our planes, which had already seen a lot of service, were not in condition to perform the feats we asked of them. The security of our routes was at the mercy of the slightest technical malfunction.

At that time, in Israel, the situation had taken a turn for the worse. An Egyptian column of 150 vehicles was approaching Tel-Aviv. Our troops could delay the advance for a while by blowing up a bridge about 19 miles south of the city, but immediate action was required if we wanted to stop it definitively.

Four ME-109 fighter planes, recently acquired in Czechoslovakia, were thrown into the battle for the first time. They attacked the Egyptian column, each carrying four 150 lb. bombs. They did not do very much damage; but the Egyptians, surprised by this attack from the air, thought it prudent to retreat to positions they had already held for some time before our ground reinforcements could counterattack.

During the operation, one of our planes, piloted by Eddy Cohen had been shot down. An ex-lieutenant of the South African Air Force, he came to Palestine in 1947 to join one of the settlements. It took him a year to get used to the new conditions of life, so different from life in South Africa. It was a difficult year—fate prevented him from gathering the fruits of his struggle for the new way of life.

The other three ME-109's were constantly in action from then on.

A few days later, as two Egyptian bombers were flying over Tel-Aviv, one of our fighter planes appeared in the sky. To the surprise of everyone watching, it shot down both of them. The pleasant result was that the Egyptians from then on adopted hit-and-run tactics, that never caused much damage.

Little by little, our Air Force began to take the initiative, and often played a decisive role in battles. On June 4th, it sank one of the three Egyptian vessels which had opened fire on the coast, at Bat Yam, near Tel-Aviv. That attack cost us one plane and two Israeli pilots.

Many sorties took place until the 11th of June, the date of the first truce. Bombing, strafing, dropping supplies—a great variety of operations were included in the day's work. And the absence of enemy planes in the sky encouraged the Air

Force to dare two night operations, the bombing of Amman and Damascus. The Arab chiefs were meeting at the time in those cities to discuss the truce proposed by the United Nations and we thought that a few bombs would help them reach a decision more quickly.

In effect, on the morning of June 11th, 1948, military operations on all fronts ceased.

The truce did not facilitate the operation of our air lift since even the French could no longer defy the British and the Americans who already knew about Ajaccio and demanded that we be denied landing rights. We therefore had to seek once again the help of our Yugoslavian friends, who fortunately gave us the use of one of their airports. The Žatec-Israel flight was thereby actually shortened.

WWW
13
ΛΛΛ

The Story of the B-17 Flying Fortresses

THE MESSERSCHMITTS had allowed us to fight back in the air, but having a limited range, they could not be used for offensive operations. An air force, based only on fighters, is doomed to failure. If we wanted to win the war and win it quickly, we had to have bombers in order to be able to hit the enemy's airfields, to destroy his aircraft on the ground and, if necessary, bomb his cities. We did not, of course, believe in massacring the civilian population, but we well knew that, even without causing serious damage, a bomb dropped on Damascus or Cairo could more surely pave the way to victory than any local military success. The weapon of psychology has always been an essential one.

B-25's and A-20's, Mosquitos, Beaufighters were the ships that we needed—medium bombers, which could be used for bombing and close support. These planes had proved their efficiency and reliability during the war.

Bombers could only be found with small private companies that used them as transport planes, or with surplus military materiel dealers, especially in the United States. Al Schwimmer was charged with their purchase and delivery. He accepted this mission gladly. He was aware of the risks, but he also knew, and said, that the acquisition of bombers would turn the tide of the war in Israel. On his own, he had already gotten Leo Gardner to look into the possibility of using the Azores as a transit base for our heavy planes.

Soon four B-17's and four A-20's were located; two B-17's were in Miami, one was in Tulsa, one was in California and the four A-20's were in Oklahoma.

The two Flying Fortresses in Miami belonged to Charles T. Winters and his partner and, stripped of their military equipment, were used for transport from Miami to Puerto Rico. Both planes were in good shape. The one in California was also in flying condition, being used for high altitude photography, but the one in Tulsa, a surplus ship, required two engines to be changed and quite a lot of work on the airframe. The A-20's were surplus and not in flying condition.

The price paid for the B-17's was $15,000 apiece and for the A-20's, $6,000 each. The purchase was made quietly and in the name of a dummy corporation.

The plan of the operation called for the departure of the four B-17's together from the Miami airport. Miami was chosen for several reasons; the airport was one of the largest in the United States, home base for many small operators and one more was not likely to attract attention. B-17's were already flying in and out and an additional ship would not arouse any uninvited curiosity; there was a maintenance base on the field, owned by a Jew, who could be trusted.

In spite of these favorable conditions, it was thought preferable not to gather all four ships at Miami until the very last moment and the Tulsa and California airplanes were prepared for flight where they were. Our preparations therefore went completely unnoticed by the FBI. But it was important to act quickly, for the crew members talked easily and the slightest slip would compromise our plans.

In spite of our best efforts, only three Fortresses were ready to take off at the appointed hour. We knew that the departure of three such large planes would be bound to attract the attention of American agents and that, as a result, our last plane would be in danger of being seized. But three "birds in the hand" are worth more than four "in the bush," and zero hour was set for midnight, June 12, 1948. First stop: Puerto Rico. For the Miami–Puerto Rica run, no official authorization was required. The planes then were to proceed to the Azores, and from there to Žatec. But, in the Azores, Ajaccio was to be given as the final destination in order to avoid suspicion. Arrangements were made that Ajaccio would confirm to the Azores that the planes had landed.

Three crews, consisting of nine men each, made their last preparations. Twenty-seven men determined to succeed, boarded the ships. The first two took off beautifully. The third started to swing on the runway and only the pilot's ability avoided disaster. A tire burst! The two B-17's were circling over the field, and as a tire change could take an hour the two aircraft in the air would certainly attract attention. The captains were given orders to proceed. In the morning the third B-17 took off.

Twenty-four hours went by, and no official reaction could be noticed. All was calm on the administrative front. Suddenly, the news exploded like a bomb on the front page of New York newspapers. Three Flying Fortress B-17's, en route to Europe, have disappeared off the Azores; rescue ships announced wreckage on the ocean!

The flight of the three planes from Puerto Rico to the Azores had been routine, except for a painful adventure that befell the navigator of one of the Fortresses. This plane had been equipped for aerial photography, and a glass pane had been set into the floor to allow the cameras to function freely. Naturally, the crew had been warned of the danger this window represented. But, in the course of the flight, the navigator, forgetting the order which forbade going near it, stepped on the glass. It broke, and our man fell out into the void. At the last minute, however, he succeeded in spreading his arm and hanging on. Nobody on the plane had noticed the incident, and the poor navigator had to hold himself up, suspended between heaven and earth, for a good half-hour. Only when the captain needed him and could not find him did the others start to look for him; then he was discovered in his uncomfortable position, half-dead of fear and cold, his clothing soaked with sweat from his hideous and quite understandable panic.

The landing at the Azores, and then the take off, proceeded as normally as the flight and, as agreed, Ajaccio was given as the planes' final destination.

The disappearance trumpeted by the New York papers did not particularly worry Al; the incident of the C-46 which had also been reported missing had taught him not to lose his head. His anxiety vanished when he was able to communicate with Paris: the three planes had arrived safely in Žatec via Ajaccio. The airport in the Azores had given the alarm only because someone in Ajaccio had forgotten to confirm the arrival of the planes.

This forgetfulness had troublesome consequences. For although the papers soon lost interest in the affair, the FBI proved to be more persevering. It did not take them long to uncover the existence of a fourth Flying Fortress and the four medium A-20 bombers. Charles Winters, who had sold us two B-17's from his company and subsequently acted as volunteer pilot for one of them, was arrested on his return to the United

States. Winters was not a Jew and could have remained utterly indifferent to our cause. But he was American, that is to say, devoted to freedom, and our struggle had appealed to the sensitive being in him that was hidden under the outward appearance of a tough businessman. Interrogated by the FBI, he courageously kept silent about everything he knew. He maintained his silence even when accusations of dealing with the Russians and being a security risk were raised against him.

The charges were levelled by Assistant United States Attorney Fred W. Bolts who declared: "It is known that Stalin and his satellites are mortal enemies sworn to and now attempting to destroy this country—there is a matter which was an attack on the national security of this country. Your boy and mine may be in mortal combat with the people to whom this crowd was giving aid and comfort."

The Russian bogy was brought in again, to justify the State Department's attitude towards our struggle. A year later, on February 4, 1949, Charles T. Winters was sentenced to eighteen months in prison and a $5,000 fine. A high price to pay for a man's belief in justice and humanity.

Starting in July, we set about retrieving the fourth Flying Fortress and the four A-20's which were still in the United States. Getting them out of American territory held certain risks, but we had finally decided to attempt the undertaking using the airport at Westchester as a base of departure for the B-17.

First fuel arrangements had to be made. "Mr. Edmunds" arrived at the field and paid $2,255 in cash for five thousand gallons of high octane gasoline and three hundred gallons of lubricating oil. "Edmunds" explained that the oil and fuel would be used for a B-17 and four A-20's which would land on the field. No questions were asked, no reports were made to the Federal authorities.

On the 11th of July, a Sunday, at 6 A.M., the B-17 landed at Westchester. The ship remained on the field until the afternoon taking on 2,500 gallons of gasoline and 100 gallons of oil. In the afternoon nine men boarded the ship and the captain, Irvin Shindler gave as the destination the West Coast and back, for the purpose of flight training.

The plane was allowed to leave and the Federal authorities waited in vain for the ship's return.

Shindler was in fact supposed to head for the St. John's airport in Newfoundland. But that day weather conditions were not favorable. Having no other choice, he decided to land at Dartmouth, in Canada. He hoped to be able to account for his arrival to the Canadian authorities and, from there, continue his flight to the Azores.

In Dartmouth, the Canadians watched in amazement as the Flying Fortress landed. Shindler told them that his plane belonged to the Overseas Air Training Corps and that he was on a training flight over the United States when the weather had overtaken him and forced him to land in Canadian territory. This account would undoubtedly have satisfied everybody if, in the meantime, a Canadian Customs official had not had the unfortunate notion to take a look around inside the plane. There he came upon a cargo of arms and enough spare parts to arouse suspicion. The local authorities were alerted, and decided to confiscate the plane temporarily and detain its crew, pending a decision from Ottawa which had been informed of the incident.

From there, the State Department was notified and, on July 12, 1948, the front pages of American newspapers took up the affair with relish. Since the crew of the B-17 had been accused of attempting to smuggle a Flying Fortress into Israel, the offices of the Israeli Government were invaded the next day by a horde of reporters clamoring for details. Our representatives answered that nobody knew anything about the incident. The same evasive answer awaited reporters who had gone to the League for a Free Palestine. Everyone in both offices was telling the truth; they actually did not know anything about the adventure of the B-17.

Shindler, meanwhile, was quite aware of the gravity of the situation. The return of the plane to the United States would inevitably result in the arrest of the whole crew. It was to be feared that some of the men might talk if subjected to intensive interrogation. The entire organization would then be in danger and the realization of our projects severely compromised. There was only one way out—to get the B-17 to the Azores at all costs and at once.

The State Department, quite unwittingly, came to Shindler's aid. In an official note addressed to Ottawa, they demanded the immediate return of the plane to the United States. While, at the Westchester Airport, Customs officials were trying to find out the real owners of the plane, in Halifax, where they were being held, Shindler and his men denied having attempted to fly the plane to Israel, and themselves insistently demanded authorization to return to the United States. On July 14th, the Canadians agreed to release the crew, fining them one hundred dollars for illegal passage through Canadian territory, and the authorities at the base were ordered to leave them just enough fuel to get them back to the United States. It was also decided that a Royal Canadian Air Force plane would escort them part of the way. Our men, who obviously did not have the slightest intention of returning to the United States, were hardly overjoyed at the prospect of having a fighter plane escort. Time was getting shorter and shorter; they would have to take the first chance they got to run out on the Canadians.

Four of our men got permission to go aboard the plane on

the pretext of seeing that everything was in order. But the sudden roar of propellers alarmed the base authorities who sent a truck, sirens going full blast, to block the runway in front of the plane. Our plot had failed. Our men made a show of lingering over checking out the instruments, and then got off calmly without giving any sign of their attempted deception.

Finally, on July 17th, the Canadians authorized them to take off alone, having made them promise to head straight for Boston where a rather special reception committee was to meet them. But the committee waited for them in vain. Night passed and the B-17 still had not arrived.

After a non-stop flight of twelve hours, the B-17 had reached the Azores. On July 18th, the information bureau of the Royal Canadian Air Force released the news to the press.

How had it been possible? How had a plane with just enough fuel aboard to reach the United States been able to make a flight of 1,500 miles? Speculation mounted. Some claimed that such a flight was possible if the crew alternately cut off one of the engines, especially if the winds were favorable. Others pointed out that in any case it was difficult to gauge the amount of fuel in the auxiliary tanks of a B-17. The controversy around the adventure of the B-17 was plastered all over the front pages of newspapers as though it were a political event of major importance.

The Royal Canadian Air Force, for its part, strongly suspected its men of not having respected the letter of the orders they had received, and of having filled the plane's tanks. That's where, in reality, the truth lay. The R.C.A.F. had made the mistake of underestimating the spirit of solidarity among airmen, which can prompt them to disobey the most categorical of orders. The idea of letting a plane go down, through their fault, was unthinkable to the Canadian airmen once our men had admitted that no matter what happened they had no intention of landing in the United States, and that they would attempt the crossing under any conditions.

Unfortunately, upon arriving in the Azores, the crew of the B-17 made a grave error. Instead of refueling at once and taking off without further delay, the men, exhausted, decided to rest for a few hours. This gave the State Department time to retaliate by pursuading the Portuguese authorities to seize the B-17 and deliver its crew over to American justice.

On July 25th, nine disgruntled men deplaned from a Pan American Clipper at a military base in the United States. The reception committee formed for Irvin Shindler and his eight crew members included FBI agents, Customs officials, members of the State Department and doctors from the Public Health Service. Thus surrounded, our men were put through a preliminary interrogation right at the base. Reporters were refused permission to interview them.

A few hours later, Shindler, walking between two FBI agents, was taken to a car and driven off to prison. Two of his companions were entrusted to Pan American guards who transferred them to Ellis Island under orders from immigrations officials, their papers not having seemed to these gentlemen to be quite in order.

Shindler was tried before a federal court on March 10, 1949. He faced a maximum sentence of two years in jail and a $10,000 fine. The assistant prosecutor, referring to the Winters case, asked for eighteen months' imprisonment. But, this time, luck was with Shindler. The judge abruptly put an end to the arguments, declaring "manifestly the accused is not one of those people who are determined to break the laws of their country . . . ," he dismissed the case.

The B-17 was not so lucky. Held under confiscation in the

Azores, its career finally came to an end in a scrap metal heap.

All the efforts of our men to put this bomber at the disposal of the fighters in Israel, all the risks they had taken and the dangers they had run, had been in vain.

14

Film Production
on a Grand Scale

HAVING ORDERED A truce, the UN announced that it was
sending an international commission to Palestine "to imple-
ment a return to peace." A Swede, Count Bernadotte, pre-
sided over the commission. His first act was to demand that
member nations of the UN put an immediate stop to shipments of arms to the belligerent parties. The "war" that the
State Department had declared on us after the B-17 affair was
stepped up all the more.

On June 27th, several of our planes which were still in
European airports were seized by Belgian, French and Dutch
authorities acting at the request of American Embassies. They
had been enjoined to seize all planes of American origin
whose destination appeared to be Israel and to confiscate the
passports of American air crews suspected of helping us in
our operations. An investigation was even conducted by
American and British agents in Czechoslovakia, but the
Czechs refused to say anything about our air lift. Without
doubt these agents had already gleaned various fragments of
information, but they did not have sufficient proof to provoke
an international scandal, and were unable to obtain it.

The fight between the British and American agents and our organization was entering a decisive phase. Our networks frequently reported cases where extremely seductive young ladies seemed to want to flee the Communist regime and tried to persuade our fliers to get them out of Czechoslovakia. We never knew whether these charming ambassadresses were working for the Americans, the British or, on the contrary, for the Czechs. For neither did the Czech police have any great fondness for our American pilots; they had the annoying habit of not keeping their opinions to themselves.

Seeing that their efforts to uncover the intrastructure of our air lift were in vain, the "enemy" agents resolved to address themselves directly to our organizations which were established throughout Europe. Here again, they failed. Our men were too conscious of their responsibilities to let down their guard for one second. They did their work quietly, trying above all never to attract attention.

The center of our European organization was in Geneva. It was first under the direction of Shaul Avigur, whose name will always live in the history of Israel. When Shaul left, a new man took charge of the organization, Pinchas Kozlonsky, now Pinchas Sapir, the present Minister of Finance. His driving force to provide the necessary funds for the various purchases had no bounds. Money was becoming scarce and without money, there were no arms. God only knows how he managed to dig up the hard cash which was required in this business, but he never failed us.

The Aviation section in Geneva was run by a young student, whose apartment had become the meeting and resting place for all our air crews in transit.

"It took me a while to get used to the Americans," his wife still remembers today. "They would sprawl out in the chairs with their feet on the table, smoking enormous cigars like characters in gangster movies. They frightened me, especially when my husband was away. But, little by little, I grew to understand them and admire them."

The address was only given out to a chosen few, actually, those in whom the organization had complete confidence. The others were simply given a list of telephone numbers and a password. Our telephone relay stations operated twenty-four hours a day, arranging meetings where our men received money and instructions.

This discreet system had had excellent results, in the United States as well as in Europe. Our offices were usually set up in private apartments, but sometimes also in such unlikely places as a well-known businessmen's club, a bank or even a nightclub.

Unable to break our organization in Europe, the State Department resolved to keep our planes from leaving American soil once and for all.

At the airport in Melville, the remaining two Constellations were ready to take off. We had invested a lot of money in their overhaul without exactly knowing what their fate would be. Our first request for an export license had been denied, the second one had never been answered. On July 9th, the two planes were ready for a test flight. But, a few seconds before they were to take off, a cluster of Customs officials and FBI agents swarmed onto the field and seized the planes.

That same day, July 9, 1948, also marked the end of the first truce in Palestine. The peace proposed by Count Bernadotte had been rejected both by the Arabs and by us. The UN moderator had seen fit to propose what would have been in effect a sort of vast ghetto encircled by Arab countries, with the Negev, Galilee and Jerusalem to be taken away from us! This incredible proposal provoked a violent reaction in the Stern group; Count Bernadotte was warned to leave the country at once. The Sternists accused him of fronting for the

British and it is true that the territory recovered from Israel was to be ceded to Transjordan, an ally of Great Britain.

But the truce had been useful to us. It had been widely exploited by our land and air forces. We held ourselves in readiness to resume hostilities by launching powerful offensives on all fronts.

The Messerschmitts, transport planes and light planes already in Israel gave us the seeds of air power; the three B-17's were being armed at Žatec, and the news from Great Britain was very good. There again, however, we had run into bad luck. A short while before the truce, a Mosquito fighter-bomber that Zur had acquired in England had literally disintegrated after taking off from the field in Ajaccio where it had made a stop-over. The accident, whose causes remained obscure, attracted the attention of the British authorities who, alerted by the make of the plane to our activities in their country, from then on kept a close watch on all the airports in Great Britain. Zur had succeeded in getting hold of several Beaufighters, bombers well known to our pilots, but it seemed impossible to get them off British soil without a solid alibi.

It was then that fortune smiled on us through the features of a charming young actress from New Zealand, a friend of one of the pilots Zur had engaged. This young woman had talked to her friend about a project for a film based on the glory of New Zealand's participation in the last war. Little by little, a novel idea imposed itself on Emmanuel Zur. It was decided to begin production on a film relating to the action of New Zealand pilots during the last war; then, in the logical development of a sequence especially devised for the occasion, to have the pilots take off in the Beaufighters and disappear into the English skies—along with the fictitious production.

Thanks to several contacts we had in the world of British cinema, a production company was duly formed and, behind this façade, we were able to proceed at will in signing on not actors, but the pilots we needed.

The day came for the four Beaufighters to take to the field. Everybody was ready and anxious to take off as trouble was in the air. The day before, one of the pilots crashed and was killed in a test flight. The accident caused a great deal of confusion as such an event required an official inquiry into the cause of the crash.

The script of the film required a scene of a scramble; the run to the planes to be made by mechanics, the starting of the aircraft by the pilots already in the cockpit. The taxying was the next scene with the follow up of a take off. After the take off, the planes were to fly to Scotland for further shooting as the scenery there was similar to that in New Zealand.

Everything went according to plan, but contrary to the script, all four planes took off immediately, one after the other and not in squadron formation as the script required. With the complicity of the producer, the authorities were not notified of the disappearance of the planes until they would have had plenty of time to land at the field in Ajaccio, which had once again been placed at our disposal.

But the Beaufighters, not being armed, could not be put to immediate use and our Air Force hoped that the general offensive, scheduled for the very day the truce ended, could be put off until the arrival of the B-17's from Žatec.

The ground force, on the other hand, felt that it was necessary to attack the minute the truce ended. It was of the opinion that it could get by with the support of the planes already available to the Air Force if they simultaneously bombarded the Egyptian field at El-Arish and the Arab troops on the northern and southern fronts.

On July 9th, accordingly, four Messerschmitts were ready to bear down on El-Arish. Only three flew off towards their objective, the fourth having crashed during take off. The pilot, fortunately, was unharmed. The three others were not able to locate their target and had to content themselves with dispersing enemy troops concentrated near Gaza. Only two planes returned to the base; one of the pilots, Robert Vickman, a Jewish volunteer, an ex-pilot of the United States Air Force, having either crashed in the desert or into the sea without our knowing, even today, exactly what happened to him.

On the northern front, our troops waited in vain for air support. The order to attack which had been given was countermanded at the last minute; the front line of our troops was so close to the enemy lines that it was feared that our men would be hit by fire from our own planes.

As for those of our planes which had been ordered to bomb the Egyptian positions to the south, they rather lamentably missed their objective. One of them even bombed one of our settlements, luckily not causing much damage. Another dropped its bombs into the sea.

It was a veritable festival of backfired missions; our pilots really did not have much to be proud of and the soldiers did not hesitate to tell them so.

The following days, most of our missions again were failures. The action by our Air Force decidedly was far from convincing, and we lost another ME-109 piloted by a Jewish volunteer from South Africa, Lionel Bloch. Both aircraft and pilot vanished without even engaging enemy aircraft.

But, with the arrival of the three B-17's, the tide of battle turned.

The Fortresses took off from Žatec on the 14th of July. The plan called for a raid on Cairo, Gaza and El-Arish. But for some technical snags, lack of oxygen causing the crews to pass out and antiaircraft fire over Albania, the flight was uneventful.

Number one Fortress found Cairo brimming with lights

and dropped two tons of bombs near King Farouk's palace. The number two aircraft executed its mission but number three could not locate El-Arish and dropped the bombs on military stores near Gaza. According to Arab sources all three raids had a most demoralizing effect on the enemy.

On the 15th of July, the three B-17's landed in Israel taking off a couple of hours later to bomb El-Arish. This time the raid was crowned with success.

The following four days the B-17's and the rest of the aircraft made many successful sorties with only one casualty. On the 17th, Spencer Boyd, an American non-Jewish volunteer, did not return from action.

The battle was just shifting in our favor when on July 19, 1948, the U.N. imposed another truce.

We had not succeeded in ousting the Syrians and Jordanians from our territory, nor the more solidly entrenched Egyptians to the south, who were barring the route to our settlements in the Negev, but the Haganah which, a few months earlier, had had at its disposal only a few badly organized and poorly equipped units, had now become a powerful military force.

The Air Force, having learned its lesson from its recent failures, took advantage of the return to a truce to demand autonomy and the freedom to elaborate its own battle tactics. It refused to remain an auxiliary branch of the ground army which did not understand its potentialities and rarely took into account the requirements of the pilots.

Beyond the relative freedom of action, the Air Force also demanded funds. It needed new combat planes at any price, experience having shown how easy it was to lose a plane, acquired with such difficulty, once it was put into action. We were given complete satisfaction; we obtained both a certain freedom of action and the funds necessary for our reinforcements.

Our first task was to arm the Beaufighters, but the necessary arms could only be found in a British Air Force depot.

Zur undertook, once again, to carry out the necessary operation, in the most perfect illegality. He flew off to England in a pleasure plane purchased at Toussus-le-Noble. Since he did not even have an entry permit for British territories, he elected to land at a field belonging to a private flying club near the estate of his English associate. Zur knew the staff at the club, and no one dreamed of doubting his word when he mentioned that he had taken off from another private airport in England.

Zur managed to acquire the prized parts without any great difficulty and even got hold of four spare Beaufighter engines. All this materiel was deposited at a friend's house. The most delicate part of the operation, getting the equipment out of England, still remained. It obviously was not a question of asking for an export license; only illegal procedures were open to us. Enticed by the promise of a large sum, a professional smuggler agreed to take over shipping the arms and the engines. Zur then went to Marseille where arrangements were to be made with the captain of a smuggling ship assuring the relay of the cargo to Israel. But, in Marseille, Zur discovered that the captain, having been caught red-handed with a load of American cigarettes, was in jail and that his boat had been seized by the French authorities.

Returning to Paris, Zur there received numerous messages from Israel urging him to get the arms shipment under way as quickly as possible. At that point, one of our pilots, John Harvey, came to his rescue. He said that he knew the owner of a Halifax heavy four-engined bomber who would probably charter us his plane. Zur agreed to let him take the chance, and Harvey carried out the operation from beginning to end in fine style.

Paradoxically, everything went without a hitch until the

plane arrived in the middle of the night at our base at Ekron, near Tel-Aviv! The plane had signaled its arrival in the code agreed upon, but the control tower did not answer. And, on the field, there were no lights at all. The Halifax's radio operator repeated his message on different frequencies, without result.

With all its lights on, the plane tirelessly circled the field until one of the engines went dead. The radio operator, in a panic, began sending out distress signals over every frequency. Ekron still showed no signs of life, so the pilot decided to fly over Tel-Aviv at a low altitude hoping that the General Staff of the Air Force would be aroused at hearing a plane prowling over their city. This hope was equally futile and when a second of the Halifax's engines cut off, the pilot was left with no choice; he had to make a landing on the field, come what may. He was aware that the runway at Tel-Aviv was too short for his bomber, but he knew the field well and hoped despite everything to get off with a minimum of damage. His hope was borne out. Reaching the end of the runway, which terminates in the sea, he finally was able to pivot his plane in the sand and avoid the worst. The Halifax had finished its career, but the crew was safe and the cargo was easily recovered.

Alas! If Tel-Aviv had not heard the distress signals sent out by the Halifax, other listening posts had and they hastened to contact London. The revelation of the role played by the Halifax led to many arrests in England. Most of the people who had helped Emmanuel Zur found themselves in prison.

15

Operation "Dust"

THE SECOND TRUCE lasted from July 19 to October 15, 1948. We had to take advantage of these three months to equip ourselves for resuming the fight.

The few planes we possessed we had only managed to get together by chasing all over the world, from America to South Africa, more often than not with the police at our heels, and by performing miracles to bring them back to our bases in Israel. Where were we to get more planes, with the State Department and the British and American Secret Services keeping a close watch on our every move?

Once again, we looked to Czechoslovakia. She offered to sell us some Spitfires which the English had turned over to Czech squadrons going home at the end of the war. We had no alternative but to accept them.

In France, we finally succeeded in getting back a few of the planes that had been seized at the request of the American Embassy. Two of them, transport planes, left at once for Tel-Aviv. But when they got over the city, in the middle of a blackout, a new drama took place. The pilots, unable to locate the airport, were flying over the coast a second time when they suddenly spotted the landing lights of a runway, where they landed. Imagine their surprise at finding themselves immediately surrounded on the field by soldiers—Arabs; they had landed at Gaza, in enemy territory! Thanks to the confusion caused by their unexpected arrival, our men were able to get away, but not for long. They were caught and had to wait out the war in an Egyptian prison camp. Subsequently, several light planes landed safely in Israel, but on the international scene our problems were growing more serious every day. The State Department showed itself more determined than ever to put an end to our activities at Žatec, hoping in this way to force us to accept the conditions of the Bernadotte mediation. Its agents at last accomplished their mission; with the help of information extracted from certain of our air crews who had returned to the United States, the State Department was able to compile a lengthy dossier against our organization.

By mid-July, American planes had already flown over Žatec and photographed the base. The Czechs protested vigorously, but in vain. The State Department even threatened the Czech Government with bringing the matter up before the United Nations. And, through channels, the United States let it be known that certain measures restricting the export of American products to Czechoslovakia might be lifted if the Czechs proved to be cooperative. The Czechs informed us of the American demands without, however, making reference to the tempting promises that had been offered in return. But we had already been briefed on that score by our own agents, in a less official capacity.

We were therefore not taken unawares. Without waiting for the American Government's maneuver to succeed, we had gone ahead and done the impossible; during the week preceeding the end of the truce, we flew a maximum amount of our materiel into Israel. Eleven planes had landed, one after the other, at Ekron, and unloaded about fifty tons of equipment of all sorts, including several Messerschmitts. In the course of this operation we did not lose a single plane. Considering the delapidated condition of the planes being flown by men half dead with fatigue, this was again a sort of miracle. Similarly, inside the country, the fact that our light Austers never once interrupted liaison between our nerve centers was only due to the extreme ingenuity of our mechanics. But in aviation, when spare parts are lacking, miracles never last very long. On August 3rd, the first accident claimed the lives of two of our young Israeli pilots, Emanuel Rotshtein and Zahava Levitov, one of our women pilots.

It was in America, during the course of her studies, that this young girl had learned to fly. Earlier, she had spent her youth in the camps of the Haganah where she had been taught to handle arms. Our forces being inadequate, we had not been in a position to exclude women from the ranks of our army, and like our men and our boys they had been put into combat. Even today, Israeli women are subject to military training and, while later they may turn to less frankly warlike activities, they nonetheless stand guard in our border settlements along with the members of the stronger sex.

On August 12, 1948, the Czech Government, giving in to American pressure, ordered the evacuation and shutting down of the Žatec base. Our air lift was crumbling.

Simultaneously, in Israel, we were confronted with an extremely serious problem. It had become imperative to build a landing field in the Negev Desert. The settlements that had been created in this vast territory, the first step toward returning the desert to its former fertility through a massive irrigation project, could then only survive on reserves of water and provisions which we had to supply them from outside. However, they were surrounded by Egyptian troops, and we could only get to them by air. Some of the settlements had landing strips for light planes, but these had already proved to be inadequate for our current means of transport.

Furthermore, since our General Staff anticipated that at the end of the truce the enemy would attempt a major assault on this region, it now behooved us to move in enough men and equipment not only to defend ourselves there, but also to rid the Negev of its invaders. Only our heavy planes, notably the C-46's, could effect this sort of transport operation, and they required much longer runways than were available.

On August 14th, one of our pilots, accompanied by a photographer, was given the mission to make a reconnaissance flight over the Negev in a light plane; we were hoping to get photographs of different strips of land lost among the mountains where we might be able eventually to locate a new field. The secondary aim of the mission was to photograph enemy positions around the Dead Sea and Gaza. Having accomplished its mission over the Dead Sea and the Negev, the plane was heading back up to Gaza when it ran into fire from Egyptian antiaircraft batteries. It succeeded in getting through the curtain of fire but, since the photographer was not certain of having gotten all the necessary shots, the pilot decided to fly over the enemy lines once more. This time, the plane was hit. The pilot was getting ready to land behind our lines when his engine went dead, and he had to put down in the middle of the desert, near a Bedouin encampment. Before landing, our man had managed to radio the major reconnaissance information back to his base.

The minute it landed, the Bedouins, armed and in an ugly mood, bore down on the plane. The pilot set fire to the gas tank with a shot from his revolver and our two men tried to escape under cover of the flames. But they were quickly surrounded and had to surrender, and would have been massacred had it not been for the timely arrival of two Egyptian cavalry officers.

The information transmitted by the pilot was far from encouraging: there was no possible site for a landing field among the gorges, rocks and sheer cliffs of the mountains of the Negev. We therefore decided to lengthen the runway one of our settlements already had. Its entire population was mobilized on the spot. Men, women and children, everyone able to hold a tool or drive a tractor, joined in the project. At first we only worked at night so as not to attract attention, but the terrible white dust we had to fight against obliged us finally to go at the job in broad daylight. Operation Dust was soon completed without the Egyptians having seen fit to react.

Meanwhile, we were preceding with a complete overhaul of all the transport planes then in Israel. Our mechanics, too, worked day and night so that everything would be in good working order for J-Day. A special piece of equipment was even designed to facilitate the loading and unloading of air freight.

On the morning of August 22nd, the H.Q. received the news it was waiting for: the 4,100 ft. runway was ready. On the night of the same day, a C-46 landed safely on it. Other planes soon followed. Thirty tons of equipment were transported that first night. The following day we reached a total of seventy-five tons.

The enemy still failed to react, and our air lift was working to capacity. In three weeks, our planes completed 170 flights, carrying 1,000 tons of equipment and 700 soldiers to relieve the men, women and children of the settlement against which, in spite of its terrible privations, all enemy attacks since the day of the invasion had failed.

As of September 10th, the tempo of the operation necessarily slowed down since the planes were in need of maintenance and their crews were exhausted.

However, during this time, a second runway had been built. Operations began again in full on October 10th. They lasted until the 20th, totaling 417 flights and allowing us to move 2,200 tons of equipment and 1,700 men into the Negev.

The operation had put into action six C-46's, five Dakotas and six Norsemen. If one takes into account that all flights were made at night and that we lacked landing lights on the runways, the achievement of our men takes on its full value.

The Negev was saved. This desert was to us not only a still sterile land that we dreamed of making bloom again as in Biblical times. Nor was it merely a sub-soil full of promise where we had already discovered copper beds and where we hoped to strike oil. This gigantic mass of rocks led to the Gulf of Aqaba and free access to the Red Sea, and it created between Israel and Egypt a real protective barrier.

The Wind Shifts

WHILE WE WERE WORKING in the Negev, the Egyptians had
received a number of reinforcement aircraft from Italy and
Great Britain.

Our air intelligence was worried. A comparison of our air
fighting strength and that of the Arabs showed that we were
badly outnumbered. Against thirty-five Egyptian Spitfires,
nine Sterling bombers, five Iraqi Furies and ten Syrian Harvards we could put only fifteen ME-109's, two Spitfires, three
B-17's, three Beaufighters and several light planes. It became
essential for our side to get hold of our Spitfires in Czechoslovakia. I therefore left for Prague.

Prague! That city I had loved so much was now, after the
Communist take-over, nothing but a shadow of what it had
been. It could have been a city of the dead. The stores were
empty, the atmosphere in the streets was mournful. I had the
impression of landing in a strange world ruled by fear and
suffering. Our Embassy seemed like a real oasis to me; only
there did one dare to speak freely, to laugh and make jokes.

The Czechs still were very friendly to us, but something in
their attitude had changed imperceptibly. We now realized
that the decision to close down the base at Žatec had not been
motivated by American intervention alone. One had to con-

sider a new development that must have weighed heavily in the balance—a progressive but quite clear shift in Moscow's policy toward us. The Kremlin, in effect, watched with some rancor the awakening of Jewish nationalism in all the countries of Eastern Europe and the massive immigration of Jews from the satellite countries to Israel. While not openly stating its hostility, Moscow had undoubtedly judged that the time had come to put an end to the direct support lent us by the Czechs.

Sam Pomerantz, chief technician for our operations in Czechoslovakia, was fighting not only against technical difficulties, but political ones as well. The contract for the Spitfires called for delivery and overhaul of all Spitfires in a factory at Kunovice, 248 miles from Prague. All spares, ground equipment and armament had to be delivered to the same factory where they had to be packed and shipped.

The aircraft and their equipment being dispersed at air bases and stores all over the country, it was essential for Sam to be everywhere to see for himself that all materiel was directed as promptly as possible to the factory. It happened quite often that work at Kunovice was slowed down by lack of spares which were available in a base, somewhere in the country, but the commanding officer did not consider their delivery as first priority.

Sam's temper was running high and, irritated by the slow progress of the work, he did not watch his tongue. His remarks, not very complimentary to the regime, reached the ears of the Security Police. And when during his flights he landed three times on the most restricted airfields, the Czechs accused him of being a spy and demanded his removal from Czechoslovakia.

In such an atmosphere of suspicion and distrust no operation could be successfully completed. We had to find out "the mind behind this slowdown" as it soon became obvious to us that the technical personnel at the factory in Kunovice as well as the commanding officers at the air bases were under orders to hamper our operations. We soon discovered that the "mind" was a high official both in the Ministry of Interiors and Finance, a trusted man of the Kremlin. It was serious but there had to be a way of overcoming his orders. Finding out that he was deeply disliked by other Communist officials, we did manage to gain their support against him and things started to move. It was high time as a flood of cables from home demanded the Spitfires.

The Czechs insisted on crating the aircraft and shipping them in order to keep the whole operation as secret as possible. No doubt it was a safe and sound scheme but it meant that the aircraft would not arrive in time to be used in the major battles that were shaping up.

At this point Sam Pomerantz intervened. He astonished everyone by proposing a solution whose audacity staggered the imagination: to strip the Spitfires of all equipment that was not absolutely essential and fit them with auxiliary gas tanks of sufficient capacity to allow them to make a non-stop flight to Israel. No one had ever thought of doing that. But a dispatch from Israel informed us that this plan was considered foolhardy and had been rejected. We were then forced to ask Belgrade for permission to land on Yugoslavian territory, and ran up against a categorical refusal. At the time, Yugoslavia's relations with Moscow were extremely strained and the Yugoslavs, with good reason, were afraid to aggravate them further by granting our request.

We could have given up, but we had urging us on more than tenacity—the energy of despair. We pleaded our cause with considerable eloquence, to the point where the Yugoslavs changed their minds and the airport at Podgorica, near the Albanian frontier, was put at our disposal. A unit of the Yugoslavian Air Force guarded the field and was to cooperate with our men, but it was understood that fuel as well as provisions were to be flown in from Israel.

Everything seemed to be working out for the best. All that remained was to inform the Czechs of our new arrangements and ask their approval. This they refused at first, designating several of their fliers, former Spitfire pilots, to convince us of the absurdity of our plan. It was sheer folly, they said, to try to cover even the shortest distance between Podgorica and Israel—fourteen hundred miles as the crow flies—in a plane whose range had never exceeded six hundred miles. We would inevitably have to make emergency landings, either in Greece or Cyprus, in which case the Czechoslovakian government would feel obliged to suspend all further deliveries. Czechoslovakia could not afford an international scandal and a renewal of American intervention.

We bargained hard and in the meantime the factory produced the special fuel tanks and the first Spitfires were nearing completion under Sam's supervision. Although we failed to persuade the Czechs to permit Sam to fly again, he somehow took a Spitfire in the air and completed a four and one-half hour test flight. It was quite an achievement, as yet unknown in the history of the Spitfires. Zero hour was approaching and the first six pilots were gathered on the field: Sam, Boris, Moti Alon, Jack C., Sid C., and Naftili B. The Czechs increased their security regulations and restricted the men to their hotel room. Permission for the flight was still not granted.

The operation was planned and worked out with the H.Q. in Israel and called for a combined effort of the Air Force and the Navy.

The six Spitfires were to make the flight from Kunovice to Podgorica alone. After a rest at Podgorica, the fighters would take off, a DC-4 acting as a lead ship. Navigation would be done by the lead ship which would take care to navigate to the highest degree of accuracy. More than five miles off direction required resetting the course. The lead ship would be responsible for keeping a strict watch on the fighter aircraft and in the event of a fighter ditching or pilot bailing out, it would report the position and drop a large dinghy as well as mark the spot with fluoresein. The remainder of the formation would continue its journey.

Air-sea rescue would be provided both by the Navy and the Air Force. Two vessels of the Navy would be on patrol at determined positions and a third on stand-by in port. Air-sea rescue search would be accomplished by a Dakota and a C-46. The first aircraft would patrol on an agreed course and upon the receipt of an emergency call would proceed to the indicated position. The aircraft would work in close coordination with the Navy. The second airplane would stand by.

The operation had to be controlled and coordinated by the operations' room and a special communication system was established to provide the necessary radio links between the forces concerned.

An additional problem was to fly out from Kunovice the armament and the equipment unloaded from the Spitfires. It was decided to use a Norseman which was flown for this purpose to Yugoslavia. Complying with the request of the Yugoslavs all aircraft landing in Podgorica had Israeli Air Force markings removed and used their American registration.

Panamanian registration could not be used anymore, as Panama had cancelled the registry of LAPSA on the 18th of September. The order of cancellation was signed by His Excellency Enrique A. Yimener, President of the Republic, and stated plainly that Panama was acting on information received from Monnet D. Davis, the United States Ambassador, which proved that LAPSA airplanes were "Actually dedicated to illegal operations of transport and bombing, with bases in Czechoslovakia and Palestine, and transported bombs, airplane parts and arms of various types."

Everything was ready but the permission to take off. On the 22nd of September our Ambassador was forced to make an official demand and permission was granted. A cable was dispatched home and the general alert was given.

In short, nothing had been overlooked and on September 24th, six Spitfires were able to take off from the airport at Kunovice, in Czechoslovakia. The flight to Podgorica went off without incident and the first five fighters landed amid applause from our men at the Yugoslavian airport. The cheering stopped abruptly when the sixth plane came in for the landing with its landing gear jammed. The Spitfire crashed on the ground, but fortunately the pilot was only slightly hurt.

On September 27th, the five unharmed planes flew out of Podgorica headed for Israel. More troubles set in. Two Spitfires had to land at Rhodes because of mechanical difficulties. What to do? We hesitated to run the risk of informing the Czechs of the incident; perhaps they would carry out their threat and suspend delivery of the planes still remaining at Kunovice. We thought it was better to wait, in the hope that our pilots might succeed in leaving Greece without attracting attention. This hope was short-lived: the Greeks seized the planes and arrested the pilots.

Interrogations followed interrogations but our pilots stuck to a story that they took off from Yugoslavia, never mentioning Czechoslovakia. Either the British or the American Intelligence Services was behind these interrogations as our men were kept in solitary confinement and our people in Athens could not even contact them. Did they take off from Czechoslovakia? The same question was fired at them constantly. At last with the help of some of our Greek friends they were released, but the authorities refused to release the Spitfires.

Quite soon the Czechs were in on the situation. Contrary to our expectations, they were not unduly alarmed. The mishap had given them the satisfaction of having predicted our failure and warned us about it and, through a sort of compensation, they proved to be extremely conciliatory. Our real troubles came from Belgrade which took a dim view of things, immediately forbidding further use of the field at Podgorica and even placing our men on the base under arrest.

These draconian measures were not just inspired by our pilots' unlucky landing at Rhodes. Other events were working against us. The arrival of a squadron of foreign planes in Podgorica had not gone unnoticed, and the somewhat boisterous behavior of our fliers, Americans for the most part, had given credit to the rumor that the United States was shipping arms into Yugoslavia. Moscow, which had sharp ears, had not remained deaf to the rumor and, from its corner, the Albanian press had taken great pleasure in accusing Tito of selling out his country to the Americans.

The prohibition on using the field at Podgorica was a fatal blow to us. If it did not mean the eventual loss of all our planes remaining in Czechoslovakia, it at least made it impossible for us to get them out in time to be sent into the next battle. To dismantle the planes and ship them by sea would take at least three months, and we needed them at once.

The only man who did not despair was Sam. "We shall fly non-stop." By adding three extra fuselage tanks in lieu of the radio, the range would be increased by two hours. Considering that the Kunovice-Podgorica leg was only one and one-half hours, the trip could easily be done. However, there were two dangers due to the great weight of the Spitfire—about 9,000 lbs. The aircraft in the fully loaded condition would be extremely unstable and the runway at Kunovice was marginal.

Headquarters agreed to this scheme in case the base in Yugoslavia was still closed. Sam was happy with the victory.

During this time, the campaign in the Negev had begun; combat had been raging since October 15, 1948. A few days before the end of the truce, Mr. Bevin had once again enthusiastically introduced Count Bernadotte's famous peace proposal, even though it had already been rejected by the Arabs as well as by us. This was very strange for Mr. Bevin had always refused to envisage a solution that was not satisfactory to Arabs and Jews alike. This time he obtained the accord of Transjordan, but only of Transjordan; the other Arab countries remained silent. How to explain this sudden about-face? The key to the mystery came to us over Radio Middle East, a station installed by the British on Cyprus. The announcer, in effect, urged the Arabs to accept Count Bernadotte's proposition, adding that "regardless of what support the British can give the Arabs, the Jews will win more territory if hostilities are prolonged."

Mr. Bevin, then, feared an Arab defeat. He even admitted it. But he figured that with the Negev taken from Israel and annexed to Transjordan, the British would have at their command a vast region in which to establish new bases for their military power in the Middle East.

Our own answer was the Negev campaign.

This time, our plan of operations called for the active participation of the Air Force. We counted on it to neutralize Egyptian air power, notably by bombing the base at El-Arish. Furthermore, our fighter planes were to support our ground groups' offensive actions.

Following a recent accord reached under the auspices of the U.N., the Egyptians had agreed to grant safe conduct through their lines to our convoys bringing food and medicine to our settlements in the Negev. However, when, on October 15th a convoy of sixteen trucks reached the Egyptian positions, the enemy opened fire. The two lead trucks were demolished and the convoy had to turn back.

The Israeli Army retaliated with a blistering attack launched simultaneously by the Army and the Air Force. We even decided to throw our transport planes into the battle, using them to support the troops.

During the night of October 15th, our B-17's, Beaufighters, ME-109's, Spitfires, C-46's, Dakotas, and our light planes were all sent out at once to designated objectives which they hit fairly hard, especially at El-Arish where many planes were destroyed on the ground. The enemy had been taken completely by surprise and his antiaircraft batteries only succeeded in hitting one of our planes, a Beaufighter, which nevertheless got back to our lines on one engine.

On the morning of the 16th, our troops were thrown into the offensive. Their objective was Fallouja, one of the key positions in the Egyptian defense. The fighting was very heavy from the beginning, for the enemy was strongly entrenched and protected by powerful artillery. Two ME-109's supported our infantry action. Given chase by two Egyptian Spitfires, they managed to shoot one of them down. After fierce fighting, which came to hand-to-hand combat, our troops, although badly punished by enemy artillery, succeeded in making considerable advances. However, as the arrival of Egyptian reinforcements was reported to be imminent, we threw the rest of our planes into the action. Our Flying Fortresses again bombed the base at El-Arish, inflicting heavy losses.

The next day, our troops assaulted a strategic point located at the intersection of two roads from which it would be possible to circumvent Fallouja, which could not be taken from the front.

Two days later, the strategic intersection fell into our hands. The road to the Negev was ours.

Up until now, quite miraculously, by the way, our Air Force had not suffered a single loss. Our planes, however, had been flying at low altitudes to be sure of not missing their targets, and deliberately defying antiaircraft batteries. This impunity could not last forever. One of our planes was finally hit while knocking out an enemy position. The pilot Modi Alon managed to bring it back to the base, but he crashed just before landing, and was killed. He had been the commander of our first fighter squadron, an Israeli, a former pilot in the R.A.F., one of our best men.

On October 20th, our army entered Beersheba, the city of the seven wells founded by Abraham. The South had been liberated, but the battle for the Negev was not over. The Egyptians still occupied the Fallouja sector, solidly entrenched in Fort Iraq Suweidan. We decided on a new attack. Two Beaufighters were designated to bomb the objective.

The first plane made a low passage but could not drop its bombs because of the failure of the release mechanism. The second Beaufighter made a pass, hitting the target. The first aircraft came in again for strafing, was hit and crashed. The pilot, Leonard Fitchet, a Canadian non-Jew, a true volunteer to our cause, the co-pilot, Stanley Andrews, a Jewish volunteer from the States and the navigator and bombardier, Dov Sugarman, a Jewish volunteer from England were all killed. Three young men gave their lives, three young men who had just survived a war and to whom the future belonged. The words which Andrews' sister wrote: "My youngest brother, a boy of 24, left our country, one that he loved and was proud of, to fight for your cause because he could not stand by and not help" apply to all of them. They all loved and were proud of their own countries, but being men born in freedom they came to us to help us to regain our freedom.

On the evening of the 24th, we again had to mourn for

friends. A Dakota crashed near Ekron and Lee Cantor, the pilot, a Jewish volunteer; the co-pilot, Fred Stevenson, a non-Jewish volunteer; the navigator, William Fisher, a Jewish volunteer, all three from Canada, and the radio operator, Yehuda Litman, a Jewish volunteer from England, were killed.

During the recent four days of the battle the Air Force executed 240 missions dropping 150 tons of bombs. Quite an achievement and we were proud of it.

Victory

DAY BY DAY, our troops slowly and painfully gained ground. Although the Egyptians still resisted in the Fallouja sector, the enemy had been cleaned out of the rest of the southern coast and pushed back toward Gaza. A breakthrough had also been made in the direction of the Dead Sea. The defenders of Fallouja, surrounded by our troops, abandoned by the Egyptian army which made not the slightest effort to rescue them, starved and exhausted, nevertheless fought on.

"As long as my men still have ammunition, I see no reason to give up," their chief had declared to our general when the two met to discuss negotiations for a surrender.

Our General Staff therefore prepared to make a final attack on Fallouja, and the Air Force's fondest hope was to be able to provide the assault infantry with powerful air cover. In order to do so, we needed more Spitfires.

In Prague, sadly, the situation had not changed at all. However, the Czech authorities did seem at times to be more conciliatory—an attitude which some people attributed to our recent victories in Israel, while others simply believed that the Czechs wanted to recoup our mounting debts as quickly as possible.

But when proposed, the non-stop flight and our request for

a take off field with a longer runway one hundred miles south was rejected. We asked again for a meeting with the Air Force. It was an unfortunate meeting indeed. The Air Force pilots objecting this time to flying without radios. Sam answered them that in our case the usefulness of the radio was limited to intercommunication only. When the Czechs replied that we would not be able to get any weather reports with the winter weather growing really bad, Sam retorted: "I'd rather have fuel." The Czechs did not know about our difficulties in Yugoslavia and we were loathe to let them know, fearing that it might affect their attitude too. Arguments followed but the decision was "No flight" and, therefore, no longer runway.

Having had to reject, in the end, Sam Pomerantz' plan for a non-stop flight, which really did seem too risky an undertaking, we needed above all to find a new intermediary base.

On the 15th of November we had fifteen Spitfires ready for flight; eight filled for the usual trip and seven for a long-range trip. Under the pretext of winter conditions, we asked for permission to extend the runway for 120 yds. and our request, to our utmost surprise, was granted. We did not fool the Czechs, it was obvious that unofficially they gave in, hinting here and there, that it would be the last flight. Officially we could not take off.

Our men were losing patience when, on the 7th of December, we received a cable from our man in Yugoslavia that permission was granted, but on several conditions. No more than six aircraft per flight; no living quarters in town and no contact with civilians; the entire operation was to be conducted with the utmost discretion. It was then the middle of December, the winter was exceptionally harsh, and yet our men had to move into uncomfortable underground shelters built by the Germans during the war. Their lot was not at all enviable, but at least we were able to resume operations, and that was the important thing.

On the 9th the pilots arrived and Yugoslavia re-established radio contact with us, and with Israel. The first cable dispatched to Israel with a copy to us read: "Have moved to field ready to receive you any time. Large field two miles South of Titograd not marked, only T placed. Runway South to North right side of railway coming from South. Aircraft must be marked with Yugoslav flags. Bring with you all food and cooking facilities for all crews. Also bedding. Bring mechanics equipped with all tools and rig for loading damaged Spits. Two ships must come. Bring an outfit for starting Spits. Details on field will follow. Advise when coming. No oil available." In an additional cable he asked that paint be brought to change markings for return.

The painting of Yugoslav markings was quite a surprise to everybody. We feared complications with the Czechs and political trouble, for us and Yugoslavs should the aircraft be forced to land on the way. We asked the Yugoslavs to reconsider this point and paint Israeli Air Force markings on all aircraft, including the Spitfires. The Yugoslavs agreed after lengthy discussions.

Our only remaining task was to get permission from the Czechs to fly out the fifteen Spitfires which were ready to leave for Israel. The Czechs took advantage of our request to remind us, with infinite courtesy, that we owed them quite a lot of money. Permission would be granted, they stipulated, only upon receipt of a deposit of a few hundred thousand dollars on payments due. At the time, our financial situation was far from secure. We tried to obtain a delay, on the pretext of having to verify the bills before we paid them. We promised to take care of this detail as soon as the planes had left. The Czech answer was not long in coming: no money, no permission.

I will never know where or how Pinchas Sapir found the

necessary amount, but twenty-four hours later the deposit the Czechs demanded was made.

The Czechs were so pleased with the money, that they even agreed to our airplane landing in Prague to collect some of the Spitfire armament. Officially they would state that the airplane was bringing oranges for Christmas and I well remember that in my cable home, I really insisted that at least fifty cases of oranges be loaded onto the aircraft. With the scarcity of food in Czechoslovakia, I hoped to achieve a lot with fifty cases of our oranges.

Alas! We had permission to take off but we could not move, the weather being so bad that even radio contact with our base in Yugoslavia had been interrupted. A blizzard was raging throughout Europe and we began to doubt that we would be able to carry through our plans before winter really set in.

On December 16th, radio contact with Yugoslavia was restored, and we learned that the weather there was equally foul; our men began to feel that they would freeze to death in their underground shelters.

During the evening hours the DC-4 landed in Prague carrying oranges. We asked for news from home—it was good. The Air Force was doing well but unfortunately there were some more losses. Three men, Oliver Holton, an American non-Jewish volunteer, an ex-fighter pilot of the celebrated Eagle Squadron of the Battle of Britain, Ralph Mooler, a Jewish volunteer from Canada, and Alvin Levy, a Jewish volunteer from the States, were killed in a flight over the Sea of Galilee.

On the 17th, the weather began to improve. We at once notified Podgorica and Israel that, conditions permitting, the Spitfires would take off on the morning of the eighteenth.

At dawn on December 18th, all our pilots assembled in the little waiting room at the field. The weather was still bad, but the forecast was good. In the hangar, our mechanics checked over the six Spitfires scheduled to take off first. Outside the windows we could see buildings and the field covered with a thick blanket of snow, while from the low-hanging sky huge flakes still fell. But, at eight o'clock, the snow stopped; in an instant all our "slaves" were mobilized to clear the runway.

Sam was a bit nervous but in a good mood. So were the remaining five: George L., Bill P., Sandy G., Red F. and Moti Fine. Six determined men of whom five were experienced pilots, foreign volunteers. Only Moti was a young Israeli, with but a few hours' flying time in the Spitfire.

Nothing is more gripping than those last moments when an operation which has been ready to go for some time still hangs in the balance. Our pilots displayed an imperturbable calm.

The weather was definitely improving. Yugoslavia announced that it was clearing there as well, but that there were still storms along the route.

Sam! You could have complete confidence in him. He would give the order if there was a chance, however small, of getting through. Everyone looked at Sam, the boss. Would he give the order to take off?

Sam went up to the control tower; he wanted to get the latest weather information. When he came back, his mind had been made up: "Take off in one hour." In a final briefing, it was decided that the group should fly in as close formation as possible. Charts were taken out, and the route verified one last time.

Sam took off first, quickly followed by the five others.

I can still feel our anguish as we waited for news from Yugoslavia. But the news did not come. Scarcely an hour had gone by when we heard the sound of engines overhead. Four Spitfires came closer, flew over the field, and then landed. The pilots, caught in a snow storm, had decided to turn back.

What had happened to the two missing planes, one of which was Sam's and the other Bill P.'s? We still hoped against all hope that they had gotten through the storm and that, soon, Yugoslavia would radio their arrival.

I doubt if anyone slept that night. I know that I could not get to sleep. We were all war veterans, we had seen many of our men go off and not come back, but now this was really our fight, and victory depended to a large extent on us.

On the morning of the 19th, the first bulletin arrived: the Yugoslavs announced that two Spitfires had crashed in the mountains, that one pilot was dead, and the other injured. The dead one was Sam.

On the 19th, the weather was clear. Twelve Spitfires were again ready for take off: G.L., Sandy R., Red F., John F. Mc., Arnold R., Caesar D., Red M., Sid A., Jack D., Jack C., Moti F. and Danny S. They took off in two flights, each flight six aircraft. After a flight of three hours and forty-five minutes both flights landed safely in Yugoslavia. Three days of preparations including painting of Israeli markings and on the 22nd only eleven Spitfires could take off, the twelfth having mechanical trouble. Unfortunately, one more had to return because of an engine snag. Everything went according to plan and each flight, led by a C-46, landed safely in Israel on the 22nd of December after a flight of six hours and forty-five minutes. Ten more Spitfires—it was a welcome addition to our air power.

Operation "Velveta" as we coded it was completed but Sam Pomerantz, the man who planned the operations, worked it out and carried it through, had gone. His courage and determination may serve us an example. His memory is linked not only with the first Spitfires in the Israeli Air Service but with the very existence of the Air Force, to which he contributed his life.

December 22nd was the day chosen for our forces' final

offensive! By-passing the pocket of Fallouja, our troops had just launched an assault on enemy lines towards Auja el-Hafir, the gateway to the Sinai Peninsula. They had made a breakthrough.

Our Spitfires, however, would be of no use at all without their arms, which had stayed behind in Czechoslovakia. They were to have followed immediately, by air. But how?

The Czechs refused landing rights for our heavy planes. On the other hand, there was not a single plane in Czechoslovakia capable of linking Prague with Tel-Aviv. We were losing hours, precious hours, in fruitless negotiations.

The only way out was to charter Dakotas from the Czech national company, have them transport our arms to a Yugoslav airport and, from there, relay them to Israel in our C-46's. But regrettably, relations between Czechoslovakia and Yugoslavia being what they were, no Czech plane was allowed to land in Yugoslavia.

Would we have to admit defeat? Would Sam's death have been in vain? No. That was impossible.

Before the war, the famous Bat'a had built a veritable city from shoe profits around his shoe factory at Zlin. We went to Zlin, for the Bat'a factory had earlier acquired two Dakotas which were no longer in use. The company would undoubtedly be willing to charter them to us if we paid in dollars. And if, furthermore, we could persuade it to remove the Czech identification markings from the two planes, we would perhaps have the solution we were looking for.

The Yugoslavs, when consulted, agreed to our new plan provided the operation was carried out at night and the C-46 from Israel left before daylight.

Now we only needed the consent of the Czechs. To our great surprise, they agreed to everything right away, with no objections.

Zlin is a pleasant little city, with its small airport squeezed in between the factory buildings. It was quite a feat to fly a Dakota out of this hemmed-in field during the day. To attempt it at night, in winter, when the field was covered with deep snow, seemed absolutely impossible. But it was done, nonetheless. In the glare of the floodlights we saw first one, then the other Dakota, throttles wide open, clear the wall at the end of the runway by just a few feet, but clear it. The flight went smoothly, although the unmarked Dakotas ran into some antiaircraft fire from the Albanians who were shooting at all unidentified planes flying over their territory at that time.

The arms arrived in time for our Spitfires to take part in the last phases of the operation. Auja el-Hafir, Abu-Ageila and El-Arish were captured from the Egyptians. Our forces crossed the frontiers of the Palestine of the Mandate and penetrated the Sinai Desert. The Egyptian army was in a shambles.

On January 6th, Cairo agreed to discuss terms for an armistice.

But our victory was supremely distasteful to the British. Through the intermediary of Washington, they delivered an ultimatum threatening us with armed intervention unless our troops withdrew immediately behind the frontiers established by the Mandate. His Majesty's government had apparently just learned that we were at war with Egypt and had suddenly decided to respect the letter of the clauses of the 1936 Anglo-Egyptian Treaty in which the two countries had agreed on mutual assistance in case of war or threat of war.

Not once, since the Declaration of November, 1947, had Great Britain publicly taken such a clearly pro-Arab stand. After British troops left Palestine, local British authorities had arranged to transfer certain military bases to the Arabs; but in the early stages of the fighting had never openly intervened. After the second truce, however, we had observed their planes from Cyprus making regular flights over Israel to photograph our installations. Since we suspected them of turning the photographs over to Cairo, we resolved to protect ourselves. In December, two of our planes gave chase to a British plane over Israel, and shot it down. From then on, no British aircraft ventured over our territory until the end of the Negev campaign.

But, on January 7, 1949, we learned that the British Air Command had been ordered to intervene once again. In a communiqué, the British Air Ministry claimed that R.A.F. aircraft had been attacked by Israeli fighter planes while making a reconnaissance flight over Egyptian territory to evaluate how far Israeli troops had penetrated into Egypt. The communiqué added that four R.A.F. planes had been shot down.

Despite the apparent clarity of this account, the communiqué falsified the facts, as we learned from reading captured documents and interrogating British prisoners.

In reality, on the morning of January 7, 1949, four British pilots attached to a squadron stationed in the Canal Zone had been assigned a special mission. The pilots were named Cooper, Close, McEllrow and Cook. They were told that a battle was taking place on the Egypto-Israeli frontier and that they were to determine the exact location of the battle, take photographs of respective positions of the two armies involved and bring back as much information as possible on the progress of the fighting. It was an armed reconnaissance flight and the guns in all aircraft were loaded. On the same morning two of our Spitfires left on a reconnaissance flight and were flying over the zone occupied by our troops when the pilots picked up a conversation in English over their radios. When they got above the Rafah-ugia highway, they spotted three Spitfires, presumably Egyptian, strafing a convoy of Israeli trucks. Our planes swooped down on the aggressors, shooting down two Spitfires whose pilots bailed out. At the last moment our pilots were astounded to see that their adversaries bore the markings of the R.A.F.

As soon as they got back to their base, our pilots made their report, which seemed incredible. But, a little later, our infantry reported that three enemy planes had been shot down; the first two in aerial combat, the third by the artillery. Two foreign pilots had been captured: Frank Close and McEllrow.

When questioned, Close stated that he had only been flying over the combat area. He had been flying at a low altitude "almost on deck" when he had been hit by small arms fire from the ground. McEllrow stated that he was fired at by an enemy aircraft and after his Spitfire started to burn, he bailed out. Both pilots denied having strafed the convoy of trucks.

That same day, in the afternoon, four of our Spitfires flying east of Rafah spotted eight planes in combat formation. They were silver-colored and painted with the insignia of the R.A.F. Under their wings, one could clearly distinguish their cargoes of bombs which they soon began to drop. Our Spitfires engaged them in combat and another British plane was shot down. This time the pilot did not have time to bail out. We recovered his body in Israeli territory amid the wreckage of his plane, ten miles from the Egyptian frontier.

These incidents dumbfounded us. Many of our pilots had learned their profession in the R.A.F., and were proud of its traditions. Besides, we were fighting the Arabs, not the British, and we wanted to avoid complications.

As might have been expected, the British Government's reaction was unpleasant. The Foreign Office demanded an explanation and reparations, while at the same time reinforcements arrived to strengthen the British troops stationed at Aqaba.

However, in Great Britain, public opinion disapproved of

the R.A.F. raids and of sending reinforcements into Egypt. And the United States, although it had supported Great Britain in her demand that we withdraw our troops from Egyptian territory, condemned the action of the R.A.F. without reservation.

On January 12, 1949, Egyptians and Israelis met again, this time at Rhodes, to work out conditions for an eventual armistice.

But negotiations proceeded extremely slowly and in an atmosphere of hostility. We claimed all the Negev region and the main outline of the old boundaries as defined by the Mandate. For their part, the Egyptians demanded the immediate withdrawal of our troops from the Beersheba and the whole southern portion of the Negev—demands which we considered unacceptable. We wanted peace, to be sure, but not peace at any price. In short, the negotiations were in danger of falling through since Egypt seemed to have made the annexation of Beersheba into a question of national prestige.

We each stood our ground until the U.N. delegate, who was acting as mediator, proposed that we negotiate, starting from the positions we currently held. This compromise gave the Egyptians the possibility of backing down without losing face.

The armistice was signed on February 24, 1949. The south of the Negev, except for the region around Gaza, remained in our possession. The evacuation of the Egyptian brigade surrounded at Fallouja was ordered; the last Egyptian soldiers left Israeli soil.

The signing of joint armistices with Lebanon and Transjordan did not take place until the 23rd of March and the 3rd of April respectively, which gave us time to recapture for Israel the port of Elath, on the Red Sea, until then occupied by the Transjordanians.

The armistice with Syria was signed on July 20, 1949. The war for the independence of Israel had ended in victory for us.

But it was soon evident that the peace would only be an armed peace. A few days after the 20th of July, one could, indeed, read in the Syrian newspaper *Al Ayam* statements that at least had the merit of being crystal clear: "It would be humiliating for Arabs to no longer desire the destruction of Israel. The Israelis know full well that the accords just concluded with the Arab states will not spare them from a future war which will see the return of Palestine to the Arabs."

From Bagdad to Cairo came a similar chorus of threats. The Arab leaders were trying to attenuate the bitterness of their defeat by giving voice to their old hatred. To fly the banners of Islam over Palestine remained their dream and, in spite of everything, they counted on making it come true in the near future.

18

The Day of Reckoning

ALTHOUGH PEACE had come, my modest hope of returning to Israel right away was not to be. I was ordered not to leave Prague until the expiration of the current contract, after the departure of the last Spitfire and the liquidation of all accounts.

A rather unpleasant surprise awaited us in the course of going over the above mentioned accounts. The first bills, fairly old ones, were extremely reasonable. But, after a certain date, prices had been raised to a point that seemed excessive and inexplicable to us. We felt we had been tricked, and said so. The discussions that followed were not conducted in the gentle language of diplomacy. Remarks far from polite were made by both sides and, on several occasions, negotiations were on the point of breaking off entirely.

These days have left us with a painful memory. It was hard for us to forget all that we owed the Czechs. On the whole, just about everything. Czech arms and Czech planes had enabled us to liberate the land of Israel.

But while it was clear that the aid given us by the Czechs was priceless, there nevertheless does exist a well-defined limit to the price of a specific article, whether it be a plane or a machine gun. Also, if the Czechs had kept strictly to business, or if they had acted like the Bulgarians who demanded a payment of $10,000 every time one of our planes landed on their soil, the situation would have been more clear-cut. But, on the contrary, they had talked endlessly of their devotion to our cause, their wish to support us to the end. . . . And now they expected to make a handsome profit.

I must add that the officials we were dealing with were unknown to us. Members of the Communist party had replaced our old friends, certain of whom had disappeared without our being able to find out exactly what had become of them. Our new opposite members were plainly not there to negotiate, but to dictate their conditions.

During the same period, Zionist activities in Czechoslovakia were gradually snuffed out. Emigration to Israel became difficult and Jewish institutions passed into Communist hands. Our Embassy found itself becoming more and more isolated from the Czech population, including Czech Jews. Nobody seemed to want to see us anymore, or to be seen with us: our friends, Jewish and non-Jewish, now begged us not to come to see them, not even to telephone them. Rumors, which were later confirmed, hinted at the arrest of certain friends we had in the Czech Army and Air Force.

Nobody could explain this gradual change of attitude and many reasons were given—guesses rather than logical deductions, as it is quite impossible to apply Western logic to a Communist regime.

I still had my pass and I was travelling a great deal to speed up work. One day after having taken stock of some Spitfire spares, we were invited to lunch in the officers' mess. This had not happened to us for a long time and we accepted the invitation gladly.

We enjoyed the conversation with our host who spoke good English, having spent some time during the war in England, when suddenly the door opened and a group of high-ranking officers walked in. They were mostly Russians with a few Czechs.

It was the first time that we met Russian officers on a Czech airfield. There were rumors that the Russians were taking over some of the airfields, could this base be one of them?

Our escort disappeared, saying that he would return in a few moments.

The officers were discussing in Russian the building of some new installations and since I understand Russian I could not help overhearing the conversation.

We were pretty uncomfortable and it was better to disappear as quickly as possible without attracting attention. We were ready to move when suddenly one of the Czech officers left the table and came towards us. We were asked who we were. We answered in English producing our passes. The officer then inquired politely whether we spoke Russian as he would like us to join their table. We thanked him and his friends for the kind invitation, we regretted that we did not speak Russian and we stressed that we were rather in a hurry as our Ambassador was waiting for our report. We shook hands with beautiful smiles all over our faces, our hearts down in our stomachs.

Closing the doors I heard him saying in Russian "Israelis who bought the Spitfires from us. American Jews who do not understand Russian."

It was a narrow escape but not for long. The conversation would be reported to the Security Police in Prague who knew that I spoke Russian well. A few days later my pass was withdrawn on the grounds that the job was completed, and all the spares dispatched to Kunovice.

We did not protest but we asked for a pass to Žatec only. The answer was simple—"No pass, a Czech officer will escort you whenever you want to go there."

From many other unmistakable signs, we gathered that it

would be wise for us to get out as soon as possible. The Czechs, now part of the Communist Bloc, felt that we knew too much on too many subjects. By going around airports, and through military bases and factories, which we did frequently, we obviously could acquire quite a store of information. It was of little interest to us and we did not seek it out, but we were neither blind nor deaf.

They were not very subtle. Our mail, which used to arrive quite regularly, was suddenly delayed. Sometimes they handled it carefully, sometimes they did not even bother to cover it up. The personnel of the hotel became arrogant and unfriendly. The service became bad. We had a friend, a waiter, and one morning he managed to whisper that he regretted his behavior, but he had to carry out orders. Our rooms were searched, our things were disappearing for "cleaning" and returned cleaned, although we did not ask for it. And no matter where we went we were followed.

Some of their methods were really childish. Our maid in the hotel, a plain, pleasant country girl was replaced by a beautiful creature who spoke French and English. She told us her life story. She was the daughter of a rich landowner who was in jail and she was now forced to do this degrading work. She hated Communists and she hated the regime. She was prepared to give anything for help in escaping. We listened politely without comments and we were "so sorry that we could not be of any help to her."

One night we found her in bed. We were most desolated to throw her out. She disappeared and did not bother us again.

We were forced to accept the bulk of the Czech demands. And get out of Prague! I admit that I left with no regrets, but with deep concern for many of my Czech friends who were forced to stay behind, for whom the freedom that they helped us to win became a dream of their own.

Adding Up the Score

WHEN THE YEARS of the fight for independence came to an end, years which, for many people in Israel, still are the years of the great adventure, it was possible to add up the score, to measure exactly the results of our efforts. Had we succeeded in giving Israel a real Air Force? In the armed peace ahead of us, would our air power be capable, when confronted with Arab air power, of guaranteeing our security? We were left with the Spitfires, the B-17, C-46's, Dakotas and some light airplanes to face the future.

It had been a romantic period, this period of getting wings for Israel, whatever wings we could and whenever they could be obtained. All the purchased airplanes were put to good service and did their job, although most of them could not be called military aircraft in the exact sense. Their distinguishing characteristic was their availability and we did not have much choice.

I have heard this period called the period of great adventure. It was for some, but for most of us these were times of hard work. The only purchases which smacked of adventure were Zur's in England and luckily we escaped embarking on a real adventure of "lifting" some airplanes.

It was in the beginning of '49. Some of our men reported

two Tempest fighters stationed on an airfield and conceived a scheme to steal them. It was one of those romantic schemes so appealing to us at certain periods of our life. It was not a serious plan and could end badly. Luckily enough the entire scheme was cancelled, better judgment prevailing.

It is true that some of the airplanes purchased were not exactly the ships that the Air Force wanted; with medium bombers we could do a much better job than dropping bombs from Dakotas or Rapides, or with real photographic airplanes equipped with air cameras we could take better pictures than with a hand camera through the open door of an Auster. The problem was not what we wanted, but what we could get.

The best military planning has no value if one does not have the equipment which it requires. It was much to the credit of our men, that they managed to get so much out of the equipment which was put at their disposal.

Our victory was not only due to the ability of our men, but to the fact that our enemy was inefficient and incapable of using its equipment. In other circumstances we would not have been able to cope so easily with the air situation.

In modern warfare, especially in the air, courage alone does not win battles. A man has to have the necessary equipment to face the enemy in the air. Quality of the equipment should come first, quantity second. Until the last phase of the war, we had neither quality nor quantity.

From the beginning of the war until the very end the Arabs had aircraft superior in quality and numbers and logically the air should have been theirs. The first wings of the Egyptian Air Force had been created in 1939. In the beginning, they had grand ideas: 500 aircraft were to be bought at once, a veritable airborne armada worthy of the oriental imagination. This splendid project remained in the myth stage for some time. After 1944, Egypt did acquire a considerable number of planes, for the most part from R.A.F.

bases in Egypt. The Egyptian Government also overhauled some of the many planes abandoned by the U.S. Air Force at one of the airfields it used, near Cairo. By 1947, the Egyptian Air Force had become a reality. And its power was already something to be reckoned with.

The build-up continued during the years that followed. In May of 1948, the Egyptians confiscated some Dakotas which had landed at the Cairo airport. In September of the same year, with the help of British technicians, they repaired and reconditioned twenty more Dakotas from among those left behind by the Americans. These they traded for ten Spitfires, the bargain being concluded through the intermediary of a British firm with the blessing of the R.A.F. During this same period Great Britain—which was simultaneously campaigning for an embargo on arms—also delivered some four-engined bombers to Egypt.

Then Italy became Egypt's principal source of supply. In October of 1948, the Egyptians made a deal with Fiat which netted them thirty-five fighter planes, and another with Macchi which brought them eighteen planes.

Egypt, then, was not lacking in planes when she went to war against Israel. The country also had the benefit of beautifully equipped airfields and well-trained pilots. All this was to collapse, however, under the stress of battle: the Egyptian Air Force always made a poor showing, without there ever seeming to be a plausible explanation of why this should be.

The Iraqi Air Force had been created in 1930, and two years later Iraq founded its first flying school. When the revolt against the British broke out in 1941, the Air Force joined the rebels and even made attacks on R.A.F. bases. But the R.A.F., in a surprise counterattack, destroyed most of the planes and airfields in Iraq. In 1944, however, the British contributed generously to the restoration of Iraqi Air Force, proving once again that in politics grudges are forgotten when larger interests are at stake.

In relation to Egyptian air power, Iraq's seemed very modest. It was in a position, nevertheless, to inflict heavy losses on us at the beginning of the war. But it limited its actions to a few strikes whose results were negligible. The same was true of the Syrian Air Force, which had not come into being until 1947 when developments in Palestine called for action. Following Egypt's example, Syria bought twelve Italian fighters which were unloaded in sections in Beirut. But the assembly of the aircraft was not completed until after the war was over. Transjordan had no air force, and Lebanon never bothered to use the few old models that it did have.

In July of 1949, when the armistice had been signed, the Security Council lifted the embargo on shipments of arms to the Middle East. This decision did not surprise us. We knew that the Council favored the Arab states. Certain Western statesmen, blind to the slow evolution of popular feeling against the Arab ruling classes, which were accused of being instruments of Western colonialism, still hoped to regain the lost sympathy of the Arab masses by doing favors. And so, as might have been expected, as soon as the embargo was lifted the Arab countries threw themselves into an arms race.

For our part, all we could obtain, in August of 1949, were a few export licenses for training planes, first in Canada, then in the United States. Our application to buy combat planes was refused by the State Department. In effect, the American Government meant to see to it that our military power remained equal to that of one of the Arab states, Syria or Egypt, for example, and not to that of all the Arab states combined, even though they were allied against us.

During the same period, an Egyptian mission led by Dr. El Rachman, head of the Egyptian Air Ministry, arrived in

England where it signed a contract guaranteeing Egypt the delivery of 110 Vampire and Meteor jets, several dozen Spitfires, and 22 four-engine bombers!

The signing of this contract raised a storm of protest in Great Britain. Public opinion as well as several members of Parliament openly accused the British Government of arming Egypt against Israel. But, despite attacks from the press and the questions raised in Parliament, the contract was ratified.

Egyptian pilots were sent to England to learn how to fly the jets, and the manufacturers involved gave special courses to train maintenance crews for the planes.

As for us, we could only imagine jets in our dreams. We struggled to get hold of some heavy planes in Australia but this project, like so many others, was doomed to failure.

That year, we celebrated New Year's Day with mixed feelings; the joy of victory was coupled with a great deal of anxiety. We were unarmed before the steady build-up of air power in the Arab states, and we well knew that our pilots, with their prop planes, could do nothing against the jets the enemy now had. It was absolutely imperative that we ourselves, and fast, get our own jets to restore the balance of power.

PART TWO

The National Front
in the Open

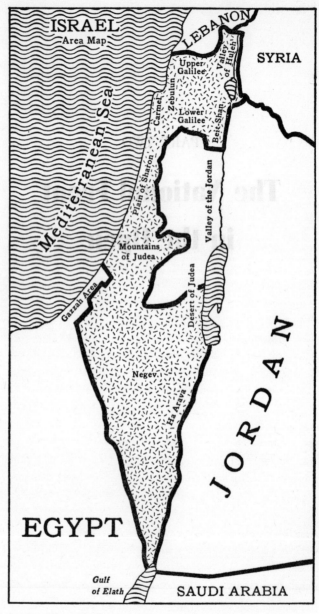

The State of Israel after the armistice of February, 1949

Israel Faces
Her Problems

ON MY RETURN to Israel, I found a country bustling with activity. The Government, with the participation of all Israeli citizens, was resolutely coping with the grave economic problems linked to the massive arrival of immigrants.

When the State of Israel was proclaimed in 1948, the Jewish population numbered 650,000 souls. By 1950 this figure had almost doubled; in the space of two years we had welcomed 500,000 immigrants!

This situation provoked, in a chain reaction, all sorts of problems, one of the most complex being the necessary assimilation of these hundreds of thousands of newcomers from all stations of life who came from all over the world. Many arrived with no money and often with no particular skills. And it was hard to ask a wealthy Jew who had just left his estate in New Zealand or the United States to have the same attitude as a Sephardi from Arabia, brutalized by centuries of poverty and subjection. As André Falk lucidly noted in his remarkable *Israël, Terre deux fois promise* (Le Seuil): "One would see in the most ordinary cafe the unreal splendor of a fairy castle, while the other suffocated in that provincial atmosphere." However, for one as well as the other, it was necessary to find employment, lodging, and to relocate them in a society which at the time was nothing but a mass in constant flux, with new arrivals pouring endlessly into it. When one realizes not only that the State of Israel was a creation *ex nihilo,* but also that the country had no industrial resources and that its cities were little more than overgrown market-places, one wonders how the government was able to solve the very real problems confronting it without any major disasters.

Another source of trouble was the fact that many of the immigrants had lived through the Nazi inferno. Some were survivors of the extermination camps—two Jews out of every thousand, others only escaped deportation by joining the underground, by going into hiding, by somehow living from day to day until the liberation. Each one of these survivors felt that life owed him something, while once again nothing but hardship lay ahead in Israel, a rugged, austere future that swept away illusions.

Finally, added to the horde of European refugees were all those who came from Iraq, from Yemen and Syria, from Egypt and North Africa. A high percentage of these were invalids, people too old to work, blind people, and a large number of retarded children.

As for our armed forces, almost all of them had been demobilized and the majority of foreign volunteers had gone home, some facing trial and jail for what they had done to help us to win our freedom. Nothing happened to the Flying Tigers who flew into China and defended the freedom of the Chinese like what awaited those men who defended the freedom of the Jews. But when Commander Auerbach declared on the witness-stand that by defending the lives of thousands of human beings in Palestine he fulfilled his elementary duty as a U.S. Naval Officer, he spoke both for the living and the dead who were flying desperately, downright foolhardy for our cause.

And again nine Americans were charged with conspiracy to violate the Neutrality Act and Export Control Law. A Grand Jury returned an indictment against Adolph Schwimmer, Roy Selk, Leon Gardner, Sam Lewis and Abraham Levin, that they unlawfully and knowingly conspired, confederated and agreed, to export illegally airplanes, spares and equipment from the United States to Panama, Czechoslovakia, Italy and Israel. There exportations were made by the defendants in willful evasion and violation of the laws of the United States with the full knowledge of the fact that no licenses for the said equipment would be granted.

A second indictment charged Miss Eleanor Rudnick, Schwimmer, Selk and Lewis with conspiring to defraud the War Surplus Administration.

As to the gravity of these charges, American opinion was divided. Those who tended to judge the affair on strictly legal terms thought that the offense was serious and merited a stiff sentence. But the majority of American citizens did not see things that way at all. In approving the conduct of our volunteers, they reaffirmed their faith in the traditional love of liberty which leads every American, whatever his beliefs, to come to the aid of peoples whose independence is threatened.

As soon as the date of the trial was set, the accused who were already in the United States, placed themselves in the hands of the law, and the others came back from Israel to answer the summons. The hearings lasted for about four months. Schwimmer, Gardner and Selk were sentenced to a fine of $10,000. All the others were acquitted. Even Schwimmer, Gardner and Selk got off lightly. The charges against them could have meant years in prison.

In Israel, during this time, the war continued under different forms. The Arabs declared a war of economic sanctions against us, and launched guerrilla actions against our frontier settlements.

The Arabs also exploited to the full the problem posed by their own refugees. Every Arab living in Israel received from his leader an order to leave the country. The result was a massive exodus which we vainly tried to stop by distributing literature throughout our cities and villages, by appeals over the radio, and by personal contacts.

The Arab leaders wanted to show Israel's neighbors the reality of war with its throngs of miserable refugees, and to prove to the whole world that no Arab was willing to accept the establishment of a Jewish State. Of the 620,000 Arabs living in Palestine, almost a half a million took the path of exile.

The Arab states bordering Israel had no idea of assimilating these refugees into their society, but planned rather on using them as a political and military weapon in a future war against Israel. To this end, they herded them into detention camps where the desired effect was soon achieved; incensed by their misery, the refugees blamed their fate on Israel, and their thirst for revenge was carefully nurtured.

The Arabs remaining in Israel were not much better disposed to us. How could they be, when their lives had been disrupted and their families were starving to death in camps across the border? "Do not cooperate with the Jews," was their leader's order of the day. "The hour of revenge is at hand."

This hostility was deepened by Egypt's decision to close the Suez Canal to Israeli shipping, a decision which Egypt justified by stating that the Judeo-Egyptian armistice was in the end nothing but a state of war.

We therefore had good reason to remain on our guard.

21

Paris

MARCH, 1950. I left Israel once again to take charge of our Air Force purchases in Europe. My headquarters were to be Paris. I went back joyfully to this city where, as a young student, I had spent several memorable years. Since childhood, I had learned to think of France not only as the cradle of culture and liberty, but also as the intellectual exemplar for other countries. And it was in France that, for the first time, I had been invited into the intimacy of a Christian family not as a barely tolerable intruder but as a friend. Until then, I had only known the oppressive atmosphere of Poland, the racial hate and Jew-baiting which were the daily fare there.

I owed a lot to France, my entire education, really. It was at the Sorbonne that I first came into contact with the splendors of Western civilization, at the Louvre and at painters' studios that art had grown to have an exciting meaning for me. And the interminable discussions in the cafés of the Latin Quarter had profoundly influenced me, especially the socialist ideas we argued about. In this friendly atmosphere, devoid of all prejudice, my inhibitions and my grievances against Gentiles soon were just unpleasant memories.

When, a few years later, I had to flee the Nazis, France

gave me refuge, and I will never forget the kindness shown me then by the modest schoolteacher of a Breton village. And it was in France again that, when I knocked at the door of an isolated farm house in the middle of the night, I was welcomed in by an old peasant woman who put me up, gave me clothes, and even gave me a little money.

And here I was in France again, in Paris. I remembered that in 1939, when I suddenly had to leave my hotel room in the Latin Quarter to join the Polish army in France, I had left everything I owned in the care of the hotel-keeper. In particular I had left photographs of my family. With the exception of my brother, all my family had since been massacred by the Nazis. Would these precious souvenirs, the thought of which had stayed with me the length of those dark years, still be there?

The hotel had not changed at all. A young woman, whom I hardly recognized, greeted me: when I had been a student, she had just been a little girl. Then Mr. André, the proprietor came. He stared at me for a moment, shook his head several times, blinked his eyes, and finally exclaimed: "Mister Ben!" He embraced me like a member of his family finally returned to the fold. And my suitcases? They were still there, along with those of other students who had no doubt disappeared forever in the turmoil of war. We sat in his parlor and talked about everything over a few bottles of red wine until dawn.

Mr. André was the sort of middle-class Frenchman who is suspicious of his leaders, prefers to vote against a thing, endlessly finds quantities of things to criticize, regularly questions the fate of his country, but is passionately patriotic. As a landlord, he had not always been accommodating. He insisted on being paid with the strictest punctuality and jealously watched to make sure that we did not use too much electricity, forbidding us, for example, to do any ironing or cooking in our rooms. But when the war was declared and the

Polish students, of whom I was one, were cut off from their country and began to run out of money, he proved to be very understanding. He never bothered us when we were behind in the rent and often, when we got home at night, made sure we had had something to eat.

Mr. André had not changed a hair and I realized that France, made up of millions of "Mr. André's," had not changed either.

I set out to find my old friends, the companions with whom I had studied for exams, played cards, and gone all over the French provinces. I found some of them in the air force and the aircraft industries, and we immediately resumed relationships that the war had interrupted.

They painted a bleak picture of the innumerable difficulties the French aircraft industry was up against. Successively bombed by the Germans and the Allies, French factories by 1945 were nothing but a mass of ruins. Those which still operated produced only obsolete models. Since 1940, French aeronautical engineers had been diverted into other industries and had lost all contact with the rapid developments in world aviation. The Nazis had not trusted them, and no French engineer had even been employed in one of the German research centers. After the Liberation, the French aircraft industry had to start from projects it had begun in 1939 and it seemed that, without the aid of the British and the Americans, it soon would flounder in its own backwardness. However, France's allies proved to be just as guarded as the Germans. According to their plans, France was supposed to be content with producing or assembling American and British planes already in service.

Both the British and the Americans underestimated the French genius and French determination to become again the leading aircraft industry in Europe.

Behind their design desks the French engineers rolled up

their sleeves and soon more than a dozen of French designed prototypes were in the air. The trouble was that there were too many of them and none which could go into production as a fighting ship.

The French Air Force demanded fighting aircraft and not prototypes and France had to "go to Canossa" and purchase from Britain a license to produce Vampire-Jet fighters.

"France, the country of prototypes," mocked a journalist well known in aviation circles at the time. His articles which appeared in a widely read newspaper, harshly criticized the Air Ministry and the manufacturers whose archaic programs seemed to illustrate, he said, the worst aspects of French individualism. A little later, I made this man's acquaintance. Extremely dynamic, brilliant, he again held forth in bitter terms on the irresponsibility of the aviation policies of his country. At the same time, he suggested we cast our lot with the Triton SO-6000, a jet training plane, and offered to take us to Brétigny airport, near Paris, where we could judge for ourselves.

On the appointed day, after having made me and my companion wait more than an hour in a bistro near his office, he finally appeared at the wheel of a powerful pre-war sports car. He drove at a fast clip, talking and gesticulating all the way. I was afraid he was going to lose control of the car at any moment and hurtle into the traffic coming from the other direction. But, by some miracle, we got to the airport in one piece.

Three Tritons were there, lined up side by side. It was the first time I had seen a jet plane from close up. I examined it like a curious animal, listening intently to one of the factory engineers' demonstration talk. Three prototypes had been built, and all three had already logged many flight hours. But when we tried to find out if the French Air Force had any intention of producing the planes, we only got the most evasive answers.

It was more than likely that these prototypes were not going into production, but nevertheless we cabled Israel asking them to send a technical mission to Brétigny. This was done, and a group of technicians and a pilot soon joined us in France. We had to admit, unfortunately, that not having had any experience with jet planes, none of us could make any recommendations whatsoever. We therefore decided to take the advice of the French Air Ministry.

What did they think of the Triton? The question was perfectly natural, but not lacking in delicate implications, the Triton being the product of a national enterprise, financed by the Air Ministry, but obviously regarded with suspicion by that same ministry. Furthermore, if the Triton were refused us, would it be because the French were not planning to produce it, or because they did not want to sell us planes?

Our French friends advised us to put our cards on the table. We followed their advice and quickly settled the first point: the French Air Force did not intend to put the Triton into service. But in building prototypes, French technicians had not been wasting their time. They had acquired the experience necessary to carry out further research. The Triton was stricken from our plans. But although France seemed to be sympathetic to us, we still did not know whether or not she would be willing to provide us with jets in the future.

Not until June, 1950, did the Air Ministry announce that it was willing to authorize us to buy Ouragans, the latest French jets, which were going into production.

Everything seemed to be turning out for the best. Sadly, we soon discovered that despite the good will of French aviation circles and of our political friends in France, we still could not conquer the reluctance of the Quai d'Orsay. This reluctance arose from France's political obligations to the Tripartite Commission established by the United States, Great Britain and France to maintain peace in the Middle East. Besides, the French still had interests in Lebanon and Syria and had not given up hope of re-establishing her influence in these two countries. It was therefore important to French diplomats that France not seem to be overly favorable to Israel.

All this bore a strong resemblance to British policy towards us, based on similar interests and similar hopes. It soon became clear the we would not obtain the Ouragans.

22

Return to London

AT THAT PERIOD, the Israeli Air Force was trying to acquire also a plane suitable for the instruction and training of its young pilots. After much backing and filling, we had decided to cast our lot with the Dutch Fokker S-11, and I was sent to the Low Countries to complete the necessary negotiations.

I had never had any contact with the Dutch people, but I felt that I would like them. Holland had never tried to hide her sympathy for us. During the Liberation, the soldiers of the Jewish Brigade stationed in Holland were welcomed with great enthusiasm and received with open arms in every Dutch household. After the war, Holland had been the only European country to oppose the entry of German tourists into her territory. This people, which had always refused to bow to the law of the German invader and had fought it stealthily and stubbornly, was naturally sympathetic to the persecuted Jews and to Israel which had proved its willingness to fight for its independence.

My relations with the representatives of the Fokker corporation were extremely cordial from the start. The company was very anxious to sell the first planes it had produced since the war. But our relations with its directors went way beyond a simple business courtesy.

When the contract with Fokker had been signed, I had to get acquainted with the British aeronautical market.

Ever since I got to Europe, I had intended to go to England. I had many friends there to whom I was tied by memories of the war. But our men in London had informed me that I was featured on the British Police's black list. The Intelligence Service, knowing about my activities in Czechoslovakia, suspected me of being a Communist. This was too much! I had had to leave Prague in a hurry, escaping arrest for "espionage for the West," and now the West accused me of being a Communist!

I was ordered to avoid England. I obeyed, but not without asking our offices in London to clear up my case. Two months had passed since then and, not having had word from London, I decided to take the risk and leave for England anyhow. I alerted our friends in London of my imminent arrival.

In the compartment of the train taking me to London, the memory of my first contact with England in wartime came to mind. After we escaped from France, we landed in Plymouth sick and tired with a dark outlook for the future. France had fallen! How long would England be able to hold out all alone? Some charming old ladies waited on the docks of the harbor to offer us a cup of tea. Tears glistened in their eyes when they saw our ragged clothing, our wounds of fortune, and above all our swollen feet, bloody from the interminable retreat down the highways of France. The incongruity of that cup of tea offered with so much dignity to the veritable tramps that we now were had a singularly soothing effect on our nerves. We burst out laughing.

I was to find the same cordiality and sense of hospitality throughout England, Scotland, where the people of the village would come out to get us at the camp and bring us home to have a drink with them, and Wales, where we finished up our military training.

There, in Barmouth, I was billeted with a family. One day they indicated that they were put out by the fact that I did not go to church, so I told them that I was a Jew. "What's a Jew?" their seven-year-old son asked immediately. My host paused a moment to reflect and then answered, "It's a kind of Christian. A bad Christian, but not quite as bad as a Catholic." I do not know if my host quite understood the uncontrollable laughter that took hold of me at that moment, and that I was not able to stop.

In London, too, I stayed with another family and made friendships that were very dear to me. So the war, then, had given me the chance to get to know and to admire English people. For cities like London, from 1940 to 1944, really were in the front lines, and few countries endured the privations and horrors of war with the nobility and calm of the English.

Sadly, in Palestine, those same English later showed themselves in a different light. People tell me that the British soldiers there were only obeying orders. I know that, and I also know that sometimes discipline can give the appearance of inhumanity, but I cannot help adding that there are different ways of carrying out an order. The very least that one can say is that the method chosen by the British soldiers in Palestine was not always one which came from the heart.

Now, after the war, after Palestine, I was back in England. What kind of atmosphere was I going to find? A half an hour after arriving at Victoria Station a taxi let me off in front of our offices. They were bustling with activity. The methods we had had to use during the underground were nothing but a memory. Our men were in direct, permanent contact with most of the airplane manufacturers. The British we were dealing with were intensely interested in the technical problems of the war we had waged against the Arabs. And they gladly rose above the much thornier question of Judeo-British tension.

After several days in London, it became clear to me that the average Englishman disapproved heartily of Bevin's policy towards us, and that many of them even sympathized with us. The military, also, seemed to be delighted with the lesson our troops had given the Arabs.

From Glasgow we began our methodical prospecting through the British aircraft industries. We were welcomed everywhere as though we were the representatives of a great power. The English, who were used to dealing with the Arabs, even thought that in order to receive us they should stage a sort of oriental ceremony. I admit we were a little miffed at being treated like "Levantines" in this fashion, but we encountered understanding and a desire to help wherever we went. At first we were somewhat skeptical of the promises that were made to us, but they were soon followed up by concrete actions that confirmed the sincerity behind them.

I spent my all too rare moments of leisure visiting old friends, among whom were several experts on the problems of the Middle East. Needless to say, I spent hours questioning them about the British conduct in Palestine.

Almost always, my friends agreed with me in being sharply critical of the higher British officials whose influence was felt by the army as well as the Civil Service, those same officials whose arrogance, stupidity, and often total incompetence had provoked the progressive decline of the British Empire. Protected by the impenetrable walls of their clubs, their offices and residences, these men were incapable of seeing beyond what had always been their dream: pretending to be "little kings." They had a profound contempt for the rest of humanity, which nothing had ever prepared them to understand anyhow.

As I pursued my travels across Great Britain, the good will

of those who were able to help us became more and more evident. However, I was obliged to abandon a good number of my illusions when I got back to London. The officials of the Israeli Embassy, in a better position than I to know what to expect, were far from sharing my optimism. While the heads of the aviation industry might be extremely friendly to us, the Foreign Office still kept us firmly in disfavor. Here, as in France, a deplorable gap persisted between public opinion and government policy. And for the same reasons: the experts on the Arab question still hoped that their country could regain its dominant position in the Middle East. Helping us certainly was not the best way to bring about this eventual redress in the Arab nations.

In the end, the material results of our trip to England turned out to be nil. No planes were supplied to us. All that I brought back to Paris were a few moral compensations.

The Arms Race

IN JUNE OF 1950, the Arab states concluded a military pact of mutual assistance. While probable aggression by Israel was cited, the actual intention of the signers was clearly offensive.

In practical application of this pact, the Arab states at once placed large orders for war materiel in Europe, especially in England. France, still anxious to strengthen her influence in Syria, found that she had to rival Great Britain in good will and supply her share of arms to the Syrians. Once more it must be noted that politics has its reasons of which the heart may disapprove.

The only hope we had left of obtaining arms, the need for which was becoming increasingly pressing, was the change that was operating in our favor in the United States. Public opinion had become very sympathetic to us there, and extended not only to the majority of Senators but to President Truman himself as well.

It seemed to us to be a good time to approach the State Department with a request for arms. We were given to understand that three main factors governed American policy on the supply of arms: availability, security and State reasons. As far as availability was concerned the United States was short of arms and in addition to her own requirements had to take into consideration the urgent need of the North Atlantic countries.

It did no good to point out that we were only interested in surplus arms and aircraft materiel which was already in the hands of surplus dealers; we were told that exportation of this materiel would also impair the military strength of the United States.

At that time hundreds, if not thousands, of aircraft were being broken down and sent to the smelting furnaces.

On the point of security, we were accused of fostering an atmosphere of hysteria in the Middle East. According to the State Department, the Arab countries were not planning an aggression against us at all. However, if we still judged that we had good reason to be alarmed, the State Department would of course be obliged to submit our request to the Joint Chiefs of Staff. It suggested, to do this, that we prepare a complete report on our military objectives, a suggestion that we refused to comply with.

The stated reasons were based on the attitude of Israel with regard to the United States and Russia. Since there were no doubts that we were not a Soviet satellite and the State Department was well aware of our strained relations with the Soviet Union, there were no problems involved.

A short time after this refusal, our second request was definitively rejected. The Joint Chiefs of Staff, according to the State Department, felt that we already had arms in sufficient quantity, and that our air power, in particular, was greater than that of all the Arab states put together. It was useless to expect anything more: our refusal to furnish the requested information had earned us this arbitrary decision. There was no point in dwelling on this refusal: no military treaty or alliance bound us to the United States. We were a sovereign state, and our future depended in part on the well-guarded secret of our military power. All the more so since we had not asked for any military support, but simply for authorization to buy the arms we needed from the United States. But the State Department's refusal was in direct contradiction to the recommendations of the President of the United States and most of the leaders of the Republican and Democratic parties who had promised us the support of their country. It was only explicable in terms of the strong pressure exerted on American diplomacy by the British.

In the impossibility of procuring arms for ourselves, we then tried to obtain a suspension of British deliveries to the Arabs. Here again, we failed. The American State Department and the British Foreign Office considered these deliveries to be necessary to assure the protection of their respective interests in the Middle East. In short, we had to admit that the State Department as well as the Foreign Office would not have been sorry to see us go under.

But we did not admit defeat. Our contacts in the United States were many and powerful. We could count party leaders and Senators among our friends—even Cabinet members. We asked them to intervene vigorously on our behalf. Pressured on all sides, the American Secretary of State finally let a vague promise to reconsider his Department's decision be wrested from him.

In May, the first light appeared on our clouded horizon. After complex negotiations, Canada had agreed to sell us a certain amount of arms on the condition that they would never be used for purposes of aggression. Had Canada's decision had an influence on the State Department? Or had our friends finally worn down the last resistance all by themselves? It is hard to know exactly. In any event, we were soon informed that the American Government was prepared to give us partial satisfaction: only arms of a defensive nature would be released to us, and we were not to buy materiel other than what could be found on the surplus market. This last restriction, unfortunately, seemed to remove all hope of getting combat planes.

Export licenses for training and liaison planes were issued us. But, meanwhile, we found some old prop-driven Mustang P-51's at various surplus dealers which we had to take apart completely and list as spare parts for shipment.

Then the Korean War broke out. The State Department instantly found a valid reason to suspend the authorizations that had been granted us. It was true, however, that the United States might in the future need every piece of equipment that it then had.

Some of our men suggested that we return to the methods used at the time of our war for independence, that is, all the tricks of the underground. This suggestion was rejected. Our official representatives refused to believe that the United States would turn down all our requests simply to protect their petroleum interests in the Middle East. They forgot that, in today's world, it's oil that dictates the law.

We decided from then on to try our luck in various Latin American countries. There, planes were slowly deteriorating on airfields without anybody caring. One of these countries had no less than a hundred bombers! The responsible authorities seemed strongly disposed to sell us some of these craft, the profits from which would allow them to buy jets in England. An interview was arranged in New York, which ended in a verbal agreement for the sale of twenty-five planes. Our hopes, which had been raised, were nevertheless short-lived: we discovered that these planes could not be sold without the permission of the United States, where they had been bought originally.

In America, decidedly, nothing was going our way. A good many of us felt that it would have been wiser to bring all our efforts to bear on Europe instead of wasting them in the New

World. But the prestige of the United States had blinded some of our people who firmly believed that European nations, France in particular, were incapable of making a decision without the prior consent of Washington.

We in France were of a different opinion. Although the American influence was decisive in the French Foreign Office, some of the other ministries and especially the Ministry of Defense, fought for an independent French foreign policy. Behind the Ministry of Defense were the French Armed Forces.

"Impossible" Is Not in the French Vocabulary

A VISIT to the French Air Ministry suddenly revealed to us that a certain number of Mosquitos were going to be put up for sale.

After the war, France had bought various types of Mosquitos from England: fighter-bombers, night fighters and reconnaissance planes.

Those aircraft, suitable for different missions, could solve our immediate operational problems, facilitating at the same time the maintenance aspect.

The Mosquito fighter bomber armed with four 20 mm. cannons and four machine guns and capable of carrying a load of bombs was famous for its exploits during the last war. The airplane's fighting record was a long tale of famous sorties.

During our preliminary inquiries our friends in the Ministry had warned us that the French Air Force, after having a few unexplained accidents in which wings folded up in the air, suspected that the wooden structure of the aircraft was rotten; the airplanes, built for the duration of the war, were unable to withstand age and the change of climatic conditions. Since using these planes in Indo-China had proved to be disastrous, the French strongly doubted that they would be suitable for operations in the Middle East. Further inquiry revealed that what they said was true: many Mosquitos sent to the Far East had had to be abandoned because of structural failures.

These findings were hardly encouraging. However, we knew that the Mosquitos had done wonders during the war and that a large number of them were still in service in Canada as well as in England. We therefore charged our men in London with filling in the information we already had without, however, revealing the reason for our investigations. The details we received from the De Havilland firm, builders of the Mosquito, and from the R.A.F., completely contradicted what we had just heard in France. The British technicians claimed that the accidents were caused by careless maintenance, and that storage conditions for the planes were equally important. According to them, if the Mosquitos were properly stored and maintained, there was nothing to worry about. Since we had great confidence in the experience of the R.A.F., we decided to take steps towards the acquisition of the Mosquitos in France without further delay.

In 1950 all our demands for arms went through the Export Department of the Defense Ministry, which channeled them to the Air Ministry and forwarded their reply to us. It was a rather long procedure. The airman, jealous of his independence, resented the intermediary role of the soldier.

A fortnight passed without a reply, the Colonel in charge of the Export Department quite helpless in the face of the Air Ministry's silence. Only a direct meeting with the Air Ministry could break this deadlock.

The interview was granted but we had a cold, though polite,

reception, the airman refusing to discuss airplanes with an army officer, our military attaché.

I once heard about a visit of one of our army officers to the Pentagon. While talking to a high-ranking officer he noticed a book on the table marked "secret" for which he had been looking for a long time.

"May I have a look at it?" he asked the officer.

"Take it," answered the man. "If I have given it to the Air Force, there is no reason to refuse it to you."

After being informed in very general terms that there were some Mosquitos available, most of them beyond the stage of repair, the airmen informed us that orders would be issued for a complete report to be forwarded to the Defense Ministry. Neither the official tone, nor the official channels were promising and I could well imagine the length of time the drawing up of such a report would take.

I suggested a meeting with the officers concerned as between Air Force officers, we should be able to clarify problems that might emanate from the report. It would save time, the Defense Ministry not being in a position to give the right answers on the spot.

The airman looked at me and smiled. The conversation took immediately a different turn and the tone was less official. We talked about our Air Force, about our war experience and the Arab pilots. We left the Ministry with a promise that orders would be issued for a meeting to be arranged as early as possible.

A few days later I was closeted with Mosquito experts who seemed to know all the answers. No information was withheld and I felt as if I were in a conference with our own officers and not with foreign ones, who were selling equipment.

Yes, there had been a few unexplained accidents. They could be attributed either to structural failures or to pilot's fault. Careful attention had to be paid to some of the known weak spots but generally the aircraft behaved well.

I learned that most of the Mosquitos were stored at the airfield at Chateaudun, and that some of them, fighter-bombers, were stored in hangars and could be put back in perfect flying condition very cheaply. The night fighters, on the other hand, had spent several winters outdoors at the mercy of the weather, and we would do well to cross them off our list. Other Mosquitos, besides, could be found at fields in Tours and Rennes.

All these planes had arrived in France armed and fully equipped. But, subsequently, their arms had been dismounted and put in storage. Their radios and radar sets had been used to equip other planes. However, there were plenty of spare parts, notably engines, in depots, which would be very useful in overhauling the aircraft.

An inspection of the aircraft was proposed before discussing prices.

On their return from Chateaudun where they had inspected the Mosquitos, our mechanics were fairly pessimistic. They had hoped to get, at long last, some new planes for our Air Force. They said they were tired of working on all those old "crates" that had to be patched together. They were right, of course. But these "old crates" were the only planes available, and we would have to make do with them.

The purchase contract was signed, and we installed our repair shops in some abandoned hangars which the commandants of the air bases at Rennes and Chateaudun had graciously put at our disposal as well as their facilities and so solved many problems for us. A few months later, thanks to the help of Nord Aviation, we were ready to cable Israel: "First plane ready for test flight. Send pilot." They sent us the English pilot John Harvey, Emmanuel Zur's old right-hand man; this non-Jewish volunteer had chosen to stay in our ranks in spite of the armistice in Palestine.

We then entered a period of all-out work, in an atmosphere of great good-fellowship with the French Air Force. I have vivid memories of this camaraderie, of which one is especially typical.

When seven Israelis were massacred by the Syrians, our aircraft bombed the two Syrian villages from which they had been shot at.

The next morning in Paris, where I was at the time, one of our officers attached to a French base telephoned asking me to come back and meet him at once. A few hours later, he told me that all morning long his French friends had appeared to be avoiding him, and that he was very upset. Could our action in Syria be the cause of this sudden coldness? He asked me if I would look into the matter.

I went to see the commandant of the base, who himself brought up the subject of our armed intervention over the Syrian villages. I thought he seemed more nervous than usual, and he appeared to be anxious to find out more about the matter. I told him the facts as they had been reported to me, and added that all our planes had returned to their base.

"Are you positive?" he asked me.

"As far as I know, yes," I answered.

"I must inform my men of this at once," said the commandant.

The French officers believed—I then learned—that we had lost two of our planes. And, dreading the thought of having to break this news to our men, they had taken refuge in the distant attitude that had worried our officer. When the rumor turned out to be false, the rest of the day was spent in general rejoicing.

The French Ministry of Foreign Affairs, alas, did not see things in such a benign light. A little later, when we asked for an export permit for the first four planes ready to leave France, we were told that following the incident on the Syrian frontier the French Government had decided to refuse us all licenses.

One can imagine our consternation. We did not know whether this measure was to be temporary or permanent, and days went by before we were able to get them to lift the ban. A week later, we were called in by the Ministry of National Defense. We were prepared for the worst. Our anxiety mounted when the official who received us closed the doors behind us after having asked his secretary to see that we were not to be disturbed.

But the minute he opened his mouth we were reassured.

"The Ministry of Defense," he said, "has signed the contract and has every intention of honoring its signature."

We broke into smiles: then it was just a question of a temporary measure.

"Be careful, however, not to give in to future provocations, and ask your command to avoid committing any acts it might have cause to regret," he advised us.

But weeks went by, and the promised license still was not forthcoming. Work went ahead at the bases. Harvey made regular test flights of the reconditioned planes. But the sight of all those freshly painted aircraft neatly lined up on the fields, and utterly useless to us, depressed our men more and more. For their part, most of the French officers expressed their indignation at their Government's policy: they could not bear to see us cheated of the results of our long and costly labors by such arbitrary decision.

Finally, a month later, a first license was issued us, for twelve planes. They left at once. As soon as they landed in Israel, we received a telegram of congratulations from our Government which I was happy to pass along to our men. Their satisfaction was a pleasure to see.

Our Air Force expected us to send it forty planes, but we had decided to do better: we wanted, in the months to come, to send sixty planes out of France. Export licenses were now given to us without the least difficulty. Every time we applied for one, the French issued it, hoping, no doubt, that it would be the last.

John Harvey, who was responsible for all test flights, was not one to spare himself. He never took off, however, without having first inspected and checked out, down to the most minute detail, the craft that had been entrusted to him. He never gave permission for the transfer of a plane, which would be left to its own fate, without being absolutely certain that it was in perfect condition.

But one morning, having flown off as usual in a Mosquito, he had just come in low over the field and was regaining altitude again when the irretrievable occurred.

On the field, everyone was torn from his work by the sound of a deafening explosion, and then a plume of black smoke rose up into the sky. We never knew what actually happened. The reports from witnesses were confused and contradictory. Some claimed to have seen the plane burst into flames in mid-flight, others said that the engines suddenly went dead. In any event John Harvey, probably trying for a forced landing, had crashed into the side of a hill. A cruel irony of fate—that hill was the only rise of land discernible in the entire area which otherwise was as flat as the polders of Holland.

John Harvey was buried with full military honors—those paid him by our men, and those bestowed by the French Air Force.

In a little cemetery in Chateaudun, five white stones commemorated the sacrifices made by five R.A.F. pilots killed during the war. A sixth white stone, exactly like the others, was added to them. One detail, however, was different: the sixth stone bore not the emblem of the R.A.F. but that of the Israeli Air Force.

25

Still A Piston-Engined Air Force

SPITFIRES AND MUSTANGS, bought in Italy, Sweden and Great Britain, were added to the Mosquitos from France.

The operation carried out in Italy to obtain Spitfires resembled Operation Mosquito in France. Begun in 1951, the negotiations were pursued through the intermediary of the industrialist Ambrosini, with whom we had remained on excellent terms since the days of the underground. He was a man of strict integrity. The work that this affair could bring the employees of his factory interested him much more than the money. Our first contact with the Italian Air Force, in September of 1951, led us to entertain the possibility of acquiring a veritable "air fleet," tons of spare parts and a formidable quantity of spare engines. The prices mentioned were on the same level as the promises—they were extravagant.

But, once we left this dream world and got down to brass tacks, it became obvious that our opposite members had only the vaguest of notions as to the actual amount of available equipment. We had asked to visit the bases where this fabulous "air fleet" could be viewed from close up, and the

Italians had agreed without the slightest hesitation. But days passed, and the visit was systematically postponed.

For a while, it is true, the Italian security forces had opposed the idea. But once this opposition was overcome, we discovered that the promised "fleet" in fact consisted of 30 Spitfires, 20 spare engines, and a meager stock of spare parts. And, although the majority of the planes were in excellent condition, it was impossible for us to offer the Italians more than half the price they were asking. Our offer clearly offended them; from then on negotiations proceeded at a snail's pace. The Italians even tried to sell their planes to Egypt, a plan which, fortunately, was opposed by NATO.

I divided my time then between Paris and Rome, being called back regularly to Italy in the hope that the agreement under consideration might be signed from one day to the next. But each time this hope proved to be in vain. So, when nothing developed, I would go back to France. My frequent visits to Rome nevertheless allowed me to make many friends among the officers of the Italian Air Force. I remember in particular a retired colonel who had witnessed the glory and decline of his country's air power. He had shared most of Mussolini's ideas, but had never forgiven him for having drawn Italy into the war. Many pilots, young and old, all passionately dedicated to their profession, used to gather at his house. They complained bitterly that Italy had become entirely dependent on the United States because of the impossibility of finding funds to launch an aviation program purely Italian in concept.

From listening to them, I came to the conclusion that our situation, while far from brilliant, was preferable to theirs. Of course, we only had a mixed bag of generally outmoded planes, while they were piloting the latest American jets. But at least we were not dependent on anyone, and that was beyond price.

After endless discussions, the sales contract for the Spit-fires was finally signed and, on February 17, 1953, we received authorization to establish our overhaul base at Foggia.

Meanwhile, we had taken advantage of the long months of uncertainty in Italy to scour many other countries, always in search of planes which might eventually become available. We operated according to a detailed plan drawn up for us in Israel. But if some offer not foreseen by the plan was made to us, we never rejected it without first giving it serious consideration. More often than not, these propositions did not stand up under close scrutiny. The General Staffs of the smaller countries with only nominal air forces were usually eager to get rid of their old equipment. But these military men were ignorant of the political factors which sooner or later must come into play, while the diplomats were mortally afraid of finding themselves implicated in an affair involving arms shipments to the Middle East and then having to confront the British and Americans.

At the same time, however, we kept up our efforts in the United States proper. We were finally rewarded. After numerous intercessions made by our political friends, we were granted a license for three PBY's (amphibious planes), then another for twenty-five Mustangs. It was stipulated that the Mustangs must come from surplus stockpiles, and that they must be disarmed before leaving the country. It was the only major contribution of the United States to the Israeli Air Force.

But a pleasant surprise was provided by a country from which *a priori* we had expected no help at all but which turned out to be one of our most reliable sources for airplanes —Sweden.

During the war, it is true, this country had welcomed numbers of Jewish refugees in a tacit protest against the Nazi terror. But, because of its traditional neutrality, it had refrained from supplying arms to Israel as long as we still were not an independent nation.

In 1952, the Swedish Air Force had just acquired a certain number of jets, and we thought that she would probably be planning to phase out some of her propeller planes. However, remembering the refusals we had met with in the recent past, it was without any great hope that our military attaché took preliminary steps towards arranging the sale. But, thanks to the many contacts he had in influential circles in the Air Force, he rather quickly obtained a promise that some Mustang P-51's would be delivered to us, at least if the Minister of Foreign Affairs was not opposed to the sale. And, in July, 1952, the Swedish Government agreed to sell Israel twenty-five Mustangs.

The news raised a storm of protest from the Israeli Army and Navy. Citing the sorry state of their own equipment, they accused our leaders of playing favorites with the Air Force. This new purchase of planes did, in effect, curtail the budget Israel could allot to her general defense. However, in our far from brilliant financial condition at the time, this budget was way below what was required to meet the most basic needs of our armed forces anyhow. If we should be obliged to endure another war, it was obvious that the Air Force could not win it all alone; so we had to make a compromise. It was agreed that to offset the purchase of the Swedish planes we would resell the American ones we had just gotten, which still needed to be armed and reconditioned, while the Swedish craft were already armed and ready for immediate service.

All that remained was for us to go to Stockholm and effect the transfer of the twenty-five Mustangs. From the first, the efficiency of the Swedes impressed us. At the Air Ministry all the necessary information was provided at once, every question got a straightforward answer, and every problem that arose was settled within a few hours. Nothing unforeseen impeded our progress, and when we got around to the question of money, it was only to find that the prices asked were as reasonable as they could be. The contract was soon signed in an atmosphere of mutual regard.

On the other hand, carrying out the Stockholm-Israel flight presented difficulties. Winter had come, bad weather gripped Europe and we did not have pilots experienced enough to fly under such trying conditions.

Here again, the Swedish Air Ministry proved its good will and its efficiency. Swedish pilots were placed at our disposal. They would deliver the Mustangs themselves, but only on the condition that they flew at their own risk and outside of their regular service flying hours. Twenty-five Swedish pilots thus had occasion to visit Israel.

It was our last purchase of World War II airplanes; we were getting jet fighters at last.

Disappointments
and Surprises

THE MOSQUITOS, Spitfires and Mustangs had considerably increased the striking power of our Air Force. Our total number of planes was still inferior to the enemy line-up and we knew that this would always be so, since our financial resources were inferior to theirs. But while we could hold our own even with a certain numerical inferiority, we could not permit ourselves to fall too far behind in quality. The enemy had jets, and we absolutely had to have similar planes. Having jets was a vital necessity not only from the standpoint of military power, but also of prestige in the psychological warfare we were obliged to wage.

In 1950, a first attempt to obtain jets from the United States had ended, as expected, in failure. We could only hope to achieve our ends in Europe, particularly in France, Italy and Great Britain.

France then produced two types of jets—the Ouragan, built by the Dassault factories, and the Mistral, built by Sud-Aviation. The Ouragan was a purely French plane; the Mistral, a modified Vampire, was produced in France under British license.

The purchase of Mistrals was out, since a clause in the license forbade France to export them without the consent of the British Government.

We did not know too much about the Ouragan, but this plane interested us highly despite reservations voiced by our Air Force. Indeed, a good many of our high-ranking officers, veterans of the R.A.F., could not believe that the French aviation industry was capable of designing and building a jet of any merit, and they only had confidence in the already proven American and British planes. They further felt that, since our experience with jets was nil, to put into service a plane of which we were not a hundred per cent sure was sheer folly. Finally, the acquisition of a French plane would involve numerous changes in the tools and installations of our bases which were then only equipped to handle British or American planes.

Regardless of these drawbacks, political and operational reasons prevailed, and our Air Force soon sent a team of experts to France charged with drawing up a complete report on the Ouragan. Our experts visited the Dassault factories where all the desired technical information was supplied to them but, when we asked permission to take a plane up for a trial flight, it was denied to us. The mission therefore returned to Israel extremely disappointed and very skeptical as to the actual worth of the Ouragan, which, however, was to prove itself later, turning out to be particularly effective in the course of the Sinai campaign.

We did not give up so easily. We hoped that the purchase of the Ouragans would renew our ties with the French Air Force and that their support, already precious in itself, would lead to our being able to obtain more modern French planes in the future. But, despite promises which had been made to us by certain French political personalities, the Government in Paris, on July 29, 1952, officially opposed our purchase requests. The planes, we were told, were not for sale. This was an excuse. We knew perfectly well that France, on the contrary, was very anxious to sell the Ouragans. In fact, France had brought up the matter before the Tripartite Commission on the Middle East, and the British had vehemently rejected all thought of letting Israel have French planes.

But history is never without its paradoxes: a little later, the British themselves informed us of their sudden decision to deliver jets to Israel! This was surprising, to say the very least. Our first request for British jets dated back to 1950, and it had been turned down despite similar agreements signed by Britain at the time with the Arab states and the obvious desire of the manufacturers to make the sale. The atmosphere had gotten friendlier after that, it is true. We had been authorized to visit the factories of the interested firm, which had the formal assurance of the Foreign Office that there would be no objections to the sale of planes to Israel. We had gotten to the point of discussing prices and delivery dates, and we really believed that we had attained our objectives. But, after several gourmet luncheons in a spirit of complete cordiality, the Foreign Office had had the last word, and the word was: No.

Right after that, a curious piece of news had reached us: in Italy, the Macchi factories, which manufactured Vampires under a British license, had been authorized to sell us a certain number of its planes. Since the heads of the company had evidently had to solicit this authorization from Great Britain, our surprise was considerable. Could the British be willing to sell us planes through the intermediary of Italy while at the same time refusing to do so directly? It was not a hypothesis to be rejected too hastily, since any sale concluded between Great Britain and Israel could be interpreted by the Arab states as an act of hostility against them.

Alas, this entire affair was the result of a simple misunderstanding. Britain had never authorized the Macchi firm to sell us Vampires. She had merely promised to look into an Italian request on this order, which she rejected, moreover, almost immediately. This rejection the Italians took very badly. Their aircraft industry was in very bad shape, and they saw in Israel a highly interesting customer. The Macchi executives lined up the support of their Air Force and their Government and, in 1952, informed us of their intention of approaching the British Government again.

That is where matters stood when in the fall of that same year an extraordinary report reached Israel: the British had finally agreed to provide us with the planes they had denied us so many times, either directly or indirectly.

What could be the reason for this sudden about-face? the revolution that had broken out in Egypt in August of 1952? But we did not believe in a reversal of British policy towards us any more than our French and Italian friends did. The real reason was purely commercial. Great Britain thought of the Middle East as its exclusive market and was afraid of French or Italian competition. The best way to eliminate such competition would be to provide us with planes "Made in England."

A dispatch from Israel, received in Paris, enjoined us to begin negotiations for the purchase of fourteen jet Gloster Meteors in England immediately. The number fourteen coincided exactly with the number the British Foreign Office, ever mindful of the balance of power in the Middle East, had declared would be acceptable.

The welcome that greeted our mission when it arrived in England was extremely amicable. It would only take a few days, we were told, for us to be familiarized with the structural and functional characteristics of the Meteor. But the engineers and pilots at Gloster learned, to their great surprise, that we knew exactly what we wanted and that they could not get rid of us that quickly. Specifically, we wanted to incorporate certain modifications in the planes' armament which would increase its efficiency.

After the contract was signed, two teams of our pilots and mechanics left for a training period in England, one at Gloster, the other at Rolls Royce, which manufactured the Meteor's engines. The arrival of a group of Israelis caused quite a stir at the latter plant, where some Syrians were already taking training courses! Personally, we were not opposed to having our men mingle with the Syrians, but the factory, fearing complications, saw to it that contacts were avoided and everybody's feelings spared.

The first British jets arrived in Israel on June 17, 1953, and the last, one year later.

In between times, the British Government made known its intention of sending us nine additional Meteors. The proposition was all the more unexpected in that, since January, 1953, our relations with Transjordan had steadily worsened. The Transjordanians, in October of 1953, had even made several raids on our frontier settlements, where they had massacred men, women and children. And, a few months later, when a bus was attacked and eleven Israelis killed in an ambush, nine Transjordanian soldiers were made to pay with their lives for this latest aggression.

So it was that, while for three days there had been shooting in Jerusalem, Gloster signed a new contract with us approved by the government in London. It is true that during that same period the Transjordanians, for their part, received ten new British jets.

27

The Hesitation Waltz

WITH THE METEORS, the Israeli Air Force finally entered the Jet Age. However, while the Meteor was the ideal plane with which to effect the transition from propeller planes to jets, as a combat plane it was distinctly obsolete. And, since we were obliged to oppose quantity with quality, we had to provide our Air Force with much more modern planes. Our quest took us back to Sweden.

The reputation of the Swedish jet, the SAAB J-29, which was said to be the equal of the MIG-15, had reached our ears, but its actual performance remained a closely guarded secret. Our Military Attaché in Sweden got in touch with SAAB, and the firm indicated that it would be willing to sell us some J-29's provided the Swedish Government was not opposed.

We therefore began to gather locally all the necessary documentation on the J-29, for we had yet to obtain the approval of our Government, and it was not an easy decision to make. In fact, the J-29 had been designed to fill the particular needs of the Swedish Air Force which called for a high performance interceptor only, while we, for our part, required an all-round fighter, fit for interception and ground support. The decision was made, however, to acquire about twenty J-29's, provided credit arrangements could be made.

But unforeseen complications arose in Stockholm, concerning the credit arrangements. We soon discovered that one of the major shareholders of the firm was a bank heartily committed in Egypt and all the difficulties grew out of fear of Egyptian economic reprisals.

The matter was reported to the Swedish Air Board, which was ashamed of this outrageous conduct of the negotiations, and it was decided that the Swedish Air Force would undertake the sale of the J-29 to us.

The Swedish Air Board decision coincided with the French decision to release to us the new French jet fighter, the Mystère II. Having the possibility of a choice, an evaluation team left for Sweden and France to make a comparison between the two aircraft.

We were so well received by the Swedish Air Force that we had a suspicion that the Air Board wanted to make amends for somebody else's behavior. We visited factories and air squadrons and all records were put at our disposal. The Swedes were proud of the J-29, and once a decision was made to give us information, it was offered without any limitations. Our pilot who performed the test flights was most satisfied with the aircraft.

After a fortnight of enjoying Sweden, the hospitality of the air bases and the beauty of Stockholm, we left for France for evaluation of the Mystère II. The aircraft was just going into production, and we followed it from stage to stage. From an operational point of view, it met with our specifications, as it had a longer range than the J-29 and was adapted for ground missions as well as for interception. It was a more modern ship than the J-29 since it was designed and redesigned after the J-29—the French learning a great deal from the F-86.

The plane's disadvantage was its lack of service experience and the impossibility to foretell whether the production aircraft would be exactly the same as the pre-serial production ones as far as performance was concerned. On his second test flight one of our pilots went through the sound barrier, no doubt an ordinary event for the great powers, but for us one which prompted sending a special dispatch to Israel. For the first time an Israeli pilot had penetrated the supersonic universe.

Our specialists were frankly enthusiastic about the Mystère II, and, after a brief hesitation, our Government sided with their conclusions.

The future was to reveal that this decision was of far-reaching importance. The preference Israel gave to the Mystère not only resulted in business relationships with the French manufacturers; it also was at the origin of ties which, little by little, developed between France and Israel to the point of uniting the two countries in a close alliance and of creating between them, for several months, an actual community of fate.

The influence of one man was the determining factor in this affair; that man was Shimon Peres, then head of the Israeli Ministry of Defense. As had most of us, Peres had for a long time placed his hopes in the United States. But a series of bitter disappointments had taught him that the American Government would never agree to arm Israel and that, by trusting in this hypothetical aid, we were in danger of simply remaining helpless forever. Realizing that nothing much could be expected from England either, Peres had the wisdom to bring all his effort to bear on France, the only European country whose political interests in the Middle East could be in accord with ours.

The uselessness of our efforts in the United States had been illustrated, moreover, by a new adventure at the time when we were negotiating for Meteors in London. We had also approached Canada with a view to acquiring, similarly, some F-86 Sabres. The first contacts had been most promising, as

Canada had never made a secret of her sympathy to Israel anyhow. Our men in the United States and Canada were so sure of success that they even urged us to postpone signing the contract with the British for the Meteors. To hear them talk, the Canadian F-86's were already ours. Luckily Shimon Peres, an experienced man, was wise enough to advise the Israeli Government to sign the contract for the Meteors without further delay. If it were a purely Canadian affair, the Canadians would probably have made a favorable decision, but the F-86's were built in Canada under an American license, and Canada could not let us have them without the prior consent of the Americans, which most likely would not be forthcoming.

The Meteor contract was signed, months passed and the F-86's deal was still under consideration. At the end it became evident that if we wanted the F-86's the official request should be made in Washington.

Our Embassy had recommended the same from the beginning. Cables brought us encouraging news about the reaction of the State Department to our application, and on their suggestion, our Ambassador met the Assistant Secretary of State on the 13th of March, 1954. The delivery of the F-86's was discussed and a promise was given to view favorably our request.

At that time we were evaluating the Mystère in France and had come to a decision.

On the 5th of April, 1954, our Ambassador had written to Mr. Byroade recalling to him his March conversation: ". . . We desire to receive your approval in principle for the purchase of twenty-four F-86 fighter aircraft, although, as I pointed out to you, we shall be in no position to purchase the entire quantity initially. However, the receipt of the approval will permit us to prepare a procurement program over a number of years, limited by our financial means and other factors such as our ability to dispose of current equipment. We propose now to make a decision concerning the type of equipment with which to replace our present equipment and our final decision in this regard now awaits your reply to our inquiry whether the United States Government will authorize the export of such aircraft to Israel."

We had already taken our decision as far as the choice between the J-29 and the Mystère II was concerned and we now awaited the reply from the States. From a purely technical point of view the F-86 was a proven-in-combat fighter, superior to any other aircraft available in Europe.

Days passed and there was no answer from the States. We in Paris pressed for a decision. Tel-Aviv cabled Washington, and the States replied with promising cables, based on private conversations with people of the State Department and of North American who alleged that they had received the green light from the State Department, but being unable to supply the aircraft themselves, had given authorization to Canadair to deliver the airplanes to us.

On the 13th of May, our New York office even received an official proposition from North American saying "we have recently arranged with Canadair, the manufacturer of the Sabre in Canada under license from North American, to produce F-87 Sabre with the Orenda-10 engine for your government." It appeared that everything was really clear now and that at last we would receive the F-86's.

A month passed and there was no official confirmation of the export license either from the State Department or from Canada. In the meantime, in France, after the choice was made, we notified the Air Ministry about our wish to purchase the Mystère II.

The fact that the French authorities granted permission to evaluate the aircraft did not yet mean that the Foreign Office had approved the sale. As a matter of fact, they did not want to commit themselves without bringing the matter before the Three Power Commission.

It was up to the Air Ministry and to us to force the Foreign Office to make a decision. Peres became such a frequent visitor in Paris that a joke circulated relating that when once at a meeting with a friend at the airport he was asked why he was so worried, he replied "I don't remember whether I have just arrived or if I am going."

But, despite constant meetings with political party men, deputies, anybody whose good will and action could contribute to our cause, we were still facing a blank wall.

There was no way out but to approach the Air Secretary directly. Officially such a *démarche* had to be made either through the Embassy—which meant the French Foreign Office, or through the Military Attaché—meaning official channels again.

There had to be a direct approach and we found one. The Minister and his staff were waiting for us, and during the introduction, he made us laugh, introducing me to Shimon Peres.

The conversation was most satisfactory and the Minister promised to do his utmost to convince the Government to supply us the aircraft. But it took Peres some more trips to Paris and more discussions with friends to induce the Quai d'Orsay to approve the delivery of a small number of Mystère II jet fighters.

The hour of grave decision descended upon us—whether to proceed with the signature of the Mystère contract or to await release of the F-86's.

In the United States, certain of our experts begged us not to sign. They were still convinced that at any moment the State Department would authorize the purchase of the F-86's. Shimon Peres therefore pressed Washington for a definite reply.

When it came, on the 9th of July, 1954, it was a refusal, just as Peres had foreseen. It was a hard blow to our people in the States who honestly and sincerely believed in the State Department's promise.

On the 19th of August, I cabled home—"We signed and passed on to the French for signature." The contract was signed on the 19th of August, 1954; delivery of the first aircraft was promised for the beginning of 1955.

On the first of April, 1955, after five years of work in France, I left Paris to return home. On the morning of my departure I was pleasantly surprised by a call from my friend at the Ministry informing me that I was to be decorated with the French Legion of Honor on that same morning.

I was not officially either an Air Attaché or a member of the Diplomatic Corps so that this was indeed an honor accorded without precedent.

I was deeply touched by the decoration and much honored. Throughout the five years of my stay in France my friends in the Air Force made me really feel that I was not in a foreign country, but at home, my second home.

WWW
28
MMM

The Philosophy
of Revolution

"WHAT SHOULD BE our role in this troubled world and what
place has been assigned to us to fill this role?" The new
master of Egypt, Gamal Abdel-Nasser, had undertaken to
answer these two questions by publishing what amounts to a
handbook of his ambitions and those he wanted his country
to assume: *The Philosophy of Revolution.* In it he made a
passionate appeal to the Egyptians to finally fulfill their
heroic mission which he declared was dictated by geographi-
cal and historic predestination.

"When I consider our location, I perceive several circles
inside of which we shall inevitably have to confine our
activity. We cannot look at a map of the world without seeing
our place marked on it and without realizing that our role is
circumscribed by the very place we occupy.

"We first see clearly that a vast Arab circle surrounds us, a
circle that is a part of us, our history being inextricably
bound up in its history.

"Beyond it, can we ignore the existence of the African
continent to which Fate has also bound us? We must know
that a terrible battle for its future will be engaged, a battle

202

whose outcome will be fatal or favorable to us, a battle that will go with us or against us!

"Can we, finally, ignore the existence of an Islamic world to which we are united by ties created by the similarity of religion and strengthened by the realities of life in this country?

"History is full of heroes who have assigned themselves glorious roles and have acted them at decisive moments. But history is also full of glorious roles which have never found heroes worthy of acting them. It seems to me that there exists today, within the Arab circle, a role of this sort, wandering about hopelessly in search of a hero. And, I don't know why, it also seems to me that this role, weary of having wandered for so long, has stopped, exhausted, at our frontiers and given us the signal to act, to at last speak the lines it dictates to us, since nobody else is qualified to do so.

"When we consider the second circle, that of the African continent, we understand that we do not have the right to remain outside the conflict that today pits five million whites against two hundred million Africans. A higher reasoning dictates its law to us: we are in Africa. . . . In no case is it possible for us to watch, indifferent and passive, what is taking place on our continent, in the false belief that it does not concern us.

"That leaves the third circle. It spans continents and oceans since it encompasses all our co-believers who, wherever they are, turn as we do towards Mecca, speaking the same words that we speak. When I think of the hundreds of millions of beings united by one faith, I become aware of the prodigious achievements that could be made possible by the union of all Muslims. The stage is set. We alone, by virtue of the place we occupy at the center of the Arab world, are in a position to assume the leading role."

Abdel-Nasser could not play this role he so eagerly coveted

unless he procured the means, and, above all, unless he gave Egypt a military might commensurate with his ambitions. He needed arms first to assure his power inside the "circles" he spoke of, where his will to rule the Arab world was in danger of being challenged and attacked. To unify the Arab world, he would have to both eliminate Israel, that "creation of Western imperialism," and bend to *The Philosophy of Revolution* those Arab states which, like Iraq and Transjordan, were still governed by that same imperialism which "imposed an invisible and deadly siege upon the whole region."

But the destruction of Israel necessarily assumed in his eyes a primordial importance: it alone would open up to him the routes to Syria, Iraq and Transjordan. And, even if Nasser had not been so explicit in his *Philosophy of Revolution*, it would have been difficult to doubt his intentions after an interview he granted Paul Sann, publisher of the *New York Post*, on October 13, 1955. "Nasser," Sann reported, "states that he does not see the slightest possibility of compromise, however limited it might be, between the Arabs and Israel. He adds that the hatred of the Arabs for the Jews is so great that any idea of peace between them is absurd. In his opinion, his personal mission is to save the Arab world from the shame and misery of a Zionist domination."

The reconquest of Palestine must then be the first act of the play the hero of Cairo had undertaken to dramatize on the world stage. But, at that time, the hero still hesitated. Although Great Britain continued to supply him with all the arms he wanted, Abdel-Nasser still did not feel in a position to launch the glorious campaign he dreamed of. He only had three times as many jets and tanks as we had. When the curtain rose for his entrance onto the stage, he wanted to feel strong enough to crush us without fail.

But then the inevitable happened. The West, alerted by the scope of the ambitions Nasser so obligingly flaunted, ended its indulgence by no longer responding favorably to his demands for arms, which became more and more urgent. And this reluctance was reinforced when the Egyptian "Rais" made known his intention of putting his philosophy into practice beyond the realm of the Middle East, in the Sudan and French West Africa, notably.

Nasser was not caught off guard. He decided to turn resolutely towards the U.S.S.R. Ever since Peter the Great, the Russians had dreamed of opening up, beyond the Dardanelles, the gateway to the Mediterranean and the Middle East. Now, here was Nasser at last offering them a way, and his Pan-Arab policies held out attractive prospects—access to the oil in the Middle East and the possibility of extending their influence into regions until now beyond their reach. Furthermore, since negotiations between Nasser and the U.S.S.R. had escaped the vigilance of our agents as well as the attention of the West, their favorable conclusion would appear throughout the entire world as a masterpiece of secret diplomacy. And Nasser would be credited with having made a master stroke.

Indeed, when on September 27, 1955, the "Rais" informed the world that Czechoslovakia would in the future supply him with all the Soviet arms he needed, the announcement burst like a bombshell. Not without some anguish, the West wondered what price Nasser had agreed to pay in return for this aid. Was it a commitment likely to put Egypt at the mercy of Soviet pressure whenever Moscow decided to exact concessions?

But when the three Western Powers, openly admitting their fears about Soviet infiltration into a region until then under Western influence, tried to find out the details of this accord, Nasser contented himself with answering that it was the privilege of every independent nation to procure arms where it saw fit. And on the very day that Messrs. Macmillan and

Dulles met to discuss the situation, the Council of the Arab League telegraphed its "Rais" unanimous approval of the intransigent attitude adopted by the Egyptian Government. However, Nasser still had his problems. Sensing that he was not yet in a position to break completely with the West, he felt he must attenuate the repercussions of his accord with the Czechs. The ideal diversion was within his grasp. All he had to do was claim that Israel was preparing to go to war against Egypt.

On Sunday, October 3, 1955, Nasser announced to the world that his agents had obtained irrefutable proof of an impending Israeli attack which Egypt had escaped until then only because of Syria's determination to respond herself to any aggression. The secret documents which had fallen into Egyptian hands further revealed, according to Nasser, that Israel had received from the West 200 British Meteor jets, 20 Mosquito pursuit planes, 100 Sherman tanks, 15 Churchill tanks, 100 armored trucks and 70 field guns. In another report, no less confidential, this one from a British source, the eventuality of an invasion of Israel was questioned and the probability of an imminent Israeli attack on Egypt emphasized. "This report is in my office at this very moment, and I am prepared to show it to the British ambassador if he wishes to see it," the Egyptian dictator added innocently. "But at present," he concluded, "thanks to Soviet aid, we can truly call ourselves freed from the Western yoke. And, from now on, there will be no influence here other than Egypt's own."

The British Foreign Office denied the shipments of arms to Israel, but declined to comment on the intelligence document that accused Israel of preparing an attack on Egypt. This document must have existed, beyond a doubt. The question was whether it had gotten into Nasser's hands in spite of the British authorities, or with their complicity. Both in England and the States the press reported the Israeli purchase of jet fighters from France as a news item which seemed to justify Nasser's claims. On the 7th of October, the military correspondent of *The Times* stated that Israel ordered jets in France, and, across the Atlantic, Hanson Baldwin of the *New York Times* reported the same purchase.

There is no doubt that Nasser had played his cards like a champion. Even the British General Staff thought that his fears were justified! Was not it now his most sacred duty to safeguard the independence of his country? Was not he justified in preparing to meet the danger that threatened him?

Egypt therefore concentrated her troops in Gaza, studded her frontier with fortifications, installed reinforcement bases on all roads leading to Israel, trained special commandos, the *Fedayin*, in guerrilla warfare, and finally stepped up preparations of her units all over the country. This deployment of forces, of course, as the world could witness, being simply preventative measures called for by the fear of impending Israeli aggression.

The *Fedayin* units, made up mostly of Palestinian Arabs, but also formed in Syria, Jordan and Lebanon, were given the mission of attacking the military preparations of the Jewish "aggressors." Looting, burning and killing at random, they soon spread terror throughout the land of Israel. Our reprisals, and notably the destruction of the *Fedayin* headquarters at Khan Yunis, seemed to have no effect at all on Nasser, and his terrorists were ordered to continue the massacre, day after day.

On October 9, 1955, a spokesman for our Foreign Ministry issued a solemn warning to Egypt, demanding that she immediately put an end to these criminal acts. But Egypt dodged the issue, claiming that she was not responsible for acts of violence committed by a few isolated elements crossing the frontier on their own initiative. "We have no knowledge of any unusual activity in that sector," the British Foreign Office confirmed Nasser's claim.

Meanwhile, we learned the details of the agreement concluded between Egypt and Czechoslovakia. The figures were quite alarming. Nasser had obtained 100 MIG-15 jets, 48 Ilyushin bombers, 20 Ilyushin transport planes, 170 T-34 tanks, 60 heavy Stalin tanks, 200 troop carriers, 100 self-propelled guns, not to mention many other arms. How could one possibly imagine that a force of that size in the hands of a fanatical dictator would only be used to defend a frontier? We were faced with a very grave situation, that was certain. There was only one way left to avert the impending conflict: to intensify our own military effort until we equalled the Egyptians in power, for we well knew that Nasser would never engage in a battle whose outcome seemed doubtful.

The urgent request for arms that we then addressed to the United States was coolly received. Our intelligence report detailing the war materiel promised to Egypt was thought to be very exaggerated. The United States said it wanted to wait for its own intelligence report, and only then would it decide whether or not coming to our aid seemed appropriate. "Up until the present, nothing warrants our concluding that the Russian arms will seriously increase the military potential of the Egyptian forces," the State Department declared. Mr. Henry Byroade, the American Ambassador to Cairo, even thought that these shipments would reduce the tension between Egypt and Israel, since the former would no longer have to fear an Israeli attack. Of course Mr. Byroade had been among those who advised the State Department to refuse to supply us with the arms we requested. According to him, nothing in Cairo at that time gave the slightest hint of aggression!

Since our security was at stake, we could not just sit back and quietly hope for a change in American policy. Not being able to count on the United States or Britain to come to our aid even if Nasser decided to invade Israel, we had to find other ways of meeting what had become a very grave situation. Nothing less than our very survival was at stake.

Our Government first launched a solemn appeal not only to all citizens of Israel but also to all Jews all over the world. This appeal for financial help had a brief slogan: "ARMS FOR ISRAEL."

But while its success went way beyond our hopes, and the money came in from the four corners of the earth, we could not confront the Egyptian menace merely with bank notes. It was no longer even a question of reverting to the risky methods of buying arms in secrecy or of again trying to patch together surplus materiel. We now most urgently needed a real ally who would openly send us arms.

And the urgency became greater as Nasser became increasingly threatening. Egypt had set up a joint General Staff with Syria which, in the event of war, would coordinate operations. Similar plans were being worked out with the other Arab states. Nasser promoted Arab unity by daily appeals to the common hatred the Arabs had for Israel, promising the fanatics to "Soon throw the Jews into the sea." His men carried the message all over the Middle East, and at the same time the Cairo radio broadcast encouragement to North Africa in its fight against French "imperialism."

It was then that President Ben-Gurion, who was recuperating from an illness, summoned his two closest consultants, General Moshe Dayan and Shimon Peres. Ben-Gurion ordered General Dayan to make the most harsh reprisals for the attacks along the Syrian and Egyptian frontiers. Shimon Peres was charged with an extraordinary mission to France.

A Question of Honor

THE NEWS coming to us then from France was far from reassuring. The test flights of the first Mystère II, just out of the factory, had not been up to our hopes. Clearly, this plane needed some major modifications. Certain French officers attached to the Air Ministry even doubted if its shortcomings could ever be corrected and, in all frankness, advised us to abandon it in favor of the Mystère IV. Our Air Force, whose purchases I had taken charge of upon returning to Israel, recommended an immediate purchase of more Ouragans as a temporary measure, and, for the future, an exchange of Mystère II's for Mystère IV's.

The Ouragan had proved itself. It was a solidly built plane, easy to fly and to maintain. As for the Mystère IV, it was said to rival the American F-86. Our request for twelve Ouragans was met with approval by France and a contract was signed. On the 6th and 12th of October, two flights took off from a French base, all pilots being Israeli but for the two flight leaders, who were Frenchmen. The ships landed on two European airfields and although we had taken severe security precautions, the delivery could not be kept secret.

The Egyptian press exaggerated as usual the number of

aircraft received but it was done, no doubt, deliberately in order to justify once more the Czech deal.

Shimon Peres arrived in France the end of October carrying along a list of armament requirements. His task was not an easy one. Indeed, the Big Four had just met in Geneva precisely to discuss the problems arising from the situation in the Middle East. Would the French agree to ship arms to us while at the same time participating in the conference in session? It did not seem likely to us, with American and British opposition remaining inflexible and Dulles and Macmillan still believing that the Israeli Army was the most efficient combat force in the Middle East.

"Where to begin? Whom to see?" Shimon Peres wondered. In the France of the IVth Republic, governments exhibited a disconcerting instability. And while officials maintained a certain continuity in the midst of this cut-throat game, they had no reason to plead our cause to the Quai d'Orsay where British and American influence weighed heavily. French statesmen were far from agreed on what policy to adopt towards us anyhow. The Right saw in us a natural ally in its fight against the policy of conciliation in North Africa and was therefore prepared to arm us. The Left was opposed to this, thinking that it would be possible to negotiate with the Arabs and even with Nasser. The Center parties had no fixed policy, and swung from one side to the other according to the course of events.

The only people whom we could really consider as our friends were the generals, the officials of the Ministry of Defense and the officers of the Armed Forces. They regarded the politicians as the real cause of their defeat in Indo-China and were worried over the state of affairs existing in North Africa. They were accused in the past, that the Indo-China war was theirs only and now the same accusations were thrown at them pertaining to the struggle in North Africa. They were well aware of the situation in the Arab world and claimed that any Egyptian military or political victory would cause an intensification of the Arab revolt in North Africa. The defeat of Israel might mean France's defeat too.

It was to the Defense Ministry that Peres turned first. The Secretary of State for Defense was a very good friend of ours, a man who decided quickly and acted promptly.

"When would you like a reply?" he asked Shimon.

"Today, if possible," Shimon answered.

At four o'clock a meeting took place with the Defense Minister, a general with a splendid army record, who many a time expressed his support of Israel. These, however, were the days when he was fighting the Government in the seat of the Opposition.

Would he stick to his words, being a Minister now? Experience had taught us that many politicians of the Opposition who used to advocate our support in the political arena, abandoned their pledges once they reached their goal—a seat in the Government.

Not him! He listened carefully to Shimon's request, being well briefed already on the subject by the Secretary. Some of the items were granted immediately then and there, while others had to be referred to officers commanding the Army and the Air Force who were unwilling to release the equipment.

In all countries where the military budget is cut down to a minimum, where equipment is scarce and hard to replace, no commanding officer is willing to part with any. All the more so because we were asking for nothing less than the French Army's modern equipment.

Neither the Ouragan nor the Mystère IV proved to be available when the Minister discussed our requests with the Air Force. Besides, the acquisition of Mystères presented an additional problem since they did not belong exclusively to France, but to NATO as well. In an effort to find a solution to all this, the Minister suggested that Peres meet with the Air Force's Chief of Staff, an interview which Peres gratefully agreed to.

"You have already gotten twelve Ouragans and crippled one of my squadrons," the Chief of Staff remarked to Peres.

"Give us twelve more, and that squadron won't be a problem any more," Peres replied.

The Chief of Staff smiled at his answer, but maintained that it was extremely difficult for him to give up planes that were needed by the French Air Force for training future Mystère IV pilots. "And what about the Mystères?" asked Peres.

They could not be spared. There were squadrons already formed and the pilots were waiting for them. He could not keep the pilots idle; it was bad for the morale of the whole of the Air Force. In addition, the airplanes being NATO property, American Inspectors watched carefully the delivery of the ships from the factory and the French Air Force was making monthly reports as to the whereabouts of the aircraft.

"May I ask your opinion?" Peres then inquired. "Would you send your pilots to fight MIG-15's if they were flying Mystère II's?"

"No," the officer answered after a long silence. Then he added, "For my part, I am willing to send you twelve Mystère IV's, but no Ouragans. I will inform the Minister at once."

The Defense Minister, after having consulted the Prime Minister, approved the sale. However, he still needed the approval of NATO. The American General in charge of this organization happened to be in Spain, and answered that Mr. Dulles should be consulted.

"Above all, not Dulles!" Shimon Peres exclaimed.

Luckily the Minister was able to settle the matter in Paris

with the American authorities and, a few days later, he informed Peres that everything was arranged. The planes could be delivered immediately. It was almost too good to be true.

In Israel, the news was received all the more enthusiastically since tension was increasing from day to day. Units of the Egyptian Army had penetrated the demilitarized zone of Nitzana, and were harassing the agricultural settlements there.

The Israeli press, reflecting public opinion, demanded an appropriate reaction, which soon became inevitable.

On October 29, 1955, our men launched an attack on an Egyptian Army camp, Kuntilla, located four and a half miles beyond the Egyptian frontier, in the south of the Negev. Ten Egyptian soldiers were killed, and twenty-nine taken prisoner. Then, on October 30th, the Israeli Government sent Egypt a warning enjoining her to evacuate the Nitzana zone.

The first days of November arrived. When Shimon Peres finally went to the Defense Ministry to sign the contract agreed upon, he at once sensed that something was wrong. Although the Minister welcomed him cordially, he seemed visibly ill at ease. When his first question referred to the weather in Israel, Peres' suspicions were confirmed. Getting down to facts, Peres learned that the Americans had opposed releasing the Mystère IV's, and that the French Government had had to give in.

Shimon Peres left the Minister, extremely disheartened. The dispatches he was getting from Israel were not very comforting either. Egyptian Vampires were now flying over our territory and *Fedayin* bands continued their harassments.

"Tomorrow, I will start all over again at the beginning," Peres vowed.

On his list of people to see there were ministers, ex-ministers, generals, leaders of different political parties and other highly placed officials.

While our Ambassador to France scheduled an interview with the Prime Minister, Peres at the same time went to see one of his best friends, a former general and a Minister. After listening to Peres, his friend picked up the receiver and asked for the Prime Minister.

"I haven't called you since the day I left your government," said the former Minister. "But I don't think we can leave the Israeli request up in the air any longer. We promised those planes to Israel. France must keep her promises, it's a question of honor."

"I have just promised the Israeli Ambassador to take care of this matter," the Prime Minister answered.

Shimon Peres did not sleep that night. And the next day seemed as though it would never end. From a dispatch from Israel he learned that our warning to Egypt had not been just empty words. An Israeli unit had taken the offensive and routed the Egyptian troops from their positions around Nitzana. The toll: fifty dead, forty-eight captured. We had lost five men. Newspapers all over the world reported this surprising turn of events.

This time, public opinion in the free countries was unanimous in its understanding of our military action, and this no doubt facilitated our negotiations with France. For, on November 4th, Peres was informed that France had decided to provide us with twelve Mystère IV's and twelve Ouragans, thereby agreeing to come to our aid even though it meant a sacrifice of her own needs.

These twenty-four planes of course only represented a symbolic force compared to the aerial power already acquired by the Egyptians. But they were all the more precious to us, and we worked at top speed to get them to Israel.

It was hoped that the ferrying of the Mystères would

commence on the 14th of the month and the Ouragans two days later. The flight plan called for landings in two European airfields. Our people in the Paris Office and our friends in the Ministry did not spare themselves in their efforts to meet the expected date. Landing rights had to be obtained, fuel arrangements had to be made and transport airplanes with spares and ground personnel to assure the maintenance on the way had to be provided.

Notwithstanding the fact that it was forced to give up equipment which it could hardly spare, the French Air Force was more than just helpful. The relevant departments planned the operations as though they were their own. Not only transport planes, spares and mechanics were provided, but when we asked for pilots, owing to the critical military situation in Israel, the request was also granted.

Everything proceeded according to plan and Shimon was now anxious to sign the agreement and to return home.

We got the first hint that something was amiss again, when we were told that owing to the limited range of the Mystère IV, the airplanes would be unable to make the direct flight from a European airfield to Israel. A landing in Cyprus was required and the French did not consider it wise to notify the British, who would oppose the delivery of the airplanes. They suggested crating the ships.

We agreed with the French that the British should not be notified but we could not agree to the crating, as it would mean a delay of two months. It could not be done otherwise, claimed the Air Force, the drop tanks which increased the range were not yet ready.

But the most annoying fact was that the Mystères were still in the factory yard and were not flown over to the airfield of departure.

On the 8th, the cat emerged from the bag. The Americans

learned of the proposed operation and warned the French to stop it.

Apparently, there must have been a misunderstanding between the Defense Minister and the American Ambassador. While speaking to the Ambassador about other French Defense affairs, the Minister casually mentioned the proposed delivery of the Mystères to us. The Ambassador made no comment and the Minister, therefore, accepted his silence as a diplomatic consent.

All the French efforts to induce the Americans, and even an appeal to Mr. Dulles, failed.

Although all negotiations were conducted in strict secrecy, Cairo got wind of them and on the 10th of November, *Life* magazine published an interview with Abdel Nasser in which he claimed that France promised to deliver Israel 70 Mystère jet fighters, 100 tanks, 100 heavy 155 mm. guns, 150 high velocity 75 mm. anti-tank guns. Was not his duty, foreseeing the future when all these arms will be delivered to Israel, to arm Egypt! "I may assure you that I am going to use the arms to start a war against Israel," stressed the Colonel.

There were many who believed him as it was comfortable to believe to justify their behavior towards Israel. No one pointed out that the Czech arms deal was signed long before the French Government decided to deliver us arms and in very restricted quantities.

On the 12th of November, an agreement was signed with the French Government for the delivery of twelve Ouragans but excluding the Mystères.

During the same time that our friends worked hard to get us the airplanes, the Quai d'Orsay was carrying on secret negotiations with Nasser. On the 13th of November, the French Minister of Foreign Affairs let it be known that France would resume arms deliveries to Egypt, Nasser having agreed to put an end to anti-French propaganda emanating from Cairo.

In the United States, the State Department had finally admitted that the transaction between Czechoslovakia and Egypt had been more serious than they had thought. Egypt had already received from the Czechs not only an "appreciable quantity" of arms, but also bombers and fighter planes. In any case, it added, Israel did not stand a chance of obtaining American aid unless she also agreed to negotiate a compromise agreement that would reduce the tension along the Israeli-Egyptian frontier. The United States, land of freedom, influenced by Sir Anthony Eden's traditional Guildhall speech on the 9th of November, backed up his proposal as the price of peace the cession of a part of Israeli territory to Nasser, thus advocating another Munich.

We were not at all disposed to accept this capitulation and we let it be known. Hostility towards us from certain Anglo-Saxon circles deepened and Nasser took advantage of it to step up the action of his killers in our territory. Even on the Jordanian frontier, the murder of Israelis and acts of sabotage continued, in the by now habitual manner of the *Fedayin*. This time we let them go on without retaliating, fearing that any action on our part might be used as a pretext to delay the departure of the Ouragans, which were still in France. They did not actually leave until November 23rd. Bad weather forced several of them to land at an Italian military base but, luckily, the base authorities were willing to appear not to notice the incident, and, a few hours later, all the planes arrived in Israel.

New troubles flared up every day along our borders. The Syrians, also, got into the act; on December 10th they opened fire on an Israeli Police border guard and on two fishing boats crossing Lake Tiberias. It was impossible for us to continue to refrain from reacting and, on the following day, our troops launched an attack on the Syrian batteries responsible for the aggression. They were wiped out by our side which lost ten men, while fifty Syrians were put out of combat.

The British Foreign Secretary termed the raid "an unmotivated Israeli attack," and Lord Salisbury declared that as a result it would be unwise of Great Britain to interrupt her delivery of arms to Egypt! He even took the occasion to express Great Britain's disapproval to the Western countries who were supplying arms to Israel. The State Department made known that, for its part, it was studying the affair with "the greatest impartiality," while at the same time its ambassador to Cairo was going out of his way to assure Nasser of the deep sympathy of the United States.

If the Quai d'Orsay was more reserved, it was because Nasser's agents were again stirring up activity in North Africa despite the recent verbal "accords," and that Egyptian contraband materiel was being used to arm the F.L.N.

The last days of December saw the first MIGs and Ilyushins enter service in the Egyptian Air Force, and Russian tanks begin to patrol the Sinai Desert.

In a last effort at peace, Ben-Gurion offered to meet Nasser personally for a joint negotiation. But Nasser rejected the offer. That was proof enough that he wanted war and that, in confirmation of *The Philosophy of Revolution,* his aim was the destruction of Israel to build, on its ruins, a new Arab Empire. He finally had the necessary arms and "world opinion" saw in him the innocent victim of Israeli aggression!

The stage was set.

PART THREE

"Kadesh"

30

True Friends and an Occasional Ally

THE BELLS WHICH, at midnight on December 31, 1955, made hope for another year of peace echo in the hearts of most men only announced to us a future full of troubles.

On top of her Soviet equipment, Egypt had just received from Great Britain fifty-one Valentine tanks, sold to her under the false designation "tractors" through an intermediary Belgian firm. A celebrated *London Daily Mirror* reporter characterized this deal as a "political and diplomatic complaisance on a grand scale." He added, "Why don't we continue along these lines and sell the Arabs our old atomic bombs as cigarette lighters, and our old jets as vacuum cleaners, surely most efficient?" But London no longer troubled to cover up shipment of arms to Egypt. On New Year's Eve, Liverpool dockers loaded twenty-one box cars of arms destined for Alexandria. Great Britain was sending her Season's Greetings to Nasser.

Nor was King Hussein of Jordan forgotten. In a spectacular ceremony, the R.A.F. presented six Vampires to the Jordanian Air Force. Iraq's Prime Minister Nouri al Said, faithful friend of Great Britain and fierce partisan of the

British Baghdad Pact, felt he, too, was doing Great Britain and the United States a favour by accepting their military equipment. He declared quite simply in his New Year good will message: "Each arm, each plane, and each tank received by Iraq will contribute to resolving the Palestine problem in the best interests of the Arabs." Only Syria had not yet received her gift. It was to come from the U.S.S.R.; but the Syria-Czech contract, although signed, had not yet produced any deliveries.

In Israel, enemy planes were flying overhead and heavy tanks were raising dust along the roads, and news from the United States, Canada and Europe gave us no comfort. Our requests for arms were regularly rejected. Great Britain even placed an embargo on the few Meteors remaining to be delivered. This decision was most surprising considering Mr. Eden's statement in his memoirs about the continuous flow of Soviet arms into Egypt. But at that time, the British Prime Minister, admitting that such a situation "could not comfort Israel much, if, as a result, she was placed at an increasing disadvantage with Egypt," did not worry about Israel's fate.

France was still our only hope. However, for the moment, she was just a hope. Paris found herself without a government in a new turn of the parliamentary merry-go-round begun at the end of the last war, and no one could predict the results of the forthcoming elections. No decision could be made in Paris until the new Chamber of Deputies convened. Therefore, we in Tel-Aviv were more preoccupied with the outcome of the French elections than were many Frenchmen.

Meanwhile, Norway was reportedly willing to sell some obsolete Vampire jet fighters. Although we were aware that Norway had agreed upon purchase of the aircraft not to re-sell them to any foreign country without Britain's authorization, we proceeded to Oslo. We had illusions that our Socialist friends, who had often declared their support of Israel, might dare to overlook this old contract clause.

We were well received in Norway. The Norwegians, sharing our anxiety and grief, showed understanding and compassion. As in similar past situations, the Air Force was most willing to get rid of the aircraft; but the Norwegian Government hesitated. In the end the answer was—No! The refusal was due not, as was contended, to the non-resale clause in the British-Norwegian contract, but to fear of Nasser's closing the Suez Canal to Norwegian shipping. It was a bitter lesson, but more were in store for us.

On January 31, 1956, a new French Government was formed, the twenty-second since the War. Guy Mollet, the Socialist leader, became Prime Minister, and Maurice Bourgès-Maunoury, a Radical, Minister of Defense. What would be their attitude toward Israel, we asked ourselves! Some months ago Shimon Peres had sought political support from Mr. Mollet, then secretary of the Socialist Party. At that time, Mollet had said, "I won't be Bevin!" Would Mr. Mollet remember his promise? We had always enjoyed the support of the Opposition, especially the Socialist one, but it acted differently when it came to power. We had forebodings when, in his first speech before the National Assembly, Prime Minister Mollet discussed the Algerian problem at great length, but made no reference whatsoever to the Middle East.

Support for our cause came again from the Opposition. Paul Reynaud, the Independent Deputy, in response to Guy Mollet's speech, openly connected France's Algerian difficulties with the aggressive policies of Nasser. "In Morocco, in Tunisia, as in Algeria," he declared, "France is up against one and the same adversary, whose nerve center is in Cairo." Reynaud's position indicated that Paris' hostility towards Nasser was growing daily as Cairo continued to be the principal source of arms for rebel (F.L.N.) activities in

Algeria. "If we were to destroy the base, wouldn't the entire structure of the revolution crumble?" many French political and military leaders began to wonder.

But Guy Mollet seemed to be trying to solve the Algerian problem peacefully. He announced that the French Government would be willing to grant General Elections if the leaders of the Algerian revolution agreed to a cease-fire.

On the 9th of February, Mr. Robert Lacoste, a Socialist, was appointed Minister Resident in Algeria, replacing Mr. Jacques Soustelle, who wanted to keep Algeria French.

The new French Government seemed to be inclined towards conciliation in North Africa and tolerance of Arab national ambitions. Did not this road lead through Cairo? In Israel, anxiety was at a fever pitch. Guy Mollet took a position in favor of pro-Arab conciliation as President Eisenhower and Prime Minister Eden were meeting in Washington. Mr. Eden was reported seeking American support and armaments for the Baghdad Pact, especially for Iraq, and a joint Anglo-American policy towards Egypt.

What could we expect from the Conference? The State Department's refusal of arms under a new pretext, that their receipt would further endanger our security since Nasser would then order more from the U.S.S.R.

As for Mr. Eden's recent proposal to buy peace in the Middle East by forcing us to accept a new Munich, that spelled disaster.

Pierre Gilbert, the French Ambassador to Tel-Aviv, a great friend of our people, who spoke better Hebrew than many Israelis, was keenly aware of our worries. Pierre Gilbert was not one of those ambassadors who shut themselves up in their embassies, as in an ivory tower. He had daily contact with all classes of the population and was familiar with our military resources. He knew that, since we could not face Egyptian tanks with courage alone, the French Government's attitude could prove fatal to us.

With great relief and joy he shared with us the news that France, uninvited to the conference, had sent Washington and London a memorandum declaring her opposition to peace in the Middle East by the dismemberment of Israel, an act that would lead to a catastrophe. The memorandum stressed that only a firm attitude, demanding respect for the borders of Israel and the re-establishment of a balance of power between the Israelis and the Arabs, could avert the danger of an imminent conflict.

This memorandum proved that France was not about to sacrifice Israel to buy peace in Algeria. Could it also be interpreted to mean that France would be willing to re-arm us to re-establish the balance of power she spoke of? A cable demanding clarification was dispatched to the Chief of the Israeli Defense Mission in Paris.

The situation could not have been more confused. The Quai d'Orsay, pursuing a strict pro-Arab policy, was seeking appeasement of Nasser and was ready to pay a price for Egyptian non-intervention in Algeria. But Bourgès-Maunoury, the young Minister of Defense, known during the resistance for his courage and determination, was strongly opposed to any such policy. He knew that orders were going to the Algerian rebellion from Cairo and that Egyptian arms and propaganda were keeping Algeria *on fire;* for while he was Minister of Interior, a document seized from a rebel had proved Egyptian interference. He, like Paul Renaud, was persuaded that it was in Cairo that France faced her enemy, the enemy of *Algérie Française.*

Prime Minister Mollet, a Socialist in the true sense of the word, deeply believed there could be no military solution for Algeria, but that peace could be achieved by negotiations. But he was not prepared to negotiate under pressure from the rebels or Cairo. He hated Nasser, as only a Socialist can hate a dictator, and his hand was outstretched to those leaders of the rebellion not under orders from Cairo. Guy Mollet was also aware of the dangers to the Middle East and Israel posed by Soviet penetration and arms in Egypt.

On February 17th, the New French Government, ignoring the previous government's contracts, stopped all arms shipments to Egypt. Guy Mollet had not forgotten his promise to Shimon Peres: "I won't be Bevin." With the full backing of Bourgès-Maunoury and Foreign Minister Christian Pineau, who did not share the pro-Nasser attitude of some influential officials in his Ministry, Mollet authorized the signing of contracts for various war materials, including a pending one for the famous Mystère IV's. A NATO decision was still required for the delivery of the aircraft, and France took it upon herself to obtain it.

At last we had fallen upon better days. We had gained true friends, and the future brought us an unexpected ally.

Sir Anthony was endeavoring to re-establish friendly Anglo-Egyptian relations if Nasser would only give up interference in the internal affairs of Jordan and Iraq and with British oil possessions on the Persian Gulf. Nasser made promises, but the "Voice of Arabs," emanating from Cairo, incited the people of Jordan and Iraq to revolt against their kings, the "lackeys of British Imperialism," and Nasser's agents penetrated both kingdoms, spreading unrest, arming terrorist groups, and trying to win over ambitious army officers, inciting them to open rebellion. London protested. Nasser, assuring London of his good will, again made promises, but did not call off either his propaganda or subversive activities.

Not all members of Eden's party shared his attitude towards the Egyptian President. Some attacked Sir Anthony's policy of conciliation and reminded him of history's recent lesson of the dangers of appeasing an aggressive, ambitious dictator. They condemned the arms embargo on Israel and called upon Britain to help arm Israel. These deputies had no special sympathy for Israel. But they saw us as the only force capable of opposing Nasser in the Middle East and as a well-armed ally in case of an Anglo-Egyptian conflict. Unfortunately, their actual influence on the British Government was feeble; at the end of February, Mr. Eden dispatched his Foreign Secretary, Mr. Selwyn Lloyd, on a good will mission throughout the Arab world.

Arriving in Cairo, the Foreign Secretary was in for a big surprise. For weeks General Glubb, the British Commander of the Arab Legion, and his British officers had become the main target of attacks from Cairo. It soon became clear that the loyalty of the Arab officers of the Legion to King Hussein was being sapped by the siren song of the Arab "Liberator." King Hussein knew which way the wind was blowing. Spectacular anti-British measures were called for if he wanted to keep his power. General Glubb and his British officers were ordered to leave Jordan immediately and were replaced by Arab officers. Mobs cheered the King and Colonel Nasser in one breath.

Neither London nor Glubb and his staff had any inkling of the coup. It was well planned and took Britain by surprise. Reportedly, the British Foreign Secretary was dining with Colonel Nasser when the news was announced. He swallowed the bitter pill and left Cairo without delay. It was a hard blow to the British Government. If Jordan fell under Nasser's power, she would probably drag Iraq along in her wake, and the Iraqi oil, Bahrein oil—the Persian Gulf—would be lost to Great Britain.

The coup was a personal blow to Sir Anthony. He realized the futility of his efforts to come to terms with Nasser, whom he now saw as a Hitler of the Middle East.

Eden and his political advisors, as well as the French officials of the Quai d'Orsay, who had not bothered to study Nasser's *Philosophy of Revolution*, did not understand that once Nasser had embarked on the road of Arab national liberation, he had to go on and wage war against British rule in the Middle East and French rule in North Africa.

What had the Quai d'Orsay expected from Mr. Pineau's visit to Cairo on March 14th? Had they expected Nasser to admit shipping arms to Algeria and training Algerian volunteers? Had they expected him to promise not to interfere in North Africa, to abandon the concept of Arab unity under his leadership? Although Pineau had already proved that Nasser had supplied arms in the Algerian rebellion, Nasser denied it. But he did state positively that to abandon the Algerian Nationalists would be "to throw away our Arabism, everything we feel for our brothers." Thus Nasser confirmed what he had previously written.

These events did not pass unnoticed in Washington, which was neither alarmed nor concerned about British loss of influence in the Middle East and the French ejection from North Africa. There was no doubt that Washington and American public opinion, influenced by years of stories about French and British colonization, welcomed the awakening of Arab nationalism, the Algerian claim for independence and the Jordanian aspirations of freedom from British influence. There was no doubt also that oil interests had their effect upon Washington's attitude. The prospects of taking over the last remaining British oil riches in the Middle East and of the conquest of the Sahara's oil with the French out of North Africa, dazzled the American oil companies and their State Department friends. It was estimated that the Sahara could be as rich as the Middle East currently holding 72 per cent of the world's oil reserves. Some French newspapers reported that a Saudi-Arabian diplomatic bag was seized at Orly Airport.

The bag contained anti-French leaflets, printed in the United States for the Algerian rebels by American oil companies with interests in Saudi Arabia.

One might have expected that, with Mr. Dulles' hatred of Communism, the danger of Soviet influence in Egypt and the Middle East would have overcome American sentimentality about colonization and even the pressure of oil interests. But although the Secretary of State was surprised by the Czech-Egyptian arms deal, he believed there was no danger of overwhelming Communist influence, in Egypt or through Egypt, upon the Middle East. He felt that Soviet influence could be offset by a more spectacular gift than the arms deal, by a loan for the Aswan High Dam. The rain of dollars and the presence of hundreds of American specialists could certainly bring Egypt back into the American sphere of influence.

The Averted Menace

NASSER became as obsessed with the idea of the Aswan High Dam, as with the destruction of Israel. The building of the dam could bring him immortal glory—the glory of the builders of the pyramids—and the destruction of Israel, the leadership of the Arab world. The dam would provide water for permanent cultivation of another two million acres of this virtually rainless land, a seemingly large area, but actually small and insufficient considering Egypt's population growth during the dam's construction period. Upon completion of the dam, the man-acre ratio would be as bad as on the day construction had begun. But the dam's power would permit industrial expansion needed to fight the country's poverty. The estimated cost of the dam was four hundred million dollars.

Washington and London, hoping this grand project would divert Nasser's political aspirations, reacted positively to Egypt's request for a long-term loan. The two powers rationalized the Czech arms deal as a requirement to assure Egypt's integrity against "warlike" Israel. Even reports of more arms deals for Egypt and of Soviet economic penetration there did not alter Mr. Dulles' attitude. On February 11th, the President of the World Bank, Mr. Eugene Black, announced that the bank had agreed to lend Nasser 200 million dollars if there was a concurrent Anglo-American loan of 70 million dollars. Nasser did not accept a second condition attached to the loan—the bank's virtual control of Egypt's budgetary plans.

The events in Jordan deeply shook the British Government and British public opinion. Although the British press and the Opposition had called for armed intervention, Eden chose wisely to help King Hussein re-establish his popularity and succeeded in protecting British interests in Jordan. Eden's offer of moral support and financial aid enabled the King to reject Nasser and the aid offered immediately after the "revolution" by the Soviets who hoped to step into British shoes. The King's determination to preserve his integrity provoked a new spate of attacks against him from the "Voice of the Arabs" and some unrest in the Army, which wanted to follow Nasser's policy of terrorizing the Jewish population until the great day of war and the annihilation of Israel. Therefore, the King had to allow the establishment of a *Fedayin* base in Jordan. From the pocket of Gaza, the *Fedayin* could now spread their guerrilla warfare over all Israeli territory, and then cross the Jordan border, where they would receive a warm reception from the Arab Legion.

The Egyptian leader then decided to send his heroes against Israel.

We asked ourselves what lay behind this decision? We knew that the Egyptian Army and Air Force were acquiring Soviet equipment and that a military build-up, including a vast lower echelon grouping in the Sinai Desert, was slowly progressing. This build-up, having only one aim, war against Israel, was not yet complete; and the launching of *Fedayin* could be a prelude to war, but not yet.

The Israeli Government could not let this arson and murder go unpunished. Long ago it had become clear to our

Government that these acts of terror would continue as long as the Arabs felt that their own lives were not in danger. This attitude gave birth to our policy of retaliation, which the Secretary General of the United Nations called aggression. Egypt and other Arab states were not condemned when their military-trained "volunteers" murdered our people. But when we, not having our own *Fedayin*, used an army unit to strike back, world opinion rose in indignation with the result that an embargo was placed on military equipment being delivered to us.

In view of the pending delivery of the long-awaited Mystère aircraft, did we have to leave these new acts of terror unpunished? But what a surprise! Mr. Dulles not only agreed that these airplanes be delivered to Israel, but suggested to the Canadians that they sell us some F-86 Sabres. The Secretary of State evidently did not mind France's and Canada's incurring Arab wrath, so long as the United States was not directly involved.

What had made Dulles adopt this new position? Was it Washington's sudden awareness of the Soviet Union's overwhelming economic and ideological penetration of Egypt; or Nasser's turning more and more towards neutrality; or France's insistence, supported by the British, on the delivery of the aircraft; or Mr. Eden's suddenly expressed anxiety about Israel's future?

In view of the NATO decision, Israel would have preferred to refrain from any military action; but when, on April 5th, Egyptian tanks and troops moved towards the frontier, we had no alternative but to strike back. Although this new border flare-up was viewed by Washington as an immediate prelude to war, and Mr. Hammarskjöld was asked to proceed to the troubled area, on April 12th France announced that she was releasing the Mystères to Israel.

This was great news for the Israelis who already mourned

14 dead and 40 wounded. "You have proved by your acts that you are heroes, the nation can have confidence in you. The enemy has felt your power and your heroism." This was the order of the day to the killers.

The Secretary General of the United Nations was on his way to Egypt and Israel to obtain a cease-fire agreement; but it became obvious that after acquiring Soviet arms, Nasser would probably move his Army and Air Force to the newly built bases in the Sinai Desert and stage a new frontier flare-up as an excuse for a major attack. The danger of destruction became real, for we were outnumbered one to ten on the ground and in the air. We required more aircraft, more Mystères, more tanks, heavier than the French ten-ton MX, to face the enemy.

Carrying a letter from Ben-Gurion to Guy Mollet, Shimon Peres again went to France. In the letter Ben-Gurion said that peace could still be saved but only if Egypt was made to realize that she enjoyed no superiority on the ground and in the air. Ben-Gurion concluded: "The small and young Republic of Israel, in this hour of danger, turns to the great and old Republic of France in the hope that her request won't be in vain." Guy Mollet did not disappoint Israel. He gave us the arms, among them the Mystère aircraft. Again the French Army and Air Force had agreed to sacrifice their own equipment to help us.

We still required heavy tanks to face Russian "Stalin Monsters," and we learned that South Africa might be willing to sell some of the Centurions which the British had persuaded them to buy in large quantity. We thought that South Africa had no sympathy for Nasser because of his support of those Africans training in Cairo for an armed battle against both the white-dominated South African states and the newborn states leaning towards the West. We hoped that, under these circumstances, South African leaders would be happy to let us have their excess Centurions.

But the reality in South Africa was a bit different. The Foreign Minister did not seem to have any sympathy towards us. He reproached us for our ties with the new African states and our recent support of them against South Africa in the United Nations. The Foreign Minister received our Ambassador in an atmosphere of cold, open hostility. But the Army was definitely with us. I soon discovered, to my utter amazement, that the reason for their support was not our victory in the battle for independence, but our "common sufferings" during British "occupation." At the time, the main topic of conversation in Pretoria was British atrocities during the Boer War. It was amazing to see how hate could be nourished over the years, growing and growing to exaggerated proportions.

Then the day came when we proceeded to a military camp to inspect the tanks. Since the Commanding Officer of the camp was an Englishman, I was told to adopt a different name, a French one, for the "spy" would report the visit to the British. It was great fun. The tanks, unused since their arrival in South Africa, were in beautiful condition. There were also plenty of spare parts and armaments. The Ministry of Defense was most willing to get rid of a substantial quantity, for many of the nation's bridges were unable to support the heavy Centurions. South Africa required fast, maneuverable, lightly-armored, but well-armed vehicles.

Unfortunately, the Minister of Foreign Affairs had the last word, and his decision was "No!"—his reason was fear of Nasser's closing the Cairo airfield to South African air traffic.

Every day it became clearer that, were it not for Guy Mollet's action, we would have been facing a bitter battle alone and unarmed. And behind Guy Mollet had been Bourgès-Maunoury and his two aides, Abel Thomas and

Colonel Louis Mangin, who had accomplished the impossible by giving us the required arms. Foreign Minister Pineau also had backed us and assured us of noninterference by the Quai d'Orsay, which was still opposing the arms deliveries.

Behind these three courageous men, to whom Israel owes an unforgettable debt, stood the French Army and Air Force. Officers and men offered their full support in the hope that one day their equipment would teach Nasser a new lesson. I could tell many stories about how this spirit of collaboration led to friendship between our men and the French. Good feeling prevailed everywhere, but was most noticeable at the air bases where the Mystères were prepared for the ferry flights and our pilots trained.

Unquestionably, the genuine help we received from France and the French people stemmed from the nation's growing hatred of Nasser for his support of the Algerian Rebellion. The French, with 250,000 soldiers pinned down in Algeria, believed that Cairo was keeping the war going. Guy Mollet had extended his hand to the rebels by dispatching peace-seeking envoys even to Cairo to meet with Algerian leaders. He wanted peace based on negotiations leading to a cease-fire and free elections. Some of the Algerian leaders were willing, but others, sold on Nasser's idea of a French unconditional surrender in Algeria, were fiercely opposed. For Nasser, Algeria had to be the stepping stone to conquest of all North Africa, just as a destroyed Israel would be to the whole Middle East. Had not the Islamic flag once flown from the shores of the Atlantic to the Persian Gulf?

The news of the French Government's releasing Mystères to Israel, followed by Egyptian Intelligence reports of arms shipments, led Cairo to order the battle in Algeria intensified. The rebellion was turning into a real war.

But peace reigned on the Israeli-Egyptian border. The Secretary General of the United Nations claimed it as his achievement. He had been convinced once more by Nasser that the Israelis were the cause of the trouble. The warm welcome he received in Cairo and the cold, distrustful one in Tel-Aviv had a direct bearing on his thinking. The Jews were guilty of aggression once more.

Peace reigned on the border because the Egyptian dictator had learned again that Israel was ready to face his armed forces. The Egyptian casualties on April 5th were heavy, and Nasser began to feel that his Army and Air Force were not yet ready for a major show-down. He needed more arms, more equipment and so he turned once more towards Russia. His request was granted.

Peace reigned on the border because the Egyptian Embassy in Washington had reported a rising wave of anti-Egyptian feeling in the United States which might endanger the dam loan. A group of Senators and part of the press came out openly against granting the loan to the Egyptian dictator.

But in reality it was not peace—only an illusion of peace.

The Theft

A FRENCH AIR FORCE PLANE from the north of France asked permission to land on one of the southern bases. Circling the field, the crew listened in on an exchange of words which were not French. "What language are they speaking?" the pilot asked his companion. "It is Hebrew to me," answered the co-pilot.

The French use the expression "Hebrew to me!" to underline that they do not understand a word, and the crew was surprised to learn later that the language spoken had indeed been Hebrew.

The Israeli pilots were going through a conversion course to be able to ferry the Mystères. It was rather a complicated affair, requiring an intermediary base in Europe where aircraft could be refuelled and maintained to take off at dawn for Israel.

The Egyptian Secret Service in quest of intelligence on deliveries of French arms to Israel, reported to Cairo some flights of Mystères from France to Italy and stressed that investigations had been unable to determine the destination of the aircraft. Officially they were training flights landing on an intermediary base and reporting their return flights to France. All pilots seemed to be French.

It is still a mystery to me how, in spite of the many difficulties, we could keep secret deliveries of aircraft flown by our own men. No doubt we owe a great debt of gratitude to the officer commanding the intermediary base and his men who kept silent, without asking questions, without talking.

When in the beginning of May, France announced more deliveries of Mystères to Israel, Cairo newspapers reported that Israel had received 70 Mystères. This figure was based upon calculations of intelligence agents who had mixed up training flights and true deliveries. We had altogether 24 Mystères; but Nasser, believing we had 70, and aware that he no longer had superiority in the air, turned his anger against the "Western Imperialists" who dared arm his enemy.

On the 16th of May, Egypt recognized Red China. Cairo admitted that this move was Nasser's reaction to the continuing conspiracy of the Western Powers. It was a hard blow to Mr. Dulles.

On the 26th of May, came the announcement from the Cairo leaders of the Algerian revolution that the only solution in Algeria was the retreat of France and a declaration of independence.

In Jordan, Iraq and Libya, Egyptian agents, helped by Egyptian military attachés, attempted to stage local *coup d'états* against the rulers "sold to the British Imperialism." In Iraq, the young King barely escaped assassination. Cairo declared war against the West in North Africa and throughout the Middle East.

While Washington carefully watched the new developments, London notified the Secretary of State that, under the prevailing circumstances, Her Majesty's Government did not view with favor the proposed loans to Egypt.

We in Israel viewed with anxiety Nasser's efforts to conquer the Arab states. Pro-Nasser regimes all around us would increase our danger by forcing us to fight on several fronts.

From Egypt came news of the completion of the military infra-structures and of troop concentrations already equipped with Soviet weapons. From the airfields of El-Arish and the newly completed Bir Gafgafa, Soviet MIG aircraft made daily passes along the border.

Only the feeling that we had true friends in Paris, who had helped us break out of the vicious circle of isolation, let us live with the threat surrounding us. This does not mean that without France's help, we would have plunged into despair and in a daze waited to be slaughtered by the Arabs. We would have fought "on the beaches and in the streets," to quote Churchill after the defeat of France.

The danger of war was looming—war without mercy, war whose aim the enemy described as "complete annihilation of Israel." Our political and military leaders started to plan the best way of preventing it. One did not need to be a military expert to realize that once the Arab armies started rolling and their air force bombed our cities, our situation would be tragic, if not hopeless. Whatever the outcome, Israel would have lain in waste and destruction. The only way to prevent war was to destroy the Egyptian bases of attack, namely the Army bases in the Sinai Desert. Without them, Nasser would be unable to concentrate his armed forces and launch a surprise attack against us. Could Israel afford such a preventive action which would be called a war of aggression?

From a strict, military point of view, we did not have enough strength for a short, decisive strike. Egyptian forces still outnumbered us. Politically, it would be suicide.

The calm which had returned for a short time to the borders was destroyed again. There were only sporadic actions, but we lost lives and property. June had started with a new victim in Jerusalem, fired upon from over the Jordanian border.

On the 13th of June, the last British soldier left Egyptian

soil. Cairo ordered celebrations and announced the arrival of Mr. Chepilov and his advisers. It was a bad sign. The outcome of Chepilov's last visit had been the Egyptian-Czech deal. What gift was the Russian bringing now? The reports indicated more arms and large economic aid. Was the Soviet Union prepared to grant the Aswan Dam loan? With the Russians financing construction of the dam, Nasser would no longer be restrained from attacking Israel. Western intervention would be hampered by the Soviet Union.

The news that Cairo was still negotiating the World Bank loan was rather comforting. The Egyptian Ambassador was trying without success to persuade the World Bank to release Egypt from the required budgetary control. Reports of Soviet penetration had set members of both the United States House and Senate against loans to Nasser. Aware of this mounting wave of hostility and at the State Department's announcement that Egypt must conclude the loan agreement by the 1st of July, the Egyptian Ambassador took off for Cairo to persuade Nasser to accept the loan. The recall, at the same time, of the American Ambassador to Cairo, a great friend, supporter and believer in Nasser, could only reflect the Secretary of State's growing annoyance with the Egyptian Dictator.

Nasser hesitated! His acceptance of the bank's condition, to submit his budget to control of a foreign country, would be exploited by his enemies as a political defeat—the re-entry of Western Imperialism through the back door. Was not an economic control as shameful as a military one? He could not take such a step on the eve of meeting with Tito and Nehru to become a third leader of the neutralist world.

Seemingly, Tito and Nehru advised Nasser, subjected already to Soviet military domination, to accept the bank's loan to escape Soviet economic domination, as well. The Egyptian Ambassador received instructions to return to the United States to accept the loan.

The Ambassador landed in New York on July 17th, and announced that Egypt had decided to accept the loan and that he hoped to meet with Mr. Dulles as soon as possible.

It was too late!

Both the Foreign Office and the State Department announced on the 19th of July their country's refusal of the loan. The statement was released while Mr. Dulles read to the Egyptian Ambassador a note stating the reasons for refusal— Soviet activities in Egypt and Egypt's economic inability to repay the loan. When the Egyptian Ambassador returned to the Embassy to cable Cairo, the news had already been flashed throughout the world. It was not only a refusal, but a slap in the face to Nasser, an insult which could topple his regime. Worried and angry, he stepped off the airplane bringing him back from Yugoslavia. If he did not react promptly, his days were numbered. His mind was made up, but he feared involving Egypt in a military conflict with the West. Whom could he consult, if not his Soviet friends? Their answer was that neither the British nor the French armed forces were ready for a large scale military action against Nasser's well-armed army. The British and French would have to mount an expeditionary force of such scope that preparations would require some time. The Russians did not think the States would interfere; and in any case, Egypt would enjoy Russian support.

On the 21st of July, Nasser issued orders to prepare the operation called Nationalization of the Suez Canal. On the 24th of July, Egypt was ready for the take-over.

On that day Nasser made his first public appearance in Cairo, attacking the United States. Following the raw speech, the Egyptian news media paved the way for Nasser's next announced appearance in Alexandria on July 26th. Not a thing leaked out about the proposed action.

Facing tens of thousands, Nasser launched one of his most

venomous attacks against the Western Powers, Britain and France specifically. The Egyptian masses listened in silence, stupefied by the wrath of the attack, dazed by the sublime actor who well knew his public.

"This, O citizens, is the battle in which we are involved. It is a battle against Imperialism, and the methods and teaching of Imperialism, and a battle against Israel, the vanguard of Imperialism. As I told you, Arab nationalism has been set on fire from the Atlantic Ocean to the Persian Gulf."

The masses listened holding their breath.

"Today, O citizens, the Suez Canal was nationalized. Today, O citizens, we declare that our property was returned to us. We are feeling today, our glory and grandeur."

The masses exploded.

Nasser answered their shouts with hysterical laughter—laughter which shook the world.

The news reached Mr. Eden while he was dining with the King of Iraq and Iraqi leaders at Downing Street. The guests "saw clearly that here was an event which changed all perspective, and understood at once how much would depend upon the resolution with which the act of defiance was met" is Sir Anthony's description of the moment. But there is a story to it, told in London. "Hit him, hit him hard, hit him now," exclaimed Nouri Said, the Iraqi Prime Minister. The Iraqi leaders were more than anxious to get rid of the dangerous troublemaker in the Arab world.

When the guests left, Mr. Eden adjourned with some of his ministers and called in the Chiefs of Staff. Britain's vital interests in all of the Middle East were threatened. The use of force was discussed, but no decision was reached. Mr. Eden, who had dedicated his life to peace, in whose memory the horrors of war were still alive, could not be persuaded to decide on military intervention until other means, such as economic pressure, were tried. Nor was Sir Anthony convinced that the Arab world would not react violently against military action, the invasion of Egypt. The French and Americans had to be consulted, a joint action worked out.

The news reached Guy Mollet while he was fighting for new military credits in the National Assembly. The Socialist leader believed that peace in Algeria could be achieved only by France's proving that no military effort would be spared against those trying to force France into unconditional surrender. Early in the morning, the session over, the Prime Minister consulted Bourgès-Maunoury and Pineau. Nasser had to be eliminated not only for the benefit of French interests in Algeria, but for the benefit of the free world. If Hitler had been stopped during the Rhineland crisis, there would not have been a World War, Guy Mollet stressed. France was for immediate military intervention.

Public opinion in England and France was violently against Nasser. Military intervention was called for to put an end to the "odious Egyptian Hitler." The members of Mr. Eden's political party who for months had advocated a strong policy against Egypt pressured the Prime Minister to make a decision. Even the Labor Party stated that Britain should answer force with force. But Sir Anthony still hesitated. He had a long telephone conversation with Guy Mollet during the day, but was still not convinced, although he realized, as he expressed in a cable to Mr. Eisenhower on the evening of the 27th, that if Nasser could not be brought to his senses by economic and political pressure, "we must be ready, as a last resort, to use force!"

Washington accepted the theft with great calm. American interests were not involved directly. The Suez Canal, not the Panama Canal, had been seized. Washington had more urgent worries in Central America, where Mr. Dulles had gone on a mission to Peru. Upon receipt of Mr. Eden's cable, the President did not consider recalling his Secretary of

State, and delegated the State Department specialist on Arab affairs, Mr. Murphy, to proceed to London. His instructions were to prevent any military operation against Egypt and to persuade Britain and France to call a conference of maritime powers to decide the issue.

Mr. Eden left London on the 28th for a short weekend, still hesitating, but agreeing that the Chiefs of Staff work out a preliminary plan of military intervention in cooperation with the French. It was the first victory of the "Suez Group," who saw no other solution to the crisis. Foreign Secretary Lloyd and Mr. Pineau were to meet with the American Envoy arriving on the 29th.

The President of the United States underestimated British and French willingness to act firmly by using force, and Mr. Murphy brought only a vague proposal for a conference of maritime powers, the real intention of which was to stall the issue until Mr. Dulles' return from Peru. Washington wished to stand aloof from the dispute.

On the 29th, Mr. Eden returned to London, convinced of the necessity of using force. On the 30th of July, he clearly stated in the House of Commons that "Her Majesty's Government will not accept any arrangement which would leave the control of the Canal to a single power, which could exploit it purely for purposes of national policy." The statement was well understood and acclaimed by all members of the House.

The atmosphere in London and his talks with Mr. Lloyd and Pineau led Mr. Murphy to believe that without Dulles' direct intervention, Britain and France might involve the United States in a war against Egypt. Mr. Murphy cabled the President, requesting the Secretary of State's immediate arrival.

During the next few days, British and French military planners tried hard to figure out the necessary strength and availability of the intervention force. If the British could mobilize a sizeable force, the French would withdraw theirs from Algeria where every soldier, every piece of equipment was needed. Would the Minister Resident in Algeria, Mr. Lacoste, and the officer commanding the French Forces in Algeria agree to allocate troops to the planned venture? Mr. Lacoste replied that one French division in Egypt was worth more than four divisions in Algeria.

On the evening of July 31st, a French colonel arrived in London with a list of French units available for the operation.

On August 1st, Mr. Dulles arrived in London. From the first talks it became obvious to the British and French that the United States had decided not only not to get involved in armed conflict in Egypt, but to prevent her allies from starting a military operation. Several reasons lay behind this decision. It was the height of a Presidential election year. The theme of the Republican campaign for Eisenhower's re-election was "Peace and Prosperity." Needless to say, British and French intentions did not exactly fit it. A war to defend colonial interests would have had a disastrous effect on the electorate. Behind this political aspect, loomed a material one. The powerful American oil companies felt that armed conflict with Nasser would endanger their interests in the Arab world. They did not realize that the Arab world had never been so near the brink of an anti-Western revolution, an expropriation of the oil riches, those same riches which the petrol lobbies had tried to defend by supporting appeasement.

The pro-Western leaders of the Arab world remained silent during the first days after the "theft." They hoped, as Nouri Said had expressed it, that the West would hit hard and hit immediately to get rid of Nasser and all he stood for once and forever. But when no sign that the West was going to hit back came, the pro-Western Arab leaders could not but support the man who had slapped the West and whose glory the excited masses were singing.

The course of history would certainly have been different if Washington, London and Paris had agreed on a common immediate action. For Nasser was frightened by his own deed. Although he declared to his public that he would meet force with force, he knew that his Army and Air Force would be unable to face the invasion forces. On July 27th, Egypt formally tried to reassure the world that it would respect the 1888 Convention of Free Navigation. But Nasser's attitude hardened with the news from London. Even the Soviet Union had not immediately sanctioned Nasser's action. Mr. Khrushchev remembered well Mr. Eden's declaration during the Premier's April visit to England, that Britain would fight for its oil in the Middle East; and the tankers which supplied Britain passed through the Suez Canal. The Russian Premier had even stated that Russia would resort to war only if a Western attack was launched on her or one of the Warsaw Pact countries. Only when disagreement between the U.S.A. and Britain and France became obvious, did Mr. Khrushchev warn the West that the Soviet Union would oppose any settlement of the Suez Crisis by force.

Tel-Aviv, although used to Nasser's threats of war and destruction, was truly shaken by Nasser's action. Israel hoped against hope that the West would not let him get away with the theft. If it did, there would be no limit to the dictator's acts. If the West would not fight for the Canal, its own possession, how could Israel expect it to fight for her safety! Despite the daily increase of terrorist actions, for weeks we had tried to restrain ourselves from any retaliatory action in order not to hamper our arms deliveries. From the 1st of June till the 1st of August, we counted ten attacks against Israeli property, and six Israelis had lost their lives. Some of us even started to doubt the efficacy of retaliation in the long run. Under the present circumstances, with the Egyptian Army concentrated in the Sinai Desert, a military action offering him an excuse for attack would be welcomed by Nasser. Only by eradicating the evil would we be able to look forward to a bright future. It was clear to us that if Britain and France decided on military action which would bring about the downfall of Nasser, we could hope for peace; but if not, it was for us, ourselves, to assure the future. To do this we would need more arms to face the Egyptian armadas in the air, on the sea, and on the ground. The road led again to Paris.

The Pitfall of Suez

PARIS was bursting with pro-war atmosphere. Senators, deputies, the press, and the man in the street reproached Guy Mollet and his Government for not taking action on their declarations.

"Criminal impotence," Senator Michel Debree, future Prime Minister, called it; "Boasting, that makes History laugh at you," wrote the journalist, Jean Fabiani.

Shimon Peres could well expect that in such an atmosphere, France would come to our aid. Guy Mollet and Bourgès-Maunoury immediately approved our request, but asked time to make a careful study of our requirements, in consideration of France's own immediate needs. Pineau expressed his support; but not trusting his own people, he asked that all arrangements be made through the Defense Ministry. The hostility of the Quai d'Orsay still prevailed, an icy wall of indifference to our anxiety; the officials still lulled themselves with pro-Arab illusions.

Hoping France would grant us enough arms to offer us a fair chance to face Nasser, we anxiously awaited good news from London, for Allied military intervention would facilitate the achievement of our goal. Shimon had not yet discussed the problem of payment for the arms. We did not have resources to cover our needs.

It was announced that Britain and France had agreed to Mr. Dulles' proposal for a London conference, where delegates from all the interested maritime powers could discuss the Canal's future and the measures to be taken to protect their common interests. We braced ourselves for war. Our French friends tried to cheer us up by telling us that France and Britain had accepted Mr. Dulles' proposal only that world opinion might then sanction military action. It seemed so. Pineau, returning from London, spoke in the National Assembly and to the press about the "solidarity of the Western Powers," about "France marching to the end of the chosen road!" From London came the echoes of Sir Anthony's announcing in the House of Commons the movement from Britain of a number of Navy, Army and Air Force units and the calling up of about 20,000 Army reservists.

The deep impression made by the announcements had not yet died when, from over the ocean, from Washington, came Mr. Dulles' words about certain countries wanting to go to war over the Canal—war which presented a danger to world peace. He spoke of the necessity of treating Egypt with utmost fairness and made an appeal to the sober judgment of the nations involved in the dispute. He made it clear that the United States would not take upon herself any firm engagements as far as the unfortunate quarrel was concerned. Paris and London were most surprised.

The London Conference was no doubt the trap of Suez. Dulles convinced Pineau and Eden to agree to the conference, which he hoped would prevent military action and inevitably result in negotiating with Nasser. Pineau's and Eden's statements indicated that they had accepted the idea, believing that Dulles would admit the need for military action if the conference failed, as they were certain it would. Would Eden have quoted the Secretary of State? "It should be possible to create a world opinion so adverse to Nasser that he would be isolated. Then, if military operations had to be undertaken, they would be more apt to succeed, and have less grave repercussions, than if it had been undertaken precipitately." Had Dulles not said it? It is doubtful that both Pineau and Eden would have made such statements without assurance of Dulles' support.

The Arab world listened carefully to these declarations and reacted accordingly. The "Rais" had won—"The Americans are backing out"—and from Lebanon, Jordan, Iraq, Saudi Arabia and Tripoli, the anti-Nasser pro-Western rulers now dispatched cables of support, assurances of Arab unity against Anglo-French imperialism. A new organization, the Islamic Popular Congress for the support of the Egyptian Canal, called for a general protest strike in all Arab countries on the 15th of August, the eve of the Dulles-sponsored international conference.

Nasser, himself, played a game of wait and see. Worried during the first days of August about military preparations in England and France, he gained self-confidence from the news of the American attitude. Even in Great Britain, the war mood changed quickly. On the 2nd of August, the leaders of the Labor Party, supporting Mr. Eden's firm hand, stood violently against Nasser; and Mr. Gaitskell declared, "It is exactly the same as we encountered from Mussolini and Hitler. I believe we were right to react sharply to this move." But the same Labor Party leaders started their retreat on the 4th of August. *The Manchester Guardian* asked what right had Britain and France to use force against Egypt. On the 8th, twenty-four Labor Party members declared that any intervention in Egypt would be considered an act of aggression.

On the 13th, the shadow government of the Labor Party issued a warning against the use of force.

The proverbial British national unity in the face of national danger no longer existed; and the deep division in the country led the Egyptian dictator to believe the danger of war averted. True, France was still united in the desire to fight, but Nasser did not believe that France alone could undertake a military intervention with most of her armed forces tied up in Algeria.

Although Israeli ships had been refused the right of passage through the Canal, and Egyptian guns had blocked their access to the port of Eilat, Israel had not been invited to the London Conference. The State Department's excuse for not inviting the Israelis was that it would offer Cairo reason not to attend.

But Nasser had declared already that he would reject the invitation to a conference "whose aims are but imperialistic."

Israeli public opinion had no doubts that this Western attitude would encourage Nasser to commit more acts of aggression leading to the final leap.

We seemed to be right. On the 16th of August, the Conference held its first session at Lancaster House, London. That same evening, a bus on the way to Eilat was attacked and a car was blown up by a mine near Sde Boker—the casualties —four killed, fourteen wounded. While the delegates discussed how to accept a defeat, while Chepilov warned the West that military intervention would mean war, an Israeli military patrol was attacked—the casualties this time—five killed. Nasser had already taken the path of war. The Government warned the population of the gravity of the situation and called for sacrifices in the face of danger.

Ben-Gurion launched a world appeal "for money for arms," for all local sacrifices could not pay a fraction of the required armaments cost. There was a slight difference of opinion between us and the French about what was required to face the Ilyushin bombers, the MIG-15 jet fighters, the Josef Stalin 4 and T-34 tanks, the SU-100 self-propelled guns and other newest Soviet equipment. General Dayan strongly believed that the best line of defense was to break up the planned offensive before it could be launched. A long list of our needs was established, representing an amount of money about which we could not even dream. Shimon presented the list to Bourgès-Maunoury and explained our monetary situation. Maunoury, without waiting for official documents to be signed or bothering with terms of payments, gave the delivery order. The action was wholeheartedly supported by both Guy Mollet and Pineau, who feared, as we did, that the failure of the London Conference would encourage Nasser to strike his imagined decisive blow against us. The French leaders knew the potential might of the Egyptian Armed Forces, which presented a problem to the planners of the Anglo-French Expeditionary Force, and doubted that an intervention force could be mounted in time to save Israel.

Planning and preparations for military intervention continued in London and Paris, despite the fact that Britain and France had accepted the conference idea. It was not perfidy, for both Eden and Mollet were deeply convinced that Dulles would not oppose the use of force if negotiations failed. In the old bunker under the Thames, where Sir Winston Churchill had conducted World War II operations, the Anglo-French joint commission worked on details of the operation. The British had quite a good picture of the Egyptian Forces —bombing force: 45 Ilyushin, 25 Soviet bombers; fighter command: 80 MIG-15 Russian fighters, 25 Meteors and 57 Vampires. The Army was deployed as follows: an infantry brigade was supported by a squadron of heavy Stalin 4 tanks in Alexandria, an infantry brigade in Port Said, an armored division of 200 T-34 Soviet-made tanks, an infantry division and an artillery brigade in the vicinity of Cairo, an infantry division in El Kantara, an armored brigade in Ismalya, an armored brigade in Kasfari, and an infantry brigade in El Shaluffa. All these Canal Zone forces, supported by SU-100 self-propelled anti-tank guns, equipped with the newest Russian troop carriers, were in constant readiness to move either towards Cairo and Alexandria, or into the Sinai Desert. The following forces were facing Israel: an infantry division and two infantry battalions in the Gaza Zone, two infantry brigades in Rafiah supported by squadrons of tanks, two infantry battalions and an armored battalion in El-Arish, two infantry brigades supported by artillery and tank squadrons in Abu Ageila, and various units all over the desert.

In the face of these forces, the Anglo-French operation had to be carefully planned, and the problem was not an easy one considering the distances involved: 1,863 miles from Marseilles and Algeria, 2,795 miles from London, and 1,163 miles from Malta. Therefore, the planners chose Cyprus as a base for a combined operation; the Air Force destroying enemy aircraft on the ground to obtain air superiority would enable an airborne operation supported by landing of troops, the Navy assuring the sea-borne operation and the lines of supply. The British proposed the occupation of Alexandria as the starting point and coded the preliminary plan "Terrapin," which was recoded in the first days of August "Operation 700." It was a heavy operation based on the principles of the Normandy landing, and it became obvious to the French that concentration of the required equipment in Cyprus would take months. The French had their own ideas about the operation, based on their recent war experience in Indo-China and Algeria. They proposed Port Said as the operational beachhead. Discussions followed. The British agreed, and the new operation received the code name "Musketeer." Although the French were more daring in their concept of modern warfare, it was clear to them that assembling the necessary force would require time. Great Britain had to provide 100 vessels, 3 cruisers, 4 aircraft carriers, some submarines, 300 aircraft and 45,000 men. France's share was 80 vessels, 2 aircraft carriers, 200 aircraft and 30,000 men.

The delay was a severe blow to the French leaders, but rather a relief to Sir Anthony. Both international and British public opinion were against the use of force, and the Labor Party virtually roused the British people against the Government. Even some prominent members of Eden's own party supported Labor's point of view. The only comfort and support was offered by the "Suez Group." Sir Anthony had told the military to proceed, but had not pressed them for haste. He was pursuing Dulles' belief in conferences and negotiations. On August 3rd, the London Conference issued its declaration, calling for the establishment of international control over the Canal, recognizing the sovereign rights of Egypt over the Canal, guaranteeing her a fair return for its use, and proposing negotiations for a new convention. A committee was chosen to meet Nasser to persuade him to accept the conditions.

In view of these events, the French leaders decided to come to our aid. They understood that Nasser's military victory over us would mean our mass extermination. Guy Mollet set aside for the moment the problems of Suez and Algeria. "If there was no Algeria, and no Suez, I would still do what I have done to save Israel," he said after the Suez Campaign.

To avoid interference from the French Foreign Office, Bourgès-Maunoury was given the responsibility of supplying arms to Israel. Abel Thomas and Louis Mangin, as deputies of the Minister, took charge, and Air Force, Army, and Navy officers executed the deliveries. Enormous difficulties were involved, for the limited equipment available had to be divided among our requirements, the French forces in Algeria, and the French obligations to "Operation Musketeer"! The men—generals, officers of all ranks, high officials, soldiers, humble employees, pilots, ship captains—who participated in this sea and air bridge to Israel did so with secrecy, zeal and often personal sacrifice, as if France's future, not Israel's, were at stake.

In Israel, all unloading was done at night. By morning all was calm, as if the feverish activity of the previous night had been only a dream. "One day the story will be told"—words in a poem by the celebrated Israel poet, Nathan Alterman, who witnessed the unloading of a ship one night.

The spirit of our armed forces grew with each piece of equipment integrated into our units. No doubt Egypt's military power was still superior to ours; but from then on, we no longer feared the outcome of the battle. At our side stood a mighty nation, whose courage and spirit of resistance no totalitarian regime had ever succeeded in crushing.

Nasser's reaction to the London Conference was just what could be expected from a dictator—abuse of the West. Three foreign correspondents, Ann Shapley of the *Evening Standard*, Eileen Travis of the *Daily Mail*, and William Stevenson of the *Toronto Star* were expelled for publishing false news. Twenty people accused of spying for Great Britain were arrested. Among them were James Swinburne of the British Arab News Agency and Charles Pittuck, an employee of the Marconi Telegraph Company. Nor were we forgotten. On August 30th, two soldiers were killed and four wounded. This time we decided to retaliate, and during the night of August

30th, our forces inflicted heavy casualties on the enemy forces.

Nasser did not react to our retaliation. The arrival of French and British units in Cyprus was not unnoticed by the world press and Egyptian Intelligence. Although at first Nasser had rejected negotiations with the Committee, the forces in Cyprus made him change his mind. On September 3rd, the Committee, headed by Australian Prime Minister Menzies, arrived in Cairo. On the same day, Mr. Eden received a message from President Eisenhower warning Britain about using force. It was Sir Anthony's personal tragedy from the very beginning that he believed, or was made to believe, as he claimed, that "the United States would not take exception to the use of force, if all peaceful means of settlement had been exhausted."

Mr. Menzies' mission failed, as could have been expected. He reported to Eden: "Egypt is not only a dictatorship, but it has all the earmarks of a police state. The tapping of telephone lines, the installation of microphones, the creation of a vast body of security police—all these things are accepted as commonplace."

Had it not been for the Presidential elections, had it not been for the image of the "man of peace and prosperity" which the Republicans presented to the people, the United States would no doubt have taken a different stand. Mr. Dulles was as well aware as his NATO partners of Moscow's use of Nasser to further Soviet aims in the Middle East and Africa. Knowing Mr. Dulles' hatred of Communism and his reaction to Soviet political and military penetrations into pro-Western countries, one can well understand the Secretary of State's divided loyalty to his party and to the ideas he cherished. Even his own colleagues believed he shared the Anglo-French desire to "finish with Nasser."

Senator William Knowland was reported to have warned Mr. Dulles not to drag the United States into this new war in Europe. Mr. Dulles' friends were concerned about his hesitation—hesitation that became the pitfall of the Suez Campaign.

Downhill to War

THE MISSION a complete failure, Mr. Menzies' Committee left Cairo on the 9th of September. Nasser refused to hand over control of the Canal to a Western international organization, whatever it was called. He had other plans for the oil resources of the Arab states. In a leaflet addressed to the Arabs, he called for the "Formation of an Egyptian-controlled Pan-Arab marketing organization to ensure that all Middle Eastern oil is used for the benefit of Egypt and Arab countries. This Pan-Arab marketing organization will make the Arabs masters of their oil."

Nasser's rejection of the Committee's proposals seemed to the French leaders reason enough to proceed with the planned military action. Britain and France already had on Cyprus about 10,000 tons of equipment, the forward elements of the invasion forces. The remaining strength was in the process of embarkation—both fleets taking to the sea, and the Air Force waiting for take-off orders. But when Mollet and Pineau arrived in London on the 10th of September, they found Sir Anthony hesitant. It became clear to them that he would not give his consent unless he was forced into it. The extent of Eden's moral dependence upon Washington surprised the French leaders, who frankly regarded further talk with the United States as a mere waste of time.

Nasser appeared to be well informed about the build-up of Anglo-French forces on Cyprus. Cairo, considering the immediate danger of being bombed, at first restrained from any military action against Israel. But the Egyptian dictator probably thought that a spectacular action against Israel would improve the morale of his countrymen. On the 10th, an attack was launched against an Israeli Army unit on a routine training exercise. Seven soldiers were killed, two wounded.

This act of aggression, the first open *Fedayin* attack on an Israeli Army unit, had to be punished. General Dayan demanded, and got permission to strike back immediately at the *Fedayin* strongholds inside enemy territory. On the 10th, our forces attacked the stronghold of Kusseima; on the 11th, the fort of El-Rahva.

On the 11th, Guy Mollet and Pineau left London without obtaining Sir Anthony's consent to military action. They had accepted, with deep misgivings, the Secretary of State's new proposal for a new conference of the maritime powers to set up the Users' Association of the Canal, which would "Promote safe, orderly, efficient and economical transit of member-controlled vessels" through the Canal. The French thought the United States was playing for time with the intention of dragging on negotiations until a situation was reached in which military intervention would become really impossible. They questioned the States' reaction should Nasser reject the new proposal, and they received their answer from a Presidential press conference on the 11th. Eisenhower's response to a question on whether the United States would back France and Britain should these countries be obliged to resort to force was: "This country will not go to war ever, while I am occupying my present post, unless the Congress is called into session, and Congress declares such a war."

The outcome of the new conference was obvious, for the United States had announced in advance that it would not back up Anglo-French military intervention.

To fairly judge Mr. Eden, one has to consider the opposition he faced in Britain, as compared with the full support of the French enjoyed by Guy Mollet.

Had Guy Mollet declared that France had decided to abandon the idea of military intervention, he would have been swept out of office; conversely, had Mr. Eden undertaken any military action at that time, he would have faced a "revolution" in Great Britain.

"Everything but Force, but never Force," was the mood of the Suez debate in the House of Commons, opened by Sir Anthony on the 12th of September. Some voices asked the opposition to consider the price Britain would have to pay for appeasement—the price of impairment of national interests for only temporary easement. The Labor Party demanded that the matter be taken to the United Nations. The most curious aspect of the House debate was the sudden awareness of Nasser's threat to Israel.

"The Nasser story would be incredible if it were not true. He was put there by the American Ambassador in Cairo. His ban on Israel ships was acquiesced to by all, despite the order of the Security Council of the United Nations Organization. Arms were given to him, and denied to Israel. . . ." (Sir R. Bouthby)

"We are dealing with a man who not only is at war with Israel, but has sworn to destroy the country, and has imposed a blockade upon that country in defiance of the resolution of the United Nations." (Sir Victor Raixes)

Believing that no responsible Government should be bound by the United Nations' inaction to do anything to protect its own security, on the 13th, we attacked the third *Fedayin* fort, El-Garandel.

Daring military actions proved to us once more that in spite of their Soviet weapons, the enemy was not imbued with a fighting spirit. General Dayan was convinced that his army would be able to destroy the enemy forces with a well-calculated blow. The idea of securing peace for years to come by destroying the Egyptian bases in the Sinai Desert was taking shape, the theories becoming operational. Nasser's strategic concept of this war against Israel, perceived rightly by our General Staff, played a major role in the decisions which brought us victory in the Sinai Desert.

According to the disposition of Egyptian forces, Nasser could either move them into the Sinai Desert for a surprise attack against us, or lure our forces into the Sinai Desert and strike a decisive blow from bases on the Canal.

In the first case, the success of the operation would depend upon the element of surprise; and we had practically no way to forestall such an operation. Nasser could always announce large-scale maneuvers in the Sinai Desert, concentrate his forces in previously designated fortified positions, and strike. It was physically impossible for us to mobilize upon each announcement of enemy maneuvers. Nasser could destroy us economically, without a hot war. We could well expect also that our neighbors, in spite of political differences with Cairo, would seize the opportunity of an Egyptian attack to march into Israel. In such case, we were doomed.

In the second case, the initiative being ours, we could forestall any enemy plan.

There was only one man in Israel who could make such a grave decision—the man who had proclaimed and won our independence in 1948—David Ben-Gurion. But even the "Old Man," as he is called by us, hesitated. First of all, there was the political aspect of such an act. Whatever we thought, the world would judge it as an act of aggression and react accordingly. We did not worry much about the reaction of New Delhi and other trusted friends of Nasser, but we did worry about the attitudes of the United States and Soviet Russia. If Washington refused to back up the Franco-British military intervention with the Atlantic Alliance at stake and the Middle Eastern oil resources in danger, because of internal considerations only, the whole wrath of the United States would turn against us. The State Department's attitude since the creation of our State did not indicate an understanding of our problems. We certainly could not expect any benediction from the Soviet Union. We did not believe that either would interfere militarily, but led by them, the world could crush us by an economic embargo. Next, there was the military aspect of such an act. Even the most brilliant plan may have its surprises. Had Ben-Gurion the right to embark on a war which would cause the country suffering, perhaps even destruction, even though he considered it the only way to assure Israel's future? But whatever the decision, the Armed Forces must be ready and not a single act of enemy aggression could be tolerated; for non-retaliation would precipitate enemy action. Nasser considered our restraint our weakness.

The French understood our hesitations. They had learned in Indo-China and Algeria that in matters of war and peace there is no place for half measures, and our retaliatory acts were half measures indeed. Lately, they had not, as expected, resulted in even temporary appeasement. The *Fedayin* terrorist acts were increasing in their amplitude, and it became clear that they were intended to completely demoralize the population.

Nasser's prestige among the Arab nations was increasing with every passing day. The impunity of the theft, and the flat rejection of the decisions of the London Conference made it obvious that he was not afraid of the West! Would he brave

Britain and France without the full support of the mighty Soviet Armed Forces? The promised destruction of Israel was only a question of time, and Jordan not only opened her territory to the *Fedayin*, but provided her own volunteers.

On the 18th, the Jordanians opened fire on an archaeological study group in Jerusalem, at Ramat Rachel, killing four people and wounding 16. We issued a strong warning to Jordan that we would not tolerate any terrorist activities.

On the 19th of September, the second London Conference opened. The members discussed the new border incident reported by the press, and Mr. Dulles stated: "The U.S.A. does not intend to shoot our way through the Canal." Not only did the Secretary of State refuse to shoot his way through the Canal, he refused to accept even a resolution which would have imposed a solution on Nasser. He asked the Conference to make a resolution acceptable to Nasser as a basis for negotiation. The Conference became a new failure, but the Secretary of State managed to convey to the British Leader of the Opposition, and other leading British political figures the American message—"No war over Suez!" Thus, Mr. Eden was forced to refer the affair to the United Nations, and the French followed without conviction. On the 23rd, a letter was dispatched to the Security Council, requesting that the Suez problem be placed on the Council's agenda.

Throughout the whole Arab world flashed a message, "Nasser has won. Israel will be next." On the 24th, *Fedayin* from Jordan killed a woman and a tractor driver.

On the 26th, while Mr. Eden and Mr. Lloyd flew to Paris to meet the French leaders, our Government decided to make good its warning. On the night of the 25th, the fort of Houssan, over the Israel-Jordan border, suspected of being *Fedayin* headquarters was attacked. The action was successful.

Immediate reaction came from London. The Foreign Office

condemned Israel aggression against Jordan, and the representative of Her Majesty's Government in Tel-Aviv warned
General Burns, the officer commanding the United Nations
Observer Corps, that Great Britain had a defense treaty with
Jordan and would help her if Israel attacked again. No word
was mentioned of the so-called aggression being a reaction to
six dead and sixteen wounded. Then, the King stated that the
Jordanian Army concentrated on the border was ready for
any future Israeli aggression, and that Jordan was appealing
to Iraq for military help.

Mr. Eden did not fail to complain to the French about our
military action and asked for their intervention; but the
French refused, stating that Britain might also have condemned Jordanian acts of aggression. As a matter of fact, the
French were more than disappointed in their chosen ally,
whose hesitation was pulling into doubt the whole plan of
operation. They insisted again upon immediate action, but
Sir Anthony would not march. He had, however, given a firm
commitment that if the Security Council was incapable of
forcing Nasser to accept international control, he would
agree to military action. It was as vague a promise as it could
be, and the French, aware that time between decision and
action was required, insisted on settling a date for the operation. Sir Anthony refused, but agreed to place the invasion
forces in a state of emergency, which would enable their
action on short notice.

There is no doubt that this unsuccessful visit made the
French political and military leaders regret their choice of
Britain as an ally. Under the prevailing circumstances, they
would have preferred to join forces with Israel, where David
Ben-Gurion slowly reached the decision that there was no
other way to save the country, but to march into the Sinai
Desert.

Reports poured in that Egyptian units were moving from

the Canal Zone to the Sinai bases; fighter aircraft were being flown to Bir Gafgafa Airfield; a state of readiness had been declared in El Kantara, Ismalya, Kasfuri and El Shaluffa, where the main Egyptian forces were concentrated, and the infantry division at El Kantara had been reinforced by armor stationed near Cairo. Jordan announced the imminent entry of Iraqi troops to support the Arab Legion in case of Israeli aggression. But the worst news item was that the Egyptian-proposed Unified Arab Command, under Egyptian leadership, was taking shape. Cairo radio blared with increasing vehemence, foretelling our destruction. Unless we were prepared just to sit and wait until it suited our enemies to annihilate us, we had to take counteraction.

The entry of Iraqi troops into Jordan was a British sponsored plan to protect the King against pro-Nasser elements in the country. It could be a splendid plan to protect British interests in the Middle East; but it was obvious to us that in case of war, the Iraqi troops would join the Arab Legion against us. We made it clear to Britain and Jordan that we would consider the entry of Iraqi troops as *casus belli*.

On the 4th of October, the eve of the Security Council Session, five Israelis were killed and one wounded. The killers, who ambushed two cars, came over the Jordan border. Neither the British Foreign Office nor the Security Council condemned this murder. "If the United Nations Organization is incapable of assuring peace on our frontiers, Israel will take the necessary steps to protect her population," declared our Foreign Office on the 7th of October. This warning was again disregarded by Jordan, and on the 9th, two more Israelis were murdered. The Security Council, too busy with the Suez problem, did not react. But we did. On the night of the 10th, we launched a full-scale military operation against the fort at Qahquilya, over the Jordan border, a stronghold of the Arab Legion situated among villages where 20,000 people lived. The purpose of the operation was to "persuade" both the Arab Legion and the civilian population to seek peace instead of war on the frontiers. Unfortunately, the presence of the civilian population made the action most difficult, for Ben-Gurion's orders had been strict and clear—the action should be directed only against the fort, not a civilian should be hurt. The operation turned into a full-scale battle, and artillery had to be used. We inflicted heavy casualties, but our own casualties in dead and wounded were no less heavy.

The action at Qahquilya brought us nearly to an open war with Britain. During the fighting, the British Consul General in Jerusalem informed our Foreign Office that King Hussein had demanded that the Commander of the British Forces in the Middle East immediately dispatch the Royal Air Force against the Israeli forces in obligation to the British-Jordan Treaty. We did not know at that time how serious the situation was, that the Royal Air Force "was on the point of going up," as Mr. Eden admitted in his memoirs. The next morning, the British Minister, in a short interview with Prime Minister Ben-Gurion, stated flatly that if Jordan was again attacked, Britain would come to her aid. He also announced the entry of an Iraqi Division into Jordan. Ben-Gurion's answer was short and clear—if the Iraqi Division entered Jordan, Israel would be free to take action according to her judgment.

We certainly could not afford to become involved in a military conflict with Britain; but we realized, as well as did the British, that Jordan had been maneuvered by Cairo into acts of hostility. Nasser would love to involve us in an armed showdown with Britain, which would facilitate his own attack against us. What would then be Britain's reaction? Perhaps some of our long-lived enemies, the so-called heirs of Lawrence, dreamed of such a situation. Britain could restrain Jordan if she really wanted to by replying that Her Majesty's

Government would not fulfill the obligations if *Fedayin* attacks against Israel from Jordan did not cease.

On the 14th of October, the Security Council failed to produce results. The Soviet Union vetoed the Anglo-French resolution. It was a severe blow to the President of the United States, who the day before had publicly stated that "the dispute is most gratifying" and "a very great crisis is behind us." While Mr. Pineau emerged from the Council declaring there was no further basis for negotiations, and Mr. Lloyd stated that everything had been done that could be done, Mr. Dulles had a new idea to save the situation—anything to drag on the negotiations, to save peace before the elections. He suggested a meeting of the French, British and Egyptians in Geneva. But the British and French had begun to wonder about another aspect of the Suez crisis and United States insistence upon a peaceful solution. Rumors had circulated that the major American oil companies and Egyptian representatives were discussing an arrangement by which the two parties would operate the Canal with the exclusion of the French and the British for payment to Egypt during the next fifteen years of one and a half million dollars. The Secretary of State's new proposal was rejected by the British and French.

But neither the United States nor the Egyptian Governments imagined that the rejection really meant war.

The Decisive Days
of October

THE FAILURE of the Security Council to produce results offered Sir Anthony the badly needed excuse for military action. Had he not gone twice to conferences? Had he not made the requested appeal to the Security Council? He had done what could be done! But the Suez group, having watched Mr. Eden's hesitation during the past few months, was not at all convinced that even now he would take a firm stand. The group feared a new Munich enforced by Washington. Anti-American feeling was running high within the group. During the Korean crisis had not Britain and France answered the American appeal, contributing substantially to the war effort; and the British Commonwealth Division was second to none! True, the major burden of the Korean War had been borne by the United States, which had a major interest in this area. And now, when Britain and France were the interested parties, Washington was betraying the alliance. Mr. Dulles' efforts to seek a settlement at any price at the expense of his allies and Washington's pursuing only its own interests, were a great shock and surprise to supporters (quite often, against the Labor Party) of the Anglo-American Alliance. And the same Labor Party now found in Mr. Dulles an understanding and rather active supporter of their opposition to the Government. "I hope that at some future conference of the Labor Party, Secretary Dulles will be a fraternal delegate" was the bitter comment from the floor of the Commons. The group members, realizing that if Sir Anthony failed to make a decision now the intervention would be doomed, made up their minds to force the issue with him. They looked with envy towards France, admiring her constancy in this crisis and her national unity, from whence came a demand for an urgent meeting to work out details of the military and political action. The message was brought by a French general, and the Deputy Chief of Staff. Mr. Eden, tired, harassed and disappointed, finally agreed to meet the French leaders in Paris on the 16th.

On the 16th, news reached Tel-Aviv that on the 14th the first units of the Iraqi division had entered Jordan. Although the British assured the French, who passed on the message to us, that the sole purpose of the troop entry was to protect the Kingdom against a pro-Nasser *coup d'état* on the eve of the elections there, we could not but consider the event an additional threat to our independence. The prospect of a war on three fronts, Egypt, Jordan and Syria, was not a rosy one.

"What was Britain's real aim?" asked our press and, no doubt, our leaders. The question was put by Guy Mollet and his friends to Sir Anthony upon his arrival in Paris on the 16th. The British Government was involving France in a most absurd situation which could turn into a nightmare overnight. By virtue of the military action Israel might be forced to take in defense against Egypt, Tel-Aviv was becoming Britain's and France's natural ally. It would be logical to consider and to discuss the benefits which the Anglo-French invasion force could derive from mutual cooperation. But Sir

Anthony not only rejected the very thought of co-operation with Israel, but asked the French to convey to Israel a firm message and warning that Britain would help Jordan if it were attacked by Israeli forces.

Although the French could well imagine some of the complicated situations arising from Sir Anthony's position, they were ready to agree to all his demands to hasten the operation. Unfortunately, nothing could be rushed, for the military required at least three weeks. So after lengthy discussions, zero hour was set for the 5th of November.

While the British and French made their decisions, Tel-Aviv was facing her own dilemma. On the 16th, Mr. Dulles announced in Washington that the United States would give assistance to any country in the Middle East that became a victim of military aggression. We thought the warning was directed only towards Paris and London, but we were wrong. On the 17th, Mr. Dulles expressed himself in rather violent terms to our Ambassador about the steps the United States would take to prevent any military operations in the Middle East, whatever influence such steps might have on Jewish electors in the United States. Never had such a warning been issued to any of the Arab states! It was a frightening message with Marechal Hakim, Chief of Staff of the Egyptian Armed Forces, declaring in Cairo that the Egyptian Army was ready and fit for action against Israel, not only in the event Jordan was attacked, but even if there should be the slightest menace of aggression. No doubt Hakim's announcement was made for the benefit of the forthcoming elections in Jordan, but it was a clear declaration that Nasser considered himself the sole judge of the definition of the menace of aggression. It could be a perfect excuse to open hostilities at a chosen date!

Mr. Dulles did not summon the Egyptian Ambassador after Marechal Hakim's statement. He knew that a reaction would not come from Cairo, but from the Kremlin.

On the 17th, the vessel, *Athos*, transporting Egyptian arms for the Algerian rebels, was intercepted by the French Navy. The outcry in the French press was tremendous! Had Nasser not denied interference, except moral support, in the Algerian military operations? Had he not even given his word of honor as a soldier to Mr. Pineau?

"Algeria, North Africa, Israel—was there no one to stop the dictator?" asked some newspapers.

Nasser seemed to be winning. In spite of Mr. Eden's support of Jordan, in spite of British money keeping the Kingdom alive, in spite of the British "gifts" to the Arab Legion, in spite of the Iraqi troops—the pro-Nasser party had won the elections.

Had London wished to restrain Jordan from military action against us, she could have done so; but it now became obvious that now the King would have to "fulfill Nasser's wishes." Our fears were confirmed in a matter of hours. General Ali Abu-Navar, Commanding Officer of the Arab Legion, announced at a press conference that the time and place for a decisive battle against Israel would be set soon by the Arabs, and the Arabs alone. A meeting of Arab military leaders was scheduled for the 25th, to establish the Arab High Command under Marechal Hakim. The fear of encirclement now became reality. Nothing stood in the way of the Egyptian Dictator's proceeding with his plans, so well outlined in his *Mein Kampf*, the *Philosophy of Revolution*.

The very necessity of survival dictated military action, even though it would certainly incur the wrath of some nations. To build our country we had been compelled to make a sword of every plowshare with our borders infringed upon by arson and murder, our nation taunted and haunted by enemies armed first by Britain, then Russia, enemies whose sole dream was and still is, to re-enact on a grand scale in

Israel the Warsaw Ghetto Massacre. Could we stake our lives on the United Nations, or on the Tripartite Declarations? The United Nations had been created to achieve peace, but not peace at any price. What had it achieved for us in recent years, but condemnation—while we were mourning our friends and relatives! Surprised by attacks from the air, by sea and on the ground, we would be annihilated before the required procedure could go through the United Nations. Could we rely on the British Government to send troops to defend our lives—a Government which only a few weeks ago had condemned us, warned us, was ready to bomb us for mounting an operation against Jordan which was no more than a justifiable retaliation. And the United States—would they send their sons to fight for us, to die for us? Even France, under a different government from that of Guy Mollet, would not dispatch her soldiers for our protection.

Under the Tripartite Declaration we could only hope and pray, and then, when it would be too late for help, fight a hopeless battle—like our brethren in the ghettos.

David Ben-Gurion decided to take the only possible way. The Army was ready. General Dayan was convinced that by a swift action he would be able to overrun the Egyptian Forces. General Tolkowsky, O.C. of the Air Force, had no doubts that air superiority could be won. But we still lacked some equipment to execute the daring operation.

The road to Paris was taken again. All Israeli requests were granted.

On the 25th, the official decision was made and the calling up of reservists begun.

Since mobilization cannot be kept secret in a democratic country like ours, where members of foreign embassies are free to gather information, President Eisenhower was informed about the military measures and sent two messages to

Ben-Gurion demanding that he not become involved in military operations.

Ben-Gurion could have given no other answer! We shall never submit passively to the consequences of Arab aggression! Israel shall not let herself be annihilated without reacting!

PART FOUR

The Sinai Campaign

And They Have Taken Off Again

THOSE OF US who remembered the days of 1948—the Austers, the ME-109's and the Spitfires—could not but with great pride look upon the Air Force of 1956, equipped with the most modern jet fighters, manned by young pilots, all Israelis, anxious to take off to fight the enemy. Fate had granted me the opportunity to be one of the few, who since the days of 1948, had been in charge of procuring the aircraft, going through anxious days of deception and happy days of success.

Although our failures and successes were both outcomes of political circumstances, and not due to our wit, those of us who had put their faith in France, who had judged rightly that France would be the only country to come to our support, could now feel self-satisfaction in achieving our goal.

On that day, the 29th of October, 1956, the Israeli Air Force was taking off again, an Air Force convinced it would not fail in spite of the enemy's apparent air superiority. The Egyptian Air Force consisted of 200 Russian MIG-15 jet fighters, 50 Russian Ilyushin 28 jet bombers, 104 British

Vampire and Meteor jet fighters. Our Air Force consisted of 37 Mystères and 42 Ouragans and Meteors, altogether 79 jets against 304 enemy jets. We were still flying piston engine fighters—28 Mustangs and 13 Mosquitos. We had not a single jet bomber. Numerically, the enemy could crush us, but our fearless pilots knew they were better trained, that the air was theirs.

The hour was 14:00. Four Mustangs, obsolete piston aircraft, took to the air. The flight commander was one of the old guard from the Air Service of the Palmach, his second in command, an Australian of the old days who had become an Israeli, and the other two pilots youngsters to whom the days of '48 were just a tale. Strange equipment, a wire and a special hook, was towed by each plane. "Target practice," remarked one of the paratroopers lying on the ground near some transport planes. "Stupid, one does not do target shooting in time of war," answered his companion.

It was not target practice. For days the four had been training for a special mission with equipment especially designed to cut the enemy telephone wires in the Sinai Desert. Flying at only 60 miles an hour because of the equipment drag, the four penetrated Egyptian territory. One cutting device broke down. The chance of success of the important mission was reduced. But the four Mustangs carried on their flight toward their target, the telephone poles in the plain between the Mittlah Pass and the Port of Suez. Only a few minutes' flying time separated them from the MIG's based on the Canal Zone airfields. Although the Mustangs were armed, they stood no chance against the Russian jets. The cutting device of the second aircraft went. Only two Mustangs were left, but the job had to be done; the telephone communications between the Egyptian outpost of the Mittlah Pass, where our paratroopers were to be dropped, and the Canal Zone bases had to be cut. The four aircraft, flying in two pairs, made their first pass. In spite of the many hours of training, the pass was a complete failure. "To hell with the equipment." The Australian, aiming at the wires, managed to cut them with his propeller. "They are down!" reported the aircraft following him, and both pilots adopted this cutting method. It was a dangerous game. The pilots had a sensation of losing their engines during the operation and saw before them the unpleasant prospect of crashing on enemy territory. But the mission had to be accomplished! The third Mustang also adopted the "propeller procedure," but the fourth pilot developed his own method, cutting the wires with his wing. The wires were all finally cut. But when the Air Force engineers heard about it, they only wondered which of the two methods, by wing or by propeller, was more dangerous. They decided upon the "wing" one, "But fools always have luck," they added.

While the Mustangs were accomplishing their mission, the transports took off from the same airfield at exactly 15:10. At the command of one sat a girl "suffragette" of the air, a reserve captain. With her blond hair, blue eyes and ready smile, Yael had cheered the squadron, whose members were envious of their friends flying jets. The transports were slow, sluggish and at their best in straight, level flying; and the pilots had stood many a joke from the glamour boys of the shining machines with great agility at dazzling heights and tremendous speeds. But now was the hour of the "transport boys." Theirs was the main task. The Mystères only escorted them.

Yael sat there, heading west, praying for her passengers' safe landing. The paratroops behaved quietly, some smiling, some deep in thought, confident of their strength, confident of success.

As the aircraft crossed the frontier, the paratroopers could see below them their brigade column moving west also. The objective of the brigade, moving on wheels, was to join up with their comrades transported by air. The way leading from the frontier to the dropping zone, the monument at the entry of the Mittlah Pass, was a rough and difficult trek of 125 miles, a 13 hour struggle against the terrain and time.

The warning ring sounded, and the boys stood up, checking their kit and harness for the last time before the jump.

"Red"—everybody lined up, the first to jump clutching the doorframe and holding hard. "Green"—all of them had jumped.

Yael, heading home, could see the last flight dropping its passengers and heard with relief the message, "Dropping mission successfully carried out!" 39 minutes after the planes had crossed the frontier, one minute before the scheduled time, east of the monument, about 93 miles west of the Israeli frontier, the battalion commander deployed his forces. His task was to hold the area until the brigade joined up.

Night descended on the country, and the radio announcement of war took the population by surprise. Although the people had known of mobilization, nobody had believed it was for a "hot war" and not just a precautionary measure.

"What would be the enemy's reactions?" the General Staff and the citizens of Israel asked themselves. "Will Nasser retaliate by bombing our cities, our airfields?" The Russian bombers could cause much damage with their great loads without our being able to fight off a night attack. But our worries were needless. Not a single enemy bomber dropped its load on an Israeli city or airfield. Only one bomber crossed the border, and the Egyptian pilot preferred to unload his bombs somewhere in the mountains near Jerusalem, instead of risking an attack on our cities or airfields. But the Egyptian readers of Cairo's weekly, *Al Moussawar*, were presented with a different picture of the bombers' feats. "The mission of our jet bomber squadron was clear, hit the

Zionist airfield," reported the squadron leader, "when our aircraft approached the target under the cover of night, the pilots had an easy time identifying and lining up, as many lights were to be seen from all quarters. A rain of bombs hit the target. The Jews promptly turned their lights off, but too late. Our bombs hit hard, and many a fire started. Some of the fires were so big, that the second bomber wave could spare their flares." An Egyptian group captain added, "Our pilots were quarrelling amongst themselves, each wanting the honor of being the first to annihilate the Jews. But the plans called for a concentrated effort, with bombing missions to be carried out simultaneously to increase their effectiveness. Huge quantities of bombs were released on military targets. Our aircraft spread destruction, collapse and fear."

While the Egyptian Air Force in vivid imagination destroyed our cities and airfields, our ground forces actually crossed the border, seized Kutsema on the center front, opened the roads to the strongholds of Abu Ageila, and captured Ras El Nakem facing Eilat in the south. The paratroop brigade, after taking Kuntilla without a battle, captured Tmamad. Now only the stronghold of Nahal barred the way to the dropping zone.

D-Day + 1—October 30th.

The Egyptian Command reacted to the airborne operation with relative speed. Troops were ordered to cross the Canal and annihilate the attacking force. The Egyptian Air Force was also alerted; and at 7:30 A.M., four Vampires flew over the dropping zone and the advancing Paratroop brigade without attacking it. At 9:30 A.M., two MIG-15's strafed the paratroopers' positions, hitting some soldiers and a light plane on the ground. At approximately the same time, two other MIG's attacked the brigade advancing to Nahal, causing three casualties. Where was the Air Force? asked the paratroopers. The Air Force had been on the job since the early hours of the morning, attending to the allocated tasks, ground support of troops and defense of the open skies. The Mystères and Ouragans, strafing enemy positions all over the desert and enemy aircraft on the ground, had just missed the MIG's. After receiving news of the MIG attack, the Mystères and Ouragans gave constant cover to the paratroopers at the monument; and at noon, Egyptian reinforcements became game to our fighter pilots. More aircraft were called in; and the enemy, under fire from 20 mm. cannons, rockets and bombs, seemed to be completely destroyed. Only burning vehicles remained in evidence of a military force's existence there. The action was executed with such impunity, only a few minutes flying time from the Canal Zone jet bases, that one wondered whether there was really an Egyptian Air Force at all. Not a single enemy aircraft was spotted until the early hours of the afternoon, when eight Mystères, widening their patrol circle over the paratroopers, met with twelve MIG's in the vicinity of Kabrit Airfield. In this first full-scale air battle two enemy aircraft were shot down and two more noted as "probables." One of the Mystères was hit, but managed to reach the base.

This time the Egyptians admitted their first air defeat, but presented it a "bit" differently to the public. A pilot whose name was given as M.A.G. told the story: "On October 30th, we got our orders to fly to one of our positions menaced by the advance of a strong Israeli force. On the way back from the target, the sky was cloudy and the visibility limited. We flew at a tremendous speed to refuel and rejoin the battle. Suddenly a horde of Mystères broke loose from the clouds higher up. We put up a stiff fight with them, but their initial advantage in altitude was telling. I saw one of our aircraft going down in flames; a few seconds later I saw another diving, heading for Suez, then a third one was diving in flames again. I could see the pilot managed to handle the aircraft, although it was but a ball of fire and smoke." But to admit only defeat was disastrous for the morale of the Egyptian readers, and the story was followed by a yarn from Squadron Leader M.S. "During the first day of the War, we shot down ten Zionist aircraft."

Nasser, himself, had a different story to tell in the weekly *Achad Saa*. According to his story, on the 30th of October, the antiaircraft guns of Abu Ageila shot down eight Israeli aircraft.

We did lose a pilot and an aircraft. Captain Benjamin Cahane did not return from his mission in a Piper Cub. Since the first day of the campaign, the small liaison airplanes had performed wonders and their pilots displayed incredible courage. Operating from the most difficult landing strips, flying for hundreds of miles over forbidding country without navigation aids, flying through the long days and during the darkness of desert nights, they evacuated the wounded and guided lost units. Piper-borne commanders also coordinated troop movements in the fluid desert warfare. The light squadrons continued their tradition of '48 in the jet age.

The air strikes against enemy forces continued until dark; the ground forces looked with confidence to their comrades in the air.

At the Mittlah Pass, the 380 paratroopers consolidated their position and waited for the brigade to join up with them. The commanding officer of the brigade, advancing on Nahal, realized the danger of enemy reinforcements arriving under the cover of night. Sparing no effort, he joined up with his unit at 22:30, after easily capturing Nahal. But the men were exhausted and running short of supplies.

On the central front, the ground forces accomplished their pincer movement and reduced the strongholds of Abu Ageila. They had orders to take Bir-el-Musha to open the road for the junction with the paratroopers at the Mittlah Pass; to seize

Bir el Hama and roll towards Bir Gafgafa, and to bar the route to enemy armor reported to be on the move from Ismailia. On the northern front, at the news of enemy motorized infantry moving from El Kantara, our forces were ordered to capture Rafah and move on to El-Arish.

At 18:00 Israeli time, Britain and France issued an ultimatum to Egypt and Israel to stop all fighting and retreat ten miles from the Canal. Egypt was told to allow Anglo-French forces temporary occupation of the Canal Zone, Port Said, Ismailia and Suez.

While the ultimatum was being announced, and with the falling dusk, all fighter aircraft returned to base. The transport boys were taking over to drop supplies, water, fuel and ammunition to the paratroopers at the Mittlah Pass. The pilots had to fly without navigation lights, since night fighter activity was assumed. T-lighted signals on the ground marked the dropping zones, but prior to the drop, radio contact had to be established with the ground forces. All night, the transport planes did their part successfully with no losses.

D-Day + 2—October 31st.

At 03:30 the citizens of Haifa were awakened by the roar of cannons from the Egyptian frigate, *Ibrahim El Awal,* which had approached within three miles of the town undetected by the Israeli Navy. The frigate fired 220 rounds at the Haifa Port, but fortunately caused very little damage and no casualties. The French destroyer *Kersaint,* which happened to be near Haifa, was the first to spot and engage the Egyptian ship, but lost her. The *Ibrahim El Awal* tried to get back to Port Said but found the way barred by two Israeli destroyers, *Jaffa* and *Eilat,* which opened fire at a range of 9,000 yards. An exchange of fire followed, but the enemy tried to escape to Beirut. The Air Force was called in. Two Ouragans attacked and badly damaged the ship with rockets and 20 mm. cannons, and the ship's captain decided to surrender. The destroyers approached the frigate and boarded her. On board, two were dead, six wounded and 145 without a scratch.

According to the ship's log, the captain, reporting the battle to Egyptian Naval Command in Alexandria, had received orders to scuttle her before abandoning ship. The captain reported "execution of the order" and surrendered the vessel. Our boys were overjoyed! A ship surrendering to our aircraft! What a story to tell!

At the airfields, all squadrons were ready for the day's work; and according to briefings, there was plenty of it.

At the monument, the battle began at 12:20. The paratroopers did not expect much resistance from a force which apparently had been destroyed by the Air Force. Unfortunately, although the enemy's transport and armored vehicles had indeed been destroyed, the greater part of the reinforcements had escaped. Two enemy battalions lay in waiting for the paratroopers.

The Mittlah Pass offered a formidable natural defense position, perfect emplacement for weapons and concealment for men in its precipitous hills of sheer rock perforated by deep fissures and caves. The defenders were safe from anything but a direct hit. Our advancing paratroopers, under constant fire, were generally equipped with sub-machine guns, but were unable to return the enemy fire at long range from the heights above them.

The Air Force could not be much help. The enemy's position was invulnerable to air strikes. The pilots had to be content with patrolling the skies over the paratroopers, whose positions offered game to enemy aircraft. No enemy plane in sight, the six patrolling Ouragans made the mistake of widening their circle. None of them remained over the battle area. They thought the paratroopers could radio them, if necessary. Suddenly, four enemy Meteors and six MIG's appeared and attacked. A breakdown in the wireless set prevented the paratroopers' summoning help. The results of the strike were disastrous—heavy casualties in dead and wounded, a fuel and ammunition vehicle burned, a light MX tank, an ambulance and other vehicles badly damaged. "Stay over the battle zone" were the orders issued, and the air patrols then stuck to the area. On the ground, the paratroopers were taking the Pass in close combat, clearing post after post, cave after cave. The enemy fought well and bravely. It was the fiercest battle of the Sinai Campaign and lasted seven hours, during which 38 paratroopers were killed and 120 wounded. More than 150 enemy soldiers met death in the Mittlah Pass.

On the central front our jets and piston-engined aircraft were given a real opportunity to show that an air force could contribute to the ground force's efforts. To permit the Army to concentrate fully on the assault of Abu Ageila fortified camps, the Air Force undertook the task of destroying and stopping armor reaching Bir Gafgafa from Ismailia.

The P-51 boys, left idle during the first day of the Sinai battle, were screaming murder about not being called in. It was a day of tension, of alerts, of scrubbed scrambles, a day full of disappointments. If it was to be a jet war only, why were they flying the old Mustangs, spoiling ammunition, training at battle tactics all over again? This bitter frustration reigned also among the Mosquito boys. But on the morning of October 31st, the mood changed rapidly when the order to scramble came through. The first two flights took off—the target—enemy armor at Bir Gafgafa. Other flights followed. What an ideal target for the old warriors carrying an arsenal of rockets and bombs plus machine guns. Quite a show, like gun and rocket practice! But very soon enemy antiaircraft fire reminded them that the burning vehicles were not defenseless dummies. A collision of a Mustang with a 40 mm. antiaircraft bullet usually meant the end of an aircraft. Flying lower and lower in order not to miss the target, not to waste a round of ammunition, not a rocket, not a bomb, the boys proceeded methodically with the destruction of the column. "We flew in such close formation that a burst of an ammunition vehicle nearly threw us at each other, and luckily we avoided collision," reported one of the pilots. But the first aircraft was hit. The pilot turned toward home, flying on deck covered by his companion, but he could not make it, and had to crash land behind enemy lines. His companion watched him set the aircraft on fire and walk off; then he returned to the battlefield. A second Mustang was hit, but the pilot luckily landed on his last drop of engine oil with a bullet at the bottom of the oil tank and a big hole in his tail. The game went on, this armored column "free for all," but not all the pilots were lucky enough to make it. Captain Uri Shlesinger did not.

The enemy took terrible punishment, and the game lasted until evening, when the Mystères ordered the "warriors" to turn home. Swarms of MIG's, at last, had come to cover what was left of the armored column. The Egyptian armor comprised two regiments of T-34 tanks, a battalion of self-propelled guns, SU-100's, and a regiment of infantry transported in the newest Russian troop carriers. But they did not bring the expected relief to the troops in the Abu Ageila area. Except for Captain Shlesinger and Major Moshe Tadmor, also a P-51 pilot, we lost no more men, but we did lose aircraft. Had it not been for the Sinai Campaign, it would probably have taken us a long time to write off the old "warriors."

But the Mustangs could not claim to be the only ones to inflict such heavy punishment on the enemy. Ouragans, Meteors, and those famous relics of World War II, the Mosquitos, and even the training aircraft, the Harvards, armed by the Air Force engineers, took part in the air strikes over the Sinai Desert. Captain Heshel Eshel, a Harvard pilot, did not return.

The highlight of the day was an air battle between a MIG-17 and a Mystère. We had no idea of the performance of the MIG-17, and we doubted whether the Egyptians really had them. The MIG-15 was known from the air battles in Korea, from the West's intelligence data; but the MIG-17 was an enigma. It was considered far superior to the F-86 Sabre and the Mystère IV.

Two of our pilots flying over El-Arish at 20,000 feet suddenly sighted three MIG's below. Since the enemy aircraft looked much like Mystères, the two pilots dived to identify them. The enemy, becoming aware of the Mystères, broke formation. One of the MIG's disappeared immediately, but the two Mystères got on the tails of the two others. A second MIG managed to get away, but the Mystère pilot following the third one identified it, to his utter amazement, as a MIG-17. Pursuing the MIG, he closed range to 200 yards and opened up with his 30 mm. cannons. The MIG went into a spin. At 10,000 feet the Egyptian pilot steadied the aircraft and ejected. The Mystère pilot saw the aircraft dive in flames and hit the ground.

It was a great victory, but the day was not yet over. The two pilots met with fifteen other MIG's and hit one of them, but the enemy managed to escape, flying off like a wounded bird. Unfortunately both our pilots ran out of ammunition and could not finish the job.

Exactly at 17:00 hours, twenty-five hours after the expiration of the ultimatum accepted by us and rejected by Egypt, the Anglo-French forces began their attack on Egyptian airfields: Almanza and Inchas near Cairo, and Abu Soueir and Kabrit in the Canal Zone. Neither Cairo West nor Cairo East were bombed because of the presence in Cairo West of American transport planes for the evacuation of American citizens;

Cairo West was the main operational base of the Egyptian bombers which we feared most. Nasser was offered the opportunity of saving his bombing force by sending it to Upper Egypt, Luxor and Saudi Arabia.

The falling night offered a well deserved rest to the fighter pilots. The transport boys took over again, dropping supplies. But the ground forces had no rest, for the Army mounted a major assault. Abu Ageila, Yebel Livni and Bir el Hama were taken, but enemy pockets at Um Katef and Umn Shiman still resisted. On the northern front, the ground forces, breaching the minefields of the fortified camps at Rafah, began their major assault to open the road to El-Arish.

In towns and villages, on airfields and military bases, everybody braced himself for an onslaught of enemy bombers. But only two came over and again dropped their loads far from any target.

The Egyptian citizens got a different picture of what was happening at the front. A journalist of the same Cairo weekly, *Al Moussara*, reported that the Egyptian Air Force had destroyed the following enemy airfields: Lod, Haifa, Quastina, Eilat, Beersheba and Ramat David. He gave fantastic details of fires set to buildings and of destroyed planes on the ground.

In addition to the destruction of our airfields, the story claimed that Egyptian MIG pilots had suffered only one loss in shooting down seven more of our planes. It quoted the MIG-17 pilot: "After shooting down an enemy aircraft over the Sinai, I turned to engage yet another one, when the smell of smoke came to my nostrils. The smoke was penetrating into the cockpit, and I was aware that unless I did something, I would be lost. I first disengaged from the combat with the Jewish aircraft by evasive action, and then I decided to jump. I used my flying seat (ejection seat) and got to the ground

And They Have Taken Off Again • *291*

safely, to witness with sorrow how the fire was swallowing the remains of my aircraft."

Nasser described October 31st as a day of great victory for the Egyptian Air Force. He claimed that the bombers had attacked Israeli airfields twenty times, that the MIG's, especially the MIG-17's, did not relinquish their air superiority and that in an air battle of three MIG-17's against eight Mystères, three Mystères had been shot down without any loss to themselves.

By the way, we would have loved to have had so many jet airfields.

D-Day + 3—November 1st.

Aircraft took off the next morning from the airfields destroyed in Egyptian imagination. The pilots were in high spirits. They had been highly praised for the previous day's work, and the terrible MIG's were not so terrible at all in the hands of Egyptian pilots. "If Wanka would fly them, things would not look so rosy," remarked somebody, and the others agreed.

A pair of Mystères was patrolling over the paratroopers, who were resting after the battle. They could easily have pushed on to the Canal, but they had received strict orders to keep away from it, according to the terms of the ultimatum.

"Bogie, Bogie, come down to help!"—the Mystères heard the call and dived. At 15,000 feet, the pilots spotted four enemy Vampires. The enemy, searching for ground targets, was unaware of the Mystères; and to the utter amazement of the paratroopers, the four Vampires crashed in flames.

On the central and northern fronts, all the squadrons were engaged in giving close support to the ground forces, who called for airstrikes as they called for artillery support. But the penalties for their daring flying were hit engines, torn wings and downed aircraft. The lucky ones made the base, the unlucky ones made forced landings in no-man's land. The squadrons' log books are full of stories. One pilot landed with a bullet torn through the padding between his head and his rear armor plate. He had not felt anything; but when suddenly something tickled him, he found Plexiglas in his collar. Another discovered a scratch on his new crash helmet, and, of course, two holes in his canopy. A third came in with both main tires blown off by enemy guns and landed, in happy ignorance, on his wheel rims. Someone else reported how bullets had hit in front of his head, smashing the whole instrument panel, and so on and so on! Those who crashed or made forced landings behind enemy lines had other stories about their narrow escapes. Only one man did not return; wounded, he was taken prisoner.

Had it not been for some Ouragans attacking our own tanks in the heat of action, this day—the 1st of November—could have been called the day of the Sinai Campaign; for in addition to the four Vampires, the Air Force added another MIG and one Meteor to their score.

Although the armor boys were angry with their own aircraft for attacking them, the incident was soon forgiven and forgotten. The sight of burned enemy tanks and vehicles on the north and central fronts had convinced them, at last, of the Air Force's contribution to their victory. What was left of the enemy armored column on the Ismailia Bir Gafgafa was fast retreating to the Canal Zone. Our boys had not managed to catch up with them. The motorized column arriving from El Kantara had been luckier for it reached El-Arish bruised and battered, but not destroyed. All over the desert, on the roads, on the railway linking El Kantara to Gaza, on the vast sandy plains, aircraft flying over could see the wrecks of what had once been the enemy fighting force. It was as much an air victory as a ground one. Even the enemy had to admit it. But for enemy pockets in Um Katef, which had withstood all our assaults, and the garrisons of Kman Youmis and Gaza which were completely cut off, the final victory was in view. Our forces reached Nahal in the south, and Bir Gafgafa on the central front, and were approaching El-Arish.

The Egyptian High Command ordered the retreat of all Sinai Desert forces. But Nasser would not admit such a defeat, especially the defeat of his Air Force. He stated in the same weekly that on the 1st of November, air superiority was still held by the Egyptians and that Egyptian bombers had again attacked the Israeli airfields twenty times.

News from the battlefield announced victory, but heavy clouds gathering in New York indicated that military victory might turn into political defeat. In spite of Washington's warnings, in spite of Mr. Dulles' statements, we did not expect the United States to join hands with Soviet Russia to stop the "aggressors." Both Washington and Moscow seemed to have their own particular vocabulary on aggression. When American soldiers had marched into Guatemala, it was not called "aggression"; neither was it called "aggression" when Russion tanks had crushed the Hungarian revolution on the 2nd to the 5th of November.

These were the days of the mopping-up operations. All sorties were accomplished without resistance from the enemy Air Force, which had disappeared from the skies. Our aircraft performed their air strikes with complete impunity. The enemy did not offer even the will to fight.

But neither the Egyptian Air Force nor Nasser, himself, would admit it. The Egyptian Air Force claimed that our air victory was due to French Mystères having entered the battle when Israeli Mystères had been destroyed. It even asserted that the French Mystères had not held their own against the MIG's and that British Hunters and Sea Hawks had been called in to help. Nasser confirmed it by stating that British, not Israeli, aircraft had inflicted the heaviest casualties on the retreating Egyptian Army.

How could he admit that the Israeli Air Force, supposedly destroyed by his bombers and fighters, had won a victory over his invincible air armada?

By the evening of the 2nd of November, the whole of northern Sinai was in our hands. On the central front, our forces moving from Bir Gafgafa advanced to ten miles east of the Canal. On the northern front, although the enemy troops had managed to escape from Um Katef towards El-Arish and Gaza, both these places were taken. Gaza, completely isolated, had the choice of fighting to the bitter end or of surrendering. Her commanding officer decided to surrender.

We had achieved the campaign's first aim—destruction of enemy bases in the Sinai Desert—and we could now proceed with our second aim—the opening of the port of Eilat.

The Sinai Peninsula consists of that part of Sinai which lies south of a line drawn from Eilat to Port Tewfik, between the Gulf of Aqaba in the east, and the Gulf of Suez in the west. It is a mountainous area, full of precipices and cliffs, rent by ravines, with almost no roads or tracks. There is no road at all along the shores of the Gulf of Aqaba, but there is one, partly paved, partly only a beaten track, along the west coast from Port Tewfik to Rass Nastrani. In Ras Nastrani, the Gulf of Aqaba is joined with the Red Sea through narrow straits between the Peninsula and Saudi Arabia, blocked by two islands, Tiran and Sanapir. At the narrowest point, the straits are no more than 1,900 feet wide.

Nasser, deploying his forces, supported by coastal guns in the Ras Nastrani and Sharm-es-Sheikh areas and on the islands, had completely halted all shipping to Eilat, in spite of the United Nations Resolution of 1951. Ignoring our appeals, neither the big powers, nor the United Nations had even tried to enforce the resolution; and our outlet to the Red Sea was sealed off. Our forces were ready to break the seal, to render us our legal rights. But in New York, on the evening of the 2nd of November, the United States pushed through a resolution calling for a cease-fire and the withdrawal of all forces from the battle area. Mr. Dulles' resolution was adopted by the United Nations Assembly by 64 to 5 votes. The five were Britain, France, Israel, Australia and New Zealand. Canada, South Africa, Belgium, Laos, the Netherlands and Portugal abstained.

While the United Nations was voting on the resolution, Nasser declared in Cairo that all forces from the Sinai Desert had been withdrawn to defend the Canal against Anglo-French invasion. He announced that the Syrian Army had agreed to be put under Egyptian Command, a decision having no military value. From Beirut came the voice of President Camille Chamoun, proposing a conference of all Arab heads of state to discuss the situation. Except for Syria, the Arab states were playing for time, time required by England and France to abolish Nasser's dictatorship.

Would the Soviet Union interfere? News came from Moscow of Syrian President El Komatly calling for Russian help on behalf of Nasser.

The die was already cast; and in order to succeed, the operation had to be swift. A force assembled in the Negev, moved through shifting sands, virtually pushing the vehicles and reached Dahav on the shores of the Gulf of Aqaba; paratroopers reached the track along the Gulf of Suez through a desert camel path, and a third force, parachuting in, took At Tor.

With all roads of retreat cut off, the enemy decided to concentrate all forces in Sharm-es-Sheikh and make a stand there. It hoped to receive reinforcements and supplies by sea route from Suez. The frigate, *Damiat,* was already en route with fresh troops.

The frigate was intercepted by a British naval force and sunk.

We were not aware of the fact. We were rather doubtful about the true aim of the British naval forces in these waters and wondered whether they would interfere with our assault on Sharm-es-Sheikh.

The pincers were closing on the last enemy outpost. The Air Force was busy again—Pipers guiding the troops through the unknown desert, finding passages through the wilderness of sand and rock, the transport planes carrying troops and supplies, and the fighter aircraft protecting the skies and offering air support. During one air strike, one of our Mystères was hit by enemy antiaircraft fire, and the pilot was forced to eject himself. He landed about 2,000 yards from his burning aircraft, and about the same distance from enemy troops. The Egyptians watching the parachute descend did not immediately dispatch a "reception committee," but waited to search for him until the pilot had hit the ground. The pilot released the parachute, which drifted with the wind. The enemy followed its direction. Although wounded in his legs, the pilot ran for his life to the neighboring mountains and climbed a rock some 500 feet high. The other Mystères did not abandon their comrade, but continued strafing the enemy to divert attention. Shortage of fuel made them return to their base, but already a Piper Cub was on its way to rescue the pilot. The Piper pilot circled the rock, but did not see the downed pilot trying to signal him with the white sleeve he had taken from his parachute. The pilot crawled to an open space, and suddenly he froze. Two enemy soldiers were walking 20 yards away. They did not see him, but meanwhile the Piper flew away. Twilight, and the Piper was back again. The pilot waved. The Piper, spotting the waving figure, came dangerously low for identification and glided down, landing no more than 100 yards from the enemy. Then he taxied back to the hideout. Crawling with his last resources, the injured pilot reached the light rescue plane.

Our aircraft were also responsible for preventing enemy ships from reaching Sharm-es-Sheikh. On one such mission, four Mystères spotted a large warship near the straits. As the ship was sighted, she turned to escape. The Mystères dived, and the warship opened fire. It was heavy flak, but the Mystères went through it, releasing all their rockets. H.M.S. *Crane* was lucky to be only slightly damaged, and none of our aircraft was hit.

On the 5th, Sharm-es-Sheikh was taken; and in the seven days which had passed since the transport planes had crossed the Israeli frontier carrying the paratroopers to their daring action at Mittlah, the Israeli Army had destroyed and defeated the enemy in his own area, in his own bases, in his own fortified positions from which he had intended to annihilate us.

This—the end of our military campaign—was followed by a political one which forced us to retreat from all our positions. We had achieved our aims. We had opened the sea route to Eilat, and we had secured peace for our country.

But for how long? How long would it take Soviet Russia to rearm the Egyptian Army, make it ready again to attack us? What price would we pay next time for our victory?

Perhaps more than any spoken words, the defeated Army's sentiments were expressed as a "dream" by Lieutenant Colonel Al Magid in the November issue of the Egyptian Army's *Maljat El Yish* . . .

It is a dream about dropping on Israel "a small and modest Atom Bomb, not more powerful than the one dropped on Hiroshima. The time will be Wednesday," writes the gallant Lieutenant Colonel, "at four o'clock in the afternoon, on a summer's day. Wednesday is chosen since it is a normal working day, and only then shall we be sure of finding a tremendous number of people in the shops and factories. The hour is chosen for the same reason, and moreover, the impending darkness that will set when the evening comes shortly after the bombing, will render the rescue operations more difficult, if there will be anything left to rescue." Then comes the description of the operation, and the Lieutenant Colonel ends his beautiful dream, saying, "My dear reader and friend, don't you believe now that the effort to get the mighty bomb is vital and worth anything?"